C-1749   CAREER EXAMINATION SERIES

This is your
PASSBOOK for...

Crane Operator

Test Preparation Study Guide
Questions & Answers

COPYRIGHT NOTICE

This book is SOLELY intended for, is sold ONLY to, and its use is RESTRICTED to individual, bona fide applicants or candidates who qualify by virtue of having seriously filed applications for appropriate license, certificate, professional and/or promotional advancement, higher school matriculation, scholarship, or other legitimate requirements of education and/or governmental authorities.

This book is NOT intended for use, class instruction, tutoring, training, duplication, copying, reprinting, excerption, or adaptation, etc., by:

1) Other publishers
2) Proprietors and/or Instructors of "Coaching" and/or Preparatory Courses
3) Personnel and/or Training Divisions of commercial, industrial, and governmental organizations
4) Schools, colleges, or universities and/or their departments and staffs, including teachers and other personnel
5) Testing Agencies or Bureaus
6) Study groups which seek by the purchase of a single volume to copy and/or duplicate and/or adapt this material for use by the group as a whole without having purchased individual volumes for each of the members of the group
7) Et al.

Such persons would be in violation of appropriate Federal and State statutes.

PROVISION OF LICENSING AGREEMENTS – Recognized educational, commercial, industrial, and governmental institutions and organizations, and others legitimately engaged in educational pursuits, including training, testing, and measurement activities, may address request for a licensing agreement to the copyright owners, who will determine whether, and under what conditions, including fees and charges, the materials in this book may be used them. In other words, a licensing facility exists for the legitimate use of the material in this book on other than an individual basis. However, it is asseverated and affirmed here that the material in this book CANNOT be used without the receipt of the express permission of such a licensing agreement from the Publishers. Inquiries re licensing should be addressed to the company, attention rights and permissions department.

All rights reserved, including the right of reproduction in whole or in part, in any form or by any means, electronic or mechanical, including photocopying, recording, or by any information storage and retrieval system, without permission in writing from the Publisher.

Copyright © 2024 by
National Learning Corporation

212 Michael Drive, Syosset, NY 11791
(516) 921-8888 • www.passbooks.com
E-mail: info@passbooks.com

PUBLISHED IN THE UNITED STATES OF AMERICA

PASSBOOK® SERIES

THE *PASSBOOK® SERIES* has been created to prepare applicants and candidates for the ultimate academic battlefield – the examination room.

At some time in our lives, each and every one of us may be required to take an examination – for validation, matriculation, admission, qualification, registration, certification, or licensure.

Based on the assumption that every applicant or candidate has met the basic formal educational standards, has taken the required number of courses, and read the necessary texts, the *PASSBOOK® SERIES* furnishes the one special preparation which may assure passing with confidence, instead of failing with insecurity. Examination questions – together with answers – are furnished as the basic vehicle for study so that the mysteries of the examination and its compounding difficulties may be eliminated or diminished by a sure method.

This book is meant to help you pass your examination provided that you qualify and are serious in your objective.

The entire field is reviewed through the huge store of content information which is succinctly presented through a provocative and challenging approach – the question-and-answer method.

A climate of success is established by furnishing the correct answers at the end of each test.

You soon learn to recognize types of questions, forms of questions, and patterns of questioning. You may even begin to anticipate expected outcomes.

You perceive that many questions are repeated or adapted so that you can gain acute insights, which may enable you to score many sure points.

You learn how to confront new questions, or types of questions, and to attack them confidently and work out the correct answers.

You note objectives and emphases, and recognize pitfalls and dangers, so that you may make positive educational adjustments.

Moreover, you are kept fully informed in relation to new concepts, methods, practices, and directions in the field.

You discover that you are actually taking the examination all the time: you are preparing for the examination by "taking" an examination, not by reading extraneous and/or supererogatory textbooks.

In short, this PASSBOOK®, used directedly, should be an important factor in helping you to pass your test.

CRANE OPERATOR (AMPES)

DUTIES
Under supervision, operates, maintains and makes such minor repairs as are necessary to assure continued operation of cranes, gantries, shovels, draglines and like equipment, using any motive power except steam; performs related work.

SCOPE OF THE EXAMINATION
The written test will appraise candidates' knowledge of rules and regulations governing erection and dismantling of climber and tower cranes; computation of weights and materials to be lifted, safe loads on various types and sizes of rigging equipment including fiber and wire ropes, chain hoists, blocks, gin poles, shear legs, cranes and hydraulic rams; ability to handle practical crane erection problems, knowledge of safety measures and accident prevention, and related matters.

HOW TO TAKE A TEST

I. YOU MUST PASS AN EXAMINATION

A. *WHAT EVERY CANDIDATE SHOULD KNOW*

Examination applicants often ask us for help in preparing for the written test. What can I study in advance? What kinds of questions will be asked? How will the test be given? How will the papers be graded?

As an applicant for a civil service examination, you may be wondering about some of these things. Our purpose here is to suggest effective methods of advance study and to describe civil service examinations.

Your chances for success on this examination can be increased if you know how to prepare. Those "pre-examination jitters" can be reduced if you know what to expect. You can even experience an adventure in good citizenship if you know why civil service exams are given.

B. *WHY ARE CIVIL SERVICE EXAMINATIONS GIVEN?*

Civil service examinations are important to you in two ways. As a citizen, you want public jobs filled by employees who know how to do their work. As a job seeker, you want a fair chance to compete for that job on an equal footing with other candidates. The best-known means of accomplishing this two-fold goal is the competitive examination.

Exams are widely publicized throughout the nation. They may be administered for jobs in federal, state, city, municipal, town or village governments or agencies.

Any citizen may apply, with some limitations, such as the age or residence of applicants. Your experience and education may be reviewed to see whether you meet the requirements for the particular examination. When these requirements exist, they are reasonable and applied consistently to all applicants. Thus, a competitive examination may cause you some uneasiness now, but it is your privilege and safeguard.

C. *HOW ARE CIVIL SERVICE EXAMS DEVELOPED?*

Examinations are carefully written by trained technicians who are specialists in the field known as "psychological measurement," in consultation with recognized authorities in the field of work that the test will cover. These experts recommend the subject matter areas or skills to be tested; only those knowledges or skills important to your success on the job are included. The most reliable books and source materials available are used as references. Together, the experts and technicians judge the difficulty level of the questions.

Test technicians know how to phrase questions so that the problem is clearly stated. Their ethics do not permit "trick" or "catch" questions. Questions may have been tried out on sample groups, or subjected to statistical analysis, to determine their usefulness.

Written tests are often used in combination with performance tests, ratings of training and experience, and oral interviews. All of these measures combine to form the best-known means of finding the right person for the right job.

II. HOW TO PASS THE WRITTEN TEST

A. NATURE OF THE EXAMINATION

To prepare intelligently for civil service examinations, you should know how they differ from school examinations you have taken. In school you were assigned certain definite pages to read or subjects to cover. The examination questions were quite detailed and usually emphasized memory. Civil service exams, on the other hand, try to discover your present ability to perform the duties of a position, plus your potentiality to learn these duties. In other words, a civil service exam attempts to predict how successful you will be. Questions cover such a broad area that they cannot be as minute and detailed as school exam questions.

In the public service similar kinds of work, or positions, are grouped together in one "class." This process is known as *position-classification*. All the positions in a class are paid according to the salary range for that class. One class title covers all of these positions, and they are all tested by the same examination.

B. FOUR BASIC STEPS

1) Study the announcement

How, then, can you know what subjects to study? Our best answer is: "Learn as much as possible about the class of positions for which you've applied." The exam will test the knowledge, skills and abilities needed to do the work.

Your most valuable source of information about the position you want is the official exam announcement. This announcement lists the training and experience qualifications. Check these standards and apply only if you come reasonably close to meeting them.

The brief description of the position in the examination announcement offers some clues to the subjects which will be tested. Think about the job itself. Review the duties in your mind. Can you perform them, or are there some in which you are rusty? Fill in the blank spots in your preparation.

Many jurisdictions preview the written test in the exam announcement by including a section called "Knowledge and Abilities Required," "Scope of the Examination," or some similar heading. Here you will find out specifically what fields will be tested.

2) Review your own background

Once you learn in general what the position is all about, and what you need to know to do the work, ask yourself which subjects you already know fairly well and which need improvement. You may wonder whether to concentrate on improving your strong areas or on building some background in your fields of weakness. When the announcement has specified "some knowledge" or "considerable knowledge," or has used adjectives like "beginning principles of..." or "advanced ... methods," you can get a clue as to the number and difficulty of questions to be asked in any given field. More questions, and hence broader coverage, would be included for those subjects which are more important in the work. Now weigh your strengths and weaknesses against the job requirements and prepare accordingly.

3) Determine the level of the position

Another way to tell how intensively you should prepare is to understand the level of the job for which you are applying. Is it the entering level? In other words, is this the position in which beginners in a field of work are hired? Or is it an intermediate or advanced level? Sometimes this is indicated by such words as "Junior" or "Senior" in the class title. Other jurisdictions use Roman numerals to designate the level – Clerk I, Clerk II, for example. The word "Supervisor" sometimes appears in the title. If the level is not indicated by the title, check the description of duties. Will you be working under very close supervision, or will you have responsibility for independent decisions in this work?

4) Choose appropriate study materials

Now that you know the subjects to be examined and the relative amount of each subject to be covered, you can choose suitable study materials. For beginning level jobs, or even advanced ones, if you have a pronounced weakness in some aspect of your training, read a modern, standard textbook in that field. Be sure it is up to date and has general coverage. Such books are normally available at your library, and the librarian will be glad to help you locate one. For entry-level positions, questions of appropriate difficulty are chosen – neither highly advanced questions, nor those too simple. Such questions require careful thought but not advanced training.

If the position for which you are applying is technical or advanced, you will read more advanced, specialized material. If you are already familiar with the basic principles of your field, elementary textbooks would waste your time. Concentrate on advanced textbooks and technical periodicals. Think through the concepts and review difficult problems in your field.

These are all general sources. You can get more ideas on your own initiative, following these leads. For example, training manuals and publications of the government agency which employs workers in your field can be useful, particularly for technical and professional positions. A letter or visit to the government department involved may result in more specific study suggestions, and certainly will provide you with a more definite idea of the exact nature of the position you are seeking.

III. KINDS OF TESTS

Tests are used for purposes other than measuring knowledge and ability to perform specified duties. For some positions, it is equally important to test ability to make adjustments to new situations or to profit from training. In others, basic mental abilities not dependent on information are essential. Questions which test these things may not appear as pertinent to the duties of the position as those which test for knowledge and information. Yet they are often highly important parts of a fair examination. For very general questions, it is almost impossible to help you direct your study efforts. What we can do is to point out some of the more common of these general abilities needed in public service positions and describe some typical questions.

1) General information

Broad, general information has been found useful for predicting job success in some kinds of work. This is tested in a variety of ways, from vocabulary lists to questions about current events. Basic background in some field of work, such as sociology or economics, may be sampled in a group of questions. Often these are principles which have become familiar to most persons through exposure rather than through formal training. It is difficult to advise you how to study for these questions; being alert to the world around you is our best suggestion.

2) Verbal ability

An example of an ability needed in many positions is verbal or language ability. Verbal ability is, in brief, the ability to use and understand words. Vocabulary and grammar tests are typical measures of this ability. Reading comprehension or paragraph interpretation questions are common in many kinds of civil service tests. You are given a paragraph of written material and asked to find its central meaning.

3) Numerical ability

Number skills can be tested by the familiar arithmetic problem, by checking paired lists of numbers to see which are alike and which are different, or by interpreting charts and graphs. In the latter test, a graph may be printed in the test booklet which you are asked to use as the basis for answering questions.

4) Observation

A popular test for law-enforcement positions is the observation test. A picture is shown to you for several minutes, then taken away. Questions about the picture test your ability to observe both details and larger elements.

5) Following directions

In many positions in the public service, the employee must be able to carry out written instructions dependably and accurately. You may be given a chart with several columns, each column listing a variety of information. The questions require you to carry out directions involving the information given in the chart.

6) Skills and aptitudes

Performance tests effectively measure some manual skills and aptitudes. When the skill is one in which you are trained, such as typing or shorthand, you can practice. These tests are often very much like those given in business school or high school courses. For many of the other skills and aptitudes, however, no short-time preparation can be made. Skills and abilities natural to you or that you have developed throughout your lifetime are being tested.

Many of the general questions just described provide all the data needed to answer the questions and ask you to use your reasoning ability to find the answers. Your best preparation for these tests, as well as for tests of facts and ideas, is to be at your physical and mental best. You, no doubt, have your own methods of getting into an exam-taking mood and keeping "in shape." The next section lists some ideas on this subject.

IV. KINDS OF QUESTIONS

Only rarely is the "essay" question, which you answer in narrative form, used in civil service tests. Civil service tests are usually of the short-answer type. Full instructions for answering these questions will be given to you at the examination. But in case this is your first experience with short-answer questions and separate answer sheets, here is what you need to know:

1) Multiple-choice Questions

Most popular of the short-answer questions is the "multiple choice" or "best answer" question. It can be used, for example, to test for factual knowledge, ability to solve problems or judgment in meeting situations found at work.

A multiple-choice question is normally one of three types—
- It can begin with an incomplete statement followed by several possible endings. You are to find the one ending which *best* completes the statement, although some of the others may not be entirely wrong.
- It can also be a complete statement in the form of a question which is answered by choosing one of the statements listed.

- It can be in the form of a problem – again you select the best answer.

Here is an example of a multiple-choice question with a discussion which should give you some clues as to the method for choosing the right answer:

When an employee has a complaint about his assignment, the action which will *best* help him overcome his difficulty is to
   A. discuss his difficulty with his coworkers
   B. take the problem to the head of the organization
   C. take the problem to the person who gave him the assignment
   D. say nothing to anyone about his complaint

In answering this question, you should study each of the choices to find which is best. Consider choice "A" – Certainly an employee may discuss his complaint with fellow employees, but no change or improvement can result, and the complaint remains unresolved. Choice "B" is a poor choice since the head of the organization probably does not know what assignment you have been given, and taking your problem to him is known as "going over the head" of the supervisor. The supervisor, or person who made the assignment, is the person who can clarify it or correct any injustice. Choice "C" is, therefore, correct. To say nothing, as in choice "D," is unwise. Supervisors have and interest in knowing the problems employees are facing, and the employee is seeking a solution to his problem.

2) True/False Questions

The "true/false" or "right/wrong" form of question is sometimes used. Here a complete statement is given. Your job is to decide whether the statement is right or wrong.

SAMPLE: A roaming cell-phone call to a nearby city costs less than a non-roaming call to a distant city.

This statement is wrong, or false, since roaming calls are more expensive.
This is not a complete list of all possible question forms, although most of the others are variations of these common types. You will always get complete directions for answering questions. Be sure you understand *how* to mark your answers – ask questions until you do.

V. RECORDING YOUR ANSWERS

Computer terminals are used more and more today for many different kinds of exams.
For an examination with very few applicants, you may be told to record your answers in the test booklet itself. Separate answer sheets are much more common. If this separate answer sheet is to be scored by machine – and this is often the case – it is highly important that you mark your answers correctly in order to get credit.
An electronic scoring machine is often used in civil service offices because of the speed with which papers can be scored. Machine-scored answer sheets must be marked with a pencil, which will be given to you. This pencil has a high graphite content which responds to the electronic scoring machine. As a matter of fact, stray dots may register as answers, so do not let your pencil rest on the answer sheet while you are pondering the correct answer. Also, if your pencil lead breaks or is otherwise defective, ask for another.

Since the answer sheet will be dropped in a slot in the scoring machine, be careful not to bend the corners or get the paper crumpled.

The answer sheet normally has five vertical columns of numbers, with 30 numbers to a column. These numbers correspond to the question numbers in your test booklet. After each number, going across the page are four or five pairs of dotted lines. These short dotted lines have small letters or numbers above them. The first two pairs may also have a "T" or "F" above the letters. This indicates that the first two pairs only are to be used if the questions are of the true-false type. If the questions are multiple choice, disregard the "T" and "F" and pay attention only to the small letters or numbers.

Answer your questions in the manner of the sample that follows:

32. The largest city in the United States is
    A. Washington, D.C.
    B. New York City
    C. Chicago
    D. Detroit
    E. San Francisco

1) Choose the answer you think is best. (New York City is the largest, so "B" is correct.)
2) Find the row of dotted lines numbered the same as the question you are answering. (Find row number 32)
3) Find the pair of dotted lines corresponding to the answer. (Find the pair of lines under the mark "B.")
4) Make a solid black mark between the dotted lines.

VI. BEFORE THE TEST

Common sense will help you find procedures to follow to get ready for an examination. Too many of us, however, overlook these sensible measures. Indeed, nervousness and fatigue have been found to be the most serious reasons why applicants fail to do their best on civil service tests. Here is a list of reminders:

- Begin your preparation early – Don't wait until the last minute to go scurrying around for books and materials or to find out what the position is all about.
- Prepare continuously – An hour a night for a week is better than an all-night cram session. This has been definitely established. What is more, a night a week for a month will return better dividends than crowding your study into a shorter period of time.
- Locate the place of the exam – You have been sent a notice telling you when and where to report for the examination. If the location is in a different town or otherwise unfamiliar to you, it would be well to inquire the best route and learn something about the building.
- Relax the night before the test – Allow your mind to rest. Do not study at all that night. Plan some mild recreation or diversion; then go to bed early and get a good night's sleep.
- Get up early enough to make a leisurely trip to the place for the test – This way unforeseen events, traffic snarls, unfamiliar buildings, etc. will not upset you.
- Dress comfortably – A written test is not a fashion show. You will be known by number and not by name, so wear something comfortable.

- Leave excess paraphernalia at home – Shopping bags and odd bundles will get in your way. You need bring only the items mentioned in the official notice you received; usually everything you need is provided. Do not bring reference books to the exam. They will only confuse those last minutes and be taken away from you when in the test room.
- Arrive somewhat ahead of time – If because of transportation schedules you must get there very early, bring a newspaper or magazine to take your mind off yourself while waiting.
- Locate the examination room – When you have found the proper room, you will be directed to the seat or part of the room where you will sit. Sometimes you are given a sheet of instructions to read while you are waiting. Do not fill out any forms until you are told to do so; just read them and be prepared.
- Relax and prepare to listen to the instructions
- If you have any physical problem that may keep you from doing your best, be sure to tell the test administrator. If you are sick or in poor health, you really cannot do your best on the exam. You can come back and take the test some other time.

VII. AT THE TEST

The day of the test is here and you have the test booklet in your hand. The temptation to get going is very strong. Caution! There is more to success than knowing the right answers. You must know how to identify your papers and understand variations in the type of short-answer question used in this particular examination. Follow these suggestions for maximum results from your efforts:

1) Cooperate with the monitor

The test administrator has a duty to create a situation in which you can be as much at ease as possible. He will give instructions, tell you when to begin, check to see that you are marking your answer sheet correctly, and so on. He is not there to guard you, although he will see that your competitors do not take unfair advantage. He wants to help you do your best.

2) Listen to all instructions

Don't jump the gun! Wait until you understand all directions. In most civil service tests you get more time than you need to answer the questions. So don't be in a hurry. Read each word of instructions until you clearly understand the meaning. Study the examples, listen to all announcements and follow directions. Ask questions if you do not understand what to do.

3) Identify your papers

Civil service exams are usually identified by number only. You will be assigned a number; you must not put your name on your test papers. Be sure to copy your number correctly. Since more than one exam may be given, copy your exact examination title.

4) Plan your time

Unless you are told that a test is a "speed" or "rate of work" test, speed itself is usually not important. Time enough to answer all the questions will be provided, but this does not mean that you have all day. An overall time limit has been set. Divide the total time (in minutes) by the number of questions to determine the approximate time you have for each question.

5) Do not linger over difficult questions

If you come across a difficult question, mark it with a paper clip (useful to have along) and come back to it when you have been through the booklet. One caution if you do this – be sure to skip a number on your answer sheet as well. Check often to be sure that you have not lost your place and that you are marking in the row numbered the same as the question you are answering.

6) Read the questions

Be sure you know what the question asks! Many capable people are unsuccessful because they failed to *read* the questions correctly.

7) Answer all questions

Unless you have been instructed that a penalty will be deducted for incorrect answers, it is better to guess than to omit a question.

8) Speed tests

It is often better NOT to guess on speed tests. It has been found that on timed tests people are tempted to spend the last few seconds before time is called in marking answers at random – without even reading them – in the hope of picking up a few extra points. To discourage this practice, the instructions may warn you that your score will be "corrected" for guessing. That is, a penalty will be applied. The incorrect answers will be deducted from the correct ones, or some other penalty formula will be used.

9) Review your answers

If you finish before time is called, go back to the questions you guessed or omitted to give them further thought. Review other answers if you have time.

10) Return your test materials

If you are ready to leave before others have finished or time is called, take ALL your materials to the monitor and leave quietly. Never take any test material with you. The monitor can discover whose papers are not complete, and taking a test booklet may be grounds for disqualification.

VIII. EXAMINATION TECHNIQUES

1) Read the general instructions carefully. These are usually printed on the first page of the exam booklet. As a rule, these instructions refer to the timing of the examination; the fact that you should not start work until the signal and must stop work at a signal, etc. If there are any *special* instructions, such as a choice of questions to be answered, make sure that you note this instruction carefully.

2) When you are ready to start work on the examination, that is as soon as the signal has been given, read the instructions to each question booklet, underline any key words or phrases, such as *least, best, outline, describe* and the like. In this way you will tend to answer as requested rather than discover on reviewing your paper that you *listed without describing*, that you selected the *worst* choice rather than the *best* choice, etc.

3) If the examination is of the objective or multiple-choice type – that is, each question will also give a series of possible answers: A, B, C or D, and you are called upon to select the best answer and write the letter next to that answer on your answer paper – it is advisable to start answering each question in turn. There may be anywhere from 50 to 100 such questions in the three or four hours allotted and you can see how much time would be taken if you read through all the questions before beginning to answer any. Furthermore, if you come across a question or group of questions which you know would be difficult to answer, it would undoubtedly affect your handling of all the other questions.

4) If the examination is of the essay type and contains but a few questions, it is a moot point as to whether you should read all the questions before starting to answer any one. Of course, if you are given a choice – say five out of seven and the like – then it is essential to read all the questions so you can eliminate the two that are most difficult. If, however, you are asked to answer all the questions, there may be danger in trying to answer the easiest one first because you may find that you will spend too much time on it. The best technique is to answer the first question, then proceed to the second, etc.

5) Time your answers. Before the exam begins, write down the time it started, then add the time allowed for the examination and write down the time it must be completed, then divide the time available somewhat as follows:
    - If 3-1/2 hours are allowed, that would be 210 minutes. If you have 80 objective-type questions, that would be an average of 2-1/2 minutes per question. Allow yourself no more than 2 minutes per question, or a total of 160 minutes, which will permit about 50 minutes to review.
    - If for the time allotment of 210 minutes there are 7 essay questions to answer, that would average about 30 minutes a question. Give yourself only 25 minutes per question so that you have about 35 minutes to review.

6) The most important instruction is to *read each question* and make sure you know what is wanted. The second most important instruction is to *time yourself properly* so that you answer every question. The third most important instruction is to *answer every question*. Guess if you have to but include something for each question. Remember that you will receive no credit for a blank and will probably receive some credit if you write something in answer to an essay question. If you guess a letter – say "B" for a multiple-choice question – you may have guessed right. If you leave a blank as an answer to a multiple-choice question, the examiners may respect your feelings but it will not add a point to your score. Some exams may penalize you for wrong answers, so in such cases *only*, you may not want to guess unless you have some basis for your answer.

7) Suggestions
    a. Objective-type questions
        1. Examine the question booklet for proper sequence of pages and questions
        2. Read all instructions carefully
        3. Skip any question which seems too difficult; return to it after all other questions have been answered
        4. Apportion your time properly; do not spend too much time on any single question or group of questions

5. Note and underline key words – *all, most, fewest, least, best, worst, same, opposite,* etc.
6. Pay particular attention to negatives
7. Note unusual option, e.g., unduly long, short, complex, different or similar in content to the body of the question
8. Observe the use of "hedging" words – *probably, may, most likely,* etc.
9. Make sure that your answer is put next to the same number as the question
10. Do not second-guess unless you have good reason to believe the second answer is definitely more correct
11. Cross out original answer if you decide another answer is more accurate; do not erase until you are ready to hand your paper in
12. Answer all questions; guess unless instructed otherwise
13. Leave time for review

   b. Essay questions
1. Read each question carefully
2. Determine exactly what is wanted. Underline key words or phrases.
3. Decide on outline or paragraph answer
4. Include many different points and elements unless asked to develop any one or two points or elements
5. Show impartiality by giving pros and cons unless directed to select one side only
6. Make and write down any assumptions you find necessary to answer the questions
7. Watch your English, grammar, punctuation and choice of words
8. Time your answers; don't crowd material

8) Answering the essay question

Most essay questions can be answered by framing the specific response around several key words or ideas. Here are a few such key words or ideas:

M's: manpower, materials, methods, money, management
P's: purpose, program, policy, plan, procedure, practice, problems, pitfalls, personnel, public relations

   a. Six basic steps in handling problems:
1. Preliminary plan and background development
2. Collect information, data and facts
3. Analyze and interpret information, data and facts
4. Analyze and develop solutions as well as make recommendations
5. Prepare report and sell recommendations
6. Install recommendations and follow up effectiveness

   b. Pitfalls to avoid
1. *Taking things for granted* – A statement of the situation does not necessarily imply that each of the elements is necessarily true; for example, a complaint may be invalid and biased so that all that can be taken for granted is that a complaint has been registered

2. *Considering only one side of a situation* – Wherever possible, indicate several alternatives and then point out the reasons you selected the best one
3. *Failing to indicate follow up* – Whenever your answer indicates action on your part, make certain that you will take proper follow-up action to see how successful your recommendations, procedures or actions turn out to be
4. *Taking too long in answering any single question* – Remember to time your answers properly

IX. AFTER THE TEST

Scoring procedures differ in detail among civil service jurisdictions although the general principles are the same. Whether the papers are hand-scored or graded by machine we have described, they are nearly always graded by number. That is, the person who marks the paper knows only the number – never the name – of the applicant. Not until all the papers have been graded will they be matched with names. If other tests, such as training and experience or oral interview ratings have been given, scores will be combined. Different parts of the examination usually have different weights. For example, the written test might count 60 percent of the final grade, and a rating of training and experience 40 percent. In many jurisdictions, veterans will have a certain number of points added to their grades.

After the final grade has been determined, the names are placed in grade order and an eligible list is established. There are various methods for resolving ties between those who get the same final grade – probably the most common is to place first the name of the person whose application was received first. Job offers are made from the eligible list in the order the names appear on it. You will be notified of your grade and your rank as soon as all these computations have been made. This will be done as rapidly as possible.

People who are found to meet the requirements in the announcement are called "eligibles." Their names are put on a list of eligible candidates. An eligible's chances of getting a job depend on how high he stands on this list and how fast agencies are filling jobs from the list.

When a job is to be filled from a list of eligibles, the agency asks for the names of people on the list of eligibles for that job. When the civil service commission receives this request, it sends to the agency the names of the three people highest on this list. Or, if the job to be filled has specialized requirements, the office sends the agency the names of the top three persons who meet these requirements from the general list.

The appointing officer makes a choice from among the three people whose names were sent to him. If the selected person accepts the appointment, the names of the others are put back on the list to be considered for future openings.

That is the rule in hiring from all kinds of eligible lists, whether they are for typist, carpenter, chemist, or something else. For every vacancy, the appointing officer has his choice of any one of the top three eligibles on the list. This explains why the person whose name is on top of the list sometimes does not get an appointment when some of the persons lower on the list do. If the appointing officer chooses the second or third eligible, the No. 1 eligible does not get a job at once, but stays on the list until he is appointed or the list is terminated.

X. HOW TO PASS THE INTERVIEW TEST

The examination for which you applied requires an oral interview test. You have already taken the written test and you are now being called for the interview test – the final part of the formal examination.

You may think that it is not possible to prepare for an interview test and that there are no procedures to follow during an interview. Our purpose is to point out some things you can do in advance that will help you and some good rules to follow and pitfalls to avoid while you are being interviewed.

What is an interview supposed to test?

The written examination is designed to test the technical knowledge and competence of the candidate; the oral is designed to evaluate intangible qualities, not readily measured otherwise, and to establish a list showing the relative fitness of each candidate – as measured against his competitors – for the position sought. Scoring is not on the basis of "right" and "wrong," but on a sliding scale of values ranging from "not passable" to "outstanding." As a matter of fact, it is possible to achieve a relatively low score without a single "incorrect" answer because of evident weakness in the qualities being measured.

Occasionally, an examination may consist entirely of an oral test – either an individual or a group oral. In such cases, information is sought concerning the technical knowledges and abilities of the candidate, since there has been no written examination for this purpose. More commonly, however, an oral test is used to supplement a written examination.

Who conducts interviews?

The composition of oral boards varies among different jurisdictions. In nearly all, a representative of the personnel department serves as chairman. One of the members of the board may be a representative of the department in which the candidate would work. In some cases, "outside experts" are used, and, frequently, a businessman or some other representative of the general public is asked to serve. Labor and management or other special groups may be represented. The aim is to secure the services of experts in the appropriate field.

However the board is composed, it is a good idea (and not at all improper or unethical) to ascertain in advance of the interview who the members are and what groups they represent. When you are introduced to them, you will have some idea of their backgrounds and interests, and at least you will not stutter and stammer over their names.

What should be done before the interview?

While knowledge about the board members is useful and takes some of the surprise element out of the interview, there is other preparation which is more substantive. It *is* possible to prepare for an oral interview – in several ways:

1) Keep a copy of your application and review it carefully before the interview

This may be the only document before the oral board, and the starting point of the interview. Know what education and experience you have listed there, and the sequence and dates of all of it. Sometimes the board will ask you to review the highlights of your experience for them; you should not have to hem and haw doing it.

2) Study the class specification and the examination announcement

Usually, the oral board has one or both of these to guide them. The qualities, characteristics or knowledges required by the position sought are stated in these documents. They offer valuable clues as to the nature of the oral interview. For example, if the job involves supervisory responsibilities, the announcement will usually indicate that knowledge of modern supervisory methods and the qualifications of the candidate as a supervisor will be tested. If so, you can expect such questions, frequently in the form of a hypothetical situation which you are expected to solve. NEVER go into an oral without knowledge of the duties and responsibilities of the job you seek.

3) Think through each qualification required

Try to visualize the kind of questions you would ask if you were a board member. How well could you answer them? Try especially to appraise your own knowledge and background in each area, *measured against the job sought*, and identify any areas in which you are weak. Be critical and realistic – do not flatter yourself.

4) Do some general reading in areas in which you feel you may be weak

For example, if the job involves supervision and your past experience has NOT, some general reading in supervisory methods and practices, particularly in the field of human relations, might be useful. Do NOT study agency procedures or detailed manuals. The oral board will be testing your understanding and capacity, not your memory.

5) Get a good night's sleep and watch your general health and mental attitude

You will want a clear head at the interview. Take care of a cold or any other minor ailment, and of course, no hangovers.

What should be done on the day of the interview?

Now comes the day of the interview itself. Give yourself plenty of time to get there. Plan to arrive somewhat ahead of the scheduled time, particularly if your appointment is in the fore part of the day. If a previous candidate fails to appear, the board might be ready for you a bit early. By early afternoon an oral board is almost invariably behind schedule if there are many candidates, and you may have to wait. Take along a book or magazine to read, or your application to review, but leave any extraneous material in the waiting room when you go in for your interview. In any event, relax and compose yourself.

The matter of dress is important. The board is forming impressions about you – from your experience, your manners, your attitude, and your appearance. Give your personal appearance careful attention. Dress your best, but not your flashiest. Choose conservative, appropriate clothing, and be sure it is immaculate. This is a business interview, and your appearance should indicate that you regard it as such. Besides, being well groomed and properly dressed will help boost your confidence.

Sooner or later, someone will call your name and escort you into the interview room. *This is it.* From here on you are on your own. It is too late for any more preparation. But remember, you asked for this opportunity to prove your fitness, and you are here because your request was granted.

What happens when you go in?

The usual sequence of events will be as follows: The clerk (who is often the board stenographer) will introduce you to the chairman of the oral board, who will introduce you to the other members of the board. Acknowledge the introductions before you sit down. Do not be surprised if you find a microphone facing you or a stenotypist sitting by. Oral interviews are usually recorded in the event of an appeal or other review.

Usually the chairman of the board will open the interview by reviewing the highlights of your education and work experience from your application – primarily for the benefit of the other members of the board, as well as to get the material into the record. Do not interrupt or comment unless there is an error or significant misinterpretation; if that is the case, do not hesitate. But do not quibble about insignificant matters. Also, he will usually ask you some question about your education, experience or your present job – partly to get you to start talking and to establish the interviewing "rapport." He may start the actual questioning, or turn it over to one of the other members. Frequently, each member undertakes the questioning on a particular area, one in which he is perhaps most competent, so you can expect each member to participate in the examination. Because time is limited, you may also expect some rather abrupt switches in the direction the questioning takes, so do not be upset by it. Normally, a board member will not pursue a single line of questioning unless he discovers a particular strength or weakness.

After each member has participated, the chairman will usually ask whether any member has any further questions, then will ask you if you have anything you wish to add. Unless you are expecting this question, it may floor you. Worse, it may start you off on an extended, extemporaneous speech. The board is not usually seeking more information. The question is principally to offer you a last opportunity to present further qualifications or to indicate that you have nothing to add. So, if you feel that a significant qualification or characteristic has been overlooked, it is proper to point it out in a sentence or so. Do not compliment the board on the thoroughness of their examination – they have been sketchy, and you know it. If you wish, merely say, "No thank you, I have nothing further to add." This is a point where you can "talk yourself out" of a good impression or fail to present an important bit of information. Remember, *you close the interview yourself.*

The chairman will then say, "That is all, Mr. _____, thank you." Do not be startled; the interview is over, and quicker than you think. Thank him, gather your belongings and take your leave. Save your sigh of relief for the other side of the door.

How to put your best foot forward

Throughout this entire process, you may feel that the board individually and collectively is trying to pierce your defenses, seek out your hidden weaknesses and embarrass and confuse you. Actually, this is not true. They are obliged to make an appraisal of your qualifications for the job you are seeking, and they want to see you in your best light. Remember, they must interview all candidates and a non-cooperative candidate may become a failure in spite of their best efforts to bring out his qualifications. Here are 15 suggestions that will help you:

1) Be natural – Keep your attitude confident, not cocky

If you are not confident that you can do the job, do not expect the board to be. Do not apologize for your weaknesses, try to bring out your strong points. The board is interested in a positive, not negative, presentation. Cockiness will antagonize any board member and make him wonder if you are covering up a weakness by a false show of strength.

2) Get comfortable, but don't lounge or sprawl

Sit erectly but not stiffly. A careless posture may lead the board to conclude that you are careless in other things, or at least that you are not impressed by the importance of the occasion. Either conclusion is natural, even if incorrect. Do not fuss with your clothing, a pencil or an ashtray. Your hands may occasionally be useful to emphasize a point; do not let them become a point of distraction.

3) Do not wisecrack or make small talk

This is a serious situation, and your attitude should show that you consider it as such. Further, the time of the board is limited – they do not want to waste it, and neither should you.

4) Do not exaggerate your experience or abilities

In the first place, from information in the application or other interviews and sources, the board may know more about you than you think. Secondly, you probably will not get away with it. An experienced board is rather adept at spotting such a situation, so do not take the chance.

5) If you know a board member, do not make a point of it, yet do not hide it

Certainly you are not fooling him, and probably not the other members of the board. Do not try to take advantage of your acquaintanceship – it will probably do you little good.

6) Do not dominate the interview

Let the board do that. They will give you the clues – do not assume that you have to do all the talking. Realize that the board has a number of questions to ask you, and do not try to take up all the interview time by showing off your extensive knowledge of the answer to the first one.

7) Be attentive

You only have 20 minutes or so, and you should keep your attention at its sharpest throughout. When a member is addressing a problem or question to you, give him your undivided attention. Address your reply principally to him, but do not exclude the other board members.

8) Do not interrupt

A board member may be stating a problem for you to analyze. He will ask you a question when the time comes. Let him state the problem, and wait for the question.

9) Make sure you understand the question

Do not try to answer until you are sure what the question is. If it is not clear, restate it in your own words or ask the board member to clarify it for you. However, do not haggle about minor elements.

10) Reply promptly but not hastily

A common entry on oral board rating sheets is "candidate responded readily," or "candidate hesitated in replies." Respond as promptly and quickly as you can, but do not jump to a hasty, ill-considered answer.

11) Do not be peremptory in your answers

A brief answer is proper – but do not fire your answer back. That is a losing game from your point of view. The board member can probably ask questions much faster than you can answer them.

12) Do not try to create the answer you think the board member wants

He is interested in what kind of mind you have and how it works – not in playing games. Furthermore, he can usually spot this practice and will actually grade you down on it.

13) Do not switch sides in your reply merely to agree with a board member

Frequently, a member will take a contrary position merely to draw you out and to see if you are willing and able to defend your point of view. Do not start a debate, yet do not surrender a good position. If a position is worth taking, it is worth defending.

14) Do not be afraid to admit an error in judgment if you are shown to be wrong

The board knows that you are forced to reply without any opportunity for careful consideration. Your answer may be demonstrably wrong. If so, admit it and get on with the interview.

15) Do not dwell at length on your present job

The opening question may relate to your present assignment. Answer the question but do not go into an extended discussion. You are being examined for a *new* job, not your present one. As a matter of fact, try to phrase ALL your answers in terms of the job for which you are being examined.

Basis of Rating

Probably you will forget most of these "do's" and "don'ts" when you walk into the oral interview room. Even remembering them all will not ensure you a passing grade. Perhaps you did not have the qualifications in the first place. But remembering them will help you to put your best foot forward, without treading on the toes of the board members.

Rumor and popular opinion to the contrary notwithstanding, an oral board wants you to make the best appearance possible. They know you are under pressure – but they also want to see how you respond to it as a guide to what your reaction would be under the pressures of the job you seek. They will be influenced by the degree of poise you display, the personal traits you show and the manner in which you respond.

ABOUT THIS BOOK

This book contains tests divided into Examination Sections. Go through each test, answering every question in the margin. We have also attached a sample answer sheet at the back of the book that can be removed and used. At the end of each test look at the answer key and check your answers. On the ones you got wrong, look at the right answer choice and learn. Do not fill in the answers first. Do not memorize the questions and answers, but understand the answer and principles involved. On your test, the questions will likely be different from the samples. Questions are changed and new ones added. If you understand these past questions you should have success with any changes that arise. Tests may consist of several types of questions. We have additional books on each subject should more study be advisable or necessary for you. Finally, the more you study, the better prepared you will be. This book is intended to be the last thing you study before you walk into the examination room. Prior study of relevant texts is also recommended. NLC publishes some of these in our Fundamental Series. Knowledge and good sense are important factors in passing your exam. Good luck also helps. So now study this Passbook, absorb the material contained within and take that knowledge into the examination. Then do your best to pass that exam.

EXAMINATION SECTION

EXAMINATION SECTION
TEST 1

DIRECTIONS: Each question or incomplete statement is followed by several suggested answers or completions. Select the one that BEST answers the question or completes the statement. *PRINT THE LETTER OF THE CORRECT ANSWER IN THE SPACE AT THE RIGHT.*

1. The proper operation and maintenance of any crane, shovel, or dragline is CHIEFLY the responsibility of the   1.____

    A. foreman   B. oiler   C. mechanic   D. operator

2. The *angle indicator* on a power-operated crane measures the   2.____

    A. angle of the boom to the horizontal
    B. angle of the boom to the vertical
    C. tilt of the housing which covers the rotating operator's station
    D. angle between the boom and the whipline

3. On a power-operated crane, the device used to prevent the boom from being pulled over the top of the cab is the   3.____

    A. brake   B. boom stop
    C. boom point   D. base

4. The block and sheave arrangement on the boom point to which the topping lift cable is reeved for lowering and raising the boom is called the   4.____

    A. boom harness   B. cableway
    C. axle   D. bogie

5. The extension attached to the boom point of a crane to provide added length for lifting is known as a   5.____

    A. folding boom   B. lay
    C. mast   D. jib

6. The *Load Rating Chart* of a mobile crane makes no allowance for   6.____

    A. range of crane load ratings
    B. operating radii and boom angles
    C. permissible boom lengths
    D. operating speeds

7. The WEAKEST part of any crane hoist or sling should be the   7.____

    A. clip   B. link   C. hook   D. clamp

8. Of the following types of equipment, the one which is MOST often used for excavation operations where extended reach (40 to 60 feet) is an important factor is the   8.____

    A. pay loader   B. power shovel
    C. dragline   D. backhoe

9. Assume that a man is reeling wire onto a smooth-faced drum. With the man facing the drum, the wire is going from the man over the top of the drum, starting with that part of the drum at the man's right side.
   The procedure being followed by this man is

   A. *correct* as described
   B. *wrong* because the wire should be reeled under the drum
   C. *wrong* because the reeling should start at the man's left side
   D. *wrong* because wire should not be reeled onto a smoothfaced drum

10. The point at which vibration will cause the GREATEST weakness in a wire rope used on rapid hoisting rigs is, approximately, _____ to _____ feet above the load attachment.

   A. 5; 20   B. 30; 45   C. 50; 65   D. 70; 85

11. The efficiency of a clipped attachment depends on the manner in which the clips are put on the wire rope, the tightness of nuts on the clips, *and* the _____ the wire rope.

   A. diameter of   B. construction of
   C. number of clips used on   D. manufacturer of

12. Of the following types of end connections, the one which is NOT generally used for attaching a wire rope to a clamshell bucket is the

   A. socket attachment   B. spliced eye attachment
   C. clipped attachment   D. wedge socket

13. A Langlay wire rope should be used ONLY with a load that

   A. is relatively light
   B. cannot rotate as it is being lifted
   C. is supported on a float
   D. will keep the rope tight

14. Of the following materials, the one MOST commonly used to make crane brake linings is

   A. cotton fabric   B. bakelite
   C. neoprene   D. asbestos fabric

15. The MAIN reason why an operator of a diesel-powered rig must not permit the diesel engine to run out of fuel is to prevent

   A. condensation in the fuel tank
   B. damage to the fuel injection system
   C. an increase in coolant temperature
   D. damage to the oil pressure regulating valve

16. If a power shovel, equipped with an electric power plant that has a single electric motor drive, is operating sluggishly due to lack of power, it would be BEST to check the motor with a

   A. tachometer and a rheostat
   B. dwell meter
   C. voltmeter and an ammeter
   D. Bailey meter

17. An operator of a gasoline-powered rig permits the engine to idle unnecessarily for long periods of time. Of the following, the MOST probable result of this practice is that the

    A. rig will operate more smoothly
    B. lubricating oil will be diluted
    C. radiator water temperature will rise too high
    D. clutch controls will freeze

18. Before fully engaging the engine clutch to set a piece of machinery in operation, the operator should

    A. partially engage and then disengage the engine clutch to test its operation
    B. check the operating controls to be sure that the clutches are in neutral
    C. examine the gears for proper lubrication
    D. examine the main machinery, making certain that no obstruction prevents its normal operation

19. An operator of a crane wished to change over from dragline operation to a clamshell operation.
    Assuming there is no boom change, the minimum amount of time it would take three men to make the conversion would be, MOST NEARLY, in the range of _____ to _____ hours.

    A. 2; 3   B. 6; 7   C. 8; 9   D. 10; 11

20. The PRIMARY function of outrigging on a truck crane is to

    A. extend the boom length
    B. avoid wear of the hoist wire rope
    C. give side support to the truck body
    D. strengthen the structural members of the boom

21. The lowering of a load by a direct-current-powered crane is controlled by _____ braking.

    A. hydraulic   B. mechanical
    C. dynamic   D. double disc

22. The shaft which operates the valves of a gasoline engine is the _____ shaft.

    A. crank   B. distributor
    C. valve   D. cam

23. Of the following, the BEST practical way to prevent a lead plate storage battery from freezing in cold weather is to

    A. turn off all the auxiliaries when not in use
    B. keep the specific gravity of the electrolyte below 1.150
    C. keep it well charged
    D. disconnect the battery cables when the machine is not in use

24. Grades in excavation work are usually designated by

    A. degree   B. percent   C. height   D. elevation

25. Of the following, the one that is a positive mechanical device for engaging or disengaging power is the

    A. universal   B. clutch
    C. brake   D. unloader

26. Of the following, the tool or device that is commonly used to check the firing of spark plugs in a gasoline engine is a(n)

    A. tachometer
    B. ammeter
    C. screw driver with an insulated handle
    D. feeler gauge

27. If the power fails when hoisting a load, the FIRST thing an operator should do is to

    A. land the load under brake control
    B. communicate with the appointed individual in charge of operations
    C. move all clutch or other power controls to the *off* position
    D. set all brakes and locking devices

28. In a 4-stroke-cycle, full-diesel engine, the fuel is ignited by

    A. a jump spark   B. special spark plugs
    C. highly compressed air   D. hot exhaust gases

29. The function of the pre-combustion chamber on a diesel engine is to

    A. eliminate pre-ignition
    B. obtain higher compression pressures
    C. pre-cool the lubricating oil
    D. assure complete combustion of the fuel

30. The PRIMARY reason for including a thermal overload device in an electrical circuit containing a 40-horsepower A.C. motor is to

    A. increase the motor's efficiency
    B. control the speed of the motor
    C. protect the motor from overheating
    D. decrease the torque of the motor

31. The MAIN function of the intercooler in a two-stage air compressor is to

    A. cool the lubricating oil
    B. cool the air between stages of compression
    C. permit the expansion of combustion products
    D. remove impurities from the air

32. The relief valve on a gasoline-powered portable air compressor is located on the

    A. oil reserve tank
    B. suction side of the air compressor
    C. discharge side of the air compressor
    D. combustion exhaust manifold

33. In a diesel engine, the injection pump and the nozzle are lubricated by 33.____

    A. an SAE 30 oil
    B. the diesel fuel itself
    C. heat-resistant grease
    D. mineral oil

34. The SAE number is an index of a diesel lubricating oil's 34.____

    A. specific gravity
    B. film strength
    C. viscosity
    D. anti-foaming ability

35. Excessive lubrication of diesel cylinders may cause 35.____

    A. condensation in the cylinders
    B. dangerous vapors in the cylinders
    C. pre-ignition in the cylinders
    D. sticking piston rings

36. The method by which water generally enters the lubricating oil system of a diesel engine is through 36.____

    A. rain dripping down into the vents
    B. condensation of the combustion products
    C. a leaky crankcase cover
    D. radiator spill-over

37. In an operator's manual, a lubricant is designated as SUMMER SAE-140 E.P. This lubricant would MOST probably be 37.____

    A. an easy-pour lubricant
    B. a grease
    C. an extreme-pressure lubricant
    D. interchangeable with chassis grease

38. A sudden change in the color of a lubricating oil in an operating engine would MOST probably be caused by a(n) 38.____

    A. dirty filter
    B. clogged oil breather
    C. overfill of lubricating oil
    D. severe overload and heat

39. The air cleaner of an air compressor is of the oil bath type. Of the following substances, the one that it is BEST to use to clean the filter element of this cleaner is 39.____

    A. gasoline
    B. oil
    C. water spray
    D. wood alcohol

40. The shipper shaft of a shovel boom is generally located close to the boom's 40.____

    A. mid-point
    B. top
    C. bottom
    D. drum

KEY (CORRECT ANSWERS)

1. D	11. C	21. C	31. B
2. A	12. A	22. D	32. C
3. B	13. B	23. C	33. B
4. A	14. D	24. B	34. C
5. D	15. B	25. B	35. D
6. D	16. C	26. C	36. B
7. C	17. B	27. D	37. C
8. C	18. D	28. C	38. D
9. A	19. A	29. D	39. B
10. A	20. C	30. C	40. A

TEST 2

DIRECTIONS: Each question or incomplete statement is followed by several suggested answers or completions. Select the one that BEST answers the question or completes the statement. *PRINT THE LETTER OF THE CORRECT ANSWER IN THE SPACE AT THE RIGHT.*

1. A friction-type clutch is preferable to a positive-type clutch in crane applications because a

   A. positive clutch can be applied only at high speeds
   B. friction clutch needs no maintenance
   C. positive clutch cannot take loads as well as a friction clutch
   D. friction clutch can be engaged at any speed

   1._____

2. Of the following types of pumps, the one which is NOT generally found on power-driven mobile machinery is the _____ pump.

   A. piston-type rotary
   B. reciprocating type
   C. gear-type
   D. balanced vane-type

   2._____

3. The term *CFM,* as applied to the capacity of air compressors, is an abbreviation for

   A. compressor feed mechanism
   B. centrifugal force meter
   C. compression fuel machine
   D. cubic feet per minute

   3._____

4. In a certain crane, a horizontal roller chain drive provides power to the jack shaft. In order that there be proper tension in the roller chain, the chain should be adjusted so that there is

   A. no sag
   B. a small amount of sag
   C. sufficient sag to allow the chain to droop at its midpoint to the level of the center line of the driving sprocket
   D. sufficient sag so that the top chain and the bottom chain will make an angle of 60° at the driving sprocket

   4._____

5. Of the following, a switch operated by the motion of a moving part of an electrically powered machine is usually called a _____ switch.

   A. disconnect
   B. remote-control
   C. limit
   D. service

   5._____

6. The BEST type of torch to use for cutting wire rope used on a land-based construction site is the

   A. oxy-acetylene torch
   B. oxy-hydrogen lance
   C. air-propane torch
   D. oxy-butane torch

   6._____

7. Of the following gear types, the one that would NOT be used to transmit power between two parallel shafts is the _____ gear.

   A. spur
   B. herringbone
   C. helical
   D. bevel

   7._____

8. The cylinder of a 2-stroke-cycle diesel engine is scavenged by the

   A. mixture of fuel oil and exhaust gases
   B. mixture of fuel oil and intake air
   C. intake fuel
   D. combustion air

9. A COMMON cause of engine back pressure in a gasoline engine is a

   A. rusted muffler   B. blocked muffler passage
   C. loose exhaust pipe   D. corroded muffler bracket

10. A grease with a consistency number of 2 is classified as

    A. semifluid   B. hard   C. very hard   D. medium

11. The one of the following to which a micron rating would be assigned is a(n)

    A. grease   B. oil filter
    C. strainer   D. magnetic plug

12. An oil is rated as SAE 20W.
    The number 20 refers to the oil's

    A. viscosity at 0° F   B. detergent factor
    C. specific volume   D. rate of deterioration

13. Crane machinery and equipment is BEST lubricated

    A. whenever it is needed
    B. when severe vibration occurs
    C. when out of service
    D. at scheduled times

14. Of the following parts of an electric motor, the one which should be checked for proper lubrication is the

    A. bearings   B. commutator
    C. rotating field   D. windings

15. Of the following liquids, the one which is used as an electrolyte in a lead-plate storage battery is

    A. hydrochloric acid   B. salt water
    C. sulphuric acid   D. ammonia water

16. A battery hydrometer is used mainly to determine a battery's

    A. specific gravity   B. temperature
    C. resistance   D. salinity

17. The BEST method to use to remove a stuck gear from a shaft is to

    A. use a wheel puller
    B. use heavy hammer blows to loosen the gear
    C. heat the shaft and then remove the gear
    D. apply oil and rotate the gear slowly

18. Internal leakage in the hydraulic oil line piping system of a mobile unit will

    A. provide lubrication for such parts as shafts and pistons
    B. result in an oil loss from the lubrication system
    C. not cause a power loss
    D. decrease with normal wear of the parts of the unit

19. A preventive maintenance program is a program in which

    A. machinery is serviced whenever required
    B. maintenance of machinery is performed on a regular schedule
    C. the machines are maintained in such a way that there is never any down-time
    D. inspection of machinery is performed only during slack periods

20. An external gear pump consists essentially of

    A. two meshed gears in a closely fitted housing
    B. one gear which is activated by the moving fluid
    C. a piston turning a gear in an enclosed housing
    D. an inlet and outlet reciprocating valve

21. The MINIMUM width of each seizing that is wrapped around a wirerope that is to be cut should be _____ the diameter of the rope.

    A. equal to   B. 1 1/2 times
    C. 2 times   D. 3 times

22. Before cutting a 1" diameter non-preformed regular-lay 6x19 wire rope, the MINIMUM number of seizings that should be placed on each side of the spot where the wire rope is to be cut is

    A. 1   B. 2   C. 3   D. 4

23. When seizing a wire rope, a *seizing iron* is mainly used to

    A. measure the length of seizing wire
    B. straighten the seizing wire
    C. loosen a badly made seizing
    D. wrap the seizing tightly

24. Of the following materials, the one from which seizing wire is made is

    A. copper   B. annealed iron
    C. nylon   D. aluminum

25. Oil used on wire rope which goes through the sheaves and over the drum of a crane will generally

    A. cause the drum to slip
    B. increase the life of the rope
    C. gum up the sheaves
    D. cause the wire to have a slimy surface

26. As a result of insertion of a steel thimble into a spliced eye attachment of a wire rope, the   26.____

    A. load will be equally distributed to the wire rope
    B. wire rope will flatten out of shape
    C. wire strands of the rope will tend to break when load is applied
    D. holding power of the attachment will be increased

27. Wedge sockets are MOST frequently used to   27.____

    A. temporarily attach wire rope to a piece of equipment
    B. make permanent attachments of wire rope to a piece of equipment
    C. connect two different sizes of wire rope to each other
    D. adjust the length of wire rope to fit the job

28. A *left-lay, regular-lay* wire rope has   28.____

    A. the wires laid right-handed and the strands left-handed
    B. the wires laid left-handed and the strands right-handed
    C. both wires and strands laid right-handed
    D. both wires and strands laid left-handed

Questions 29 - 33.

DIRECTIONS: Questions 29 through 33 inclusive are to be answered in accordance with the following paragraphs.

Exhaust valve clearance adjustment on diesel engines is very important for proper operation of the engine. Insufficient clearance between the exhaust valve stem and the rocker arm causes a loss of compression and, after a while, burning of the valves and valve seat inserts. On the other hand, too much valve clearance will result in noisy operation of the engine.

Exhaust valves that are maintained in good operating condition will result in efficient combustion in the engine. Valve seats must be true and unpitted and valve stems must work smoothly within the valve guides. Long valve life will result from proper maintenance and operation of the engine.

Engine operating temperatures should be maintained between 160° F and 185° F. Low operating temperatures result in incomplete combustion and the deposit of fuel lacquers on valves.

29. According to the above paragraphs, too much valve clearance will cause the engine to operate   29.____

    A. slowly   B. noisily   C. smoothly   D. cold

30. On the basis of the information given in the above paragraphs, operating temperatures of a diesel engine should be between _____ F and _____ F.   30.____

    A. 125°; 130°   B. 140°; 150°
    C. 160°; 185°   D. 190°; 205°

31. According to the above paragraphs, the deposit of fuel lacquers on valves is caused by   31.____

    A. high operating temperatures
    B. insufficient valve clearance
    C. low operating temperatures
    D. efficient combustion

32. According to the above paragraphs, for efficient operation of the engine, valve seats must   32.____

    A. have sufficient clearance
    B. be true and unpitted
    C. operate at low temperatures
    D. be adjusted regularly

33. According to the above paragraphs, a loss of compression is due to insufficient clearance between the exhaust valve stem and the   33.____

    A. rocker arm   B. valve seat
    C. valve seat inserts   D. valve guides

34. The BEST of the following ways to deal with a helper assigned to you who is a chronic complainer is to   34.____

    A. tell him to stop complaining so much
    B. treat each complaint as if it were valid
    C. walk away from him when he starts to complain
    D. tell him his complaints are senseless

35. An oiler assigned to service your crane has always performed his duties diligently, but for the past several weeks he has been lax.
    Of the following actions, the BEST one to take would be to   35.____

    A. recommend his transfer
    B. report him to your superior
    C. re-assign him to office work
    D. ask him if there is anything wrong

36. Of the following, the BEST procedure for an operator to follow when breaking in a new oiler on the job is to   36.____

    A. assign work that he is capable of performing
    B. give him minor work assignments to do until he proves he is capable of doing the job
    C. praise him even though his work is not satisfactory
    D. criticize the man in a loud manner when he makes an error

37. An operator of a crane working a short distance from where you are operating, is rendered unconscious when the boom of his crane hits an electric power line.
    Of the following, after safely securing your machine, the FIRST procedure for you to follow would be to   37.____

    A. immediately apply artificial respiration to the unconscious operator
    B. call a physician
    C. determine if an electrical hazard still exists aboard the crane
    D. administer a stimulant to the unconscious operator

38. A crane engineman is operating a gasoline-powered crane and sees smoke coming from the engine.
In this situation, the operator should FIRST

    A. call his helper for assistance
    B. get the fire extinguisher
    C. shut the engine off
    D. wait for flames to appear

39. Assume that a helper has fallen off the crane and is unable to move.
The BEST procedure to follow in this instance would be to

    A. seek medical aid, letting him lie where he is
    B. place him in a sitting position
    C. give him a stimulant to drink
    D. call the other workers to remove him from the work site

40. Of the following types of fire extinguishing agents, the one that should NOT be used on an oil fire in an oil storage area is

    A. foam
    B. dry chemical
    C. carbon dioxide
    D. soda acid

KEY (CORRECT ANSWERS)

1. D	11. B	21. A	31. C
2. B	12. A	22. C	32. B
3. D	13. D	23. D	33. A
4. B	14. A	24. B	34. B
5. C	15. C	25. B	35. D
6. A	16. A	26. D	36. A
7. D	17. A	27. A	37. C
8. D	18. A	28. A	38. C
9. B	19. B	29. B	39. A
10. D	20. A	30. C	40. D

EXAMINATION SECTION
TEST 1

DIRECTIONS: Each question or incomplete statement is followed by several suggested answers or completions. Select the one that BEST answers the question or completes the statement. *PRINT THE LETTER OF THE CORRECT ANSWER IN THE SPACE AT THE RIGHT.*

1. The type of crane that requires surface rail tracks is a 1.____

    A. stiff leg derrick
    B. gantry crane
    C. rotary crane
    D. jub crane

2. Dynamic breaking is 2.____

    A. the term used when actuating a trustor brake
    B. a term used when energizing a magnetic type break
    C. closing a magnetic contactor which permits the brake to close
    D. a method of reducing the speed of some hoisting motors when lowering a load

3. Minimum tread diameter for a 6x7 steel wire rope should be *approximately* _____ times the rope diameter. 3.____

    A. 20 B. 24 C. 36 D. 42

4. The type of D.C. *motor most commonly* used for powering cranes is the 4.____

    A. shunt wound motor
    B. compound motor
    C. series wound motor
    D. cumulative compound motor

5. Two similar $\frac{1}{2}$"-6-strand wire ropes are to be spliced together. If the two ropes are to be spliced by a standard short splice, the seizings should be placed _____ feet from the ends. 5.____

    A. 2 B. 5 C. 10 D. 15

6. The type of A.C. motor *most commonly* used for powering cranes is the 6.____

    A. slip-ring type induction motor
    B. synchronous motor
    C. squirrel-cagetype, induction motor
    D. universal motor

7. A square foot of sheet steel 3/8" thick weighs 15.3 lbs. A pile of sheet steel consists of 10 sheets, each measuring 4' x 8' x 3/8". This pile weighs approximately _____ ton(s). 7.____

    A. 1 B. 1.5 C. 2 D. 2.5

8. On A.C. cranes equipped with reverse torque control on the hoist, as in magnet or bucket handling cranes, the motor brake must slow down the motor from about _____ % synch. speed to stand still and then hold the load. 8.____

    A. 35 B. 60 C. 20 D. 100

9. The wire rope which you are to use has a minimum safety factor of 5 and a breaking strength of 10,000 lbs. The maximum load in tons which you would hoist when complying with the above given data is approximately _____ ton(s).

   A. 1   B. 2   C. 3   D. 5

10. On direct current controllers where it is necessary to remove or replace blow out coils, it is very important to

    A. insert the blow out coils to give the proper polarity
    B. cross their leads before connecting them
    C. see that they are wound non-inductive
    D. see that they are not wound non-inductive

11. The blackwall hitch is used

    A. when making a temporary fastening to a hook
    B. to shorten a line
    C. for fastening a rope around a beam
    D. for towing cars

12. Worn pins and bushings in motor solenoid brakes

    A. will decrease the operating solenoid stroke
    B. will increase the operating solenoid stroke
    C. must be lubricated with graphite
    D. should not be lubricated

13. The metal used for socketing wire ropes is

    A. tin
    B. lead
    C. aluminum of the highest commercial purity
    D. zinc

14. To reverse the direction of rotation of a series-wound D.C. motor

    A. reverse both the field and the armature
    B. interchange the armature leads at the motor terminals
    C. rotate the brushes counterclockwise
    D. interchange the lines wires

15. The speed regulation of an A.C. wound rotor induction motor is best obtained by

    A. changing the stator voltage
    B. rotating the brushes on slip rings
    C. varying the resistance in the rotor circuit
    D. using a diverter

16. With the exception of slings with bridge sockets or open sockets, the length of different types of slings is taken

    A. from bearing to bearing
    B. from bearing to bearing times $\frac{1}{2}$

C. from bearing to bearing times 3/4
D. from bearing to bearing times 2

17. The size of the fuse to be used in a circuit depends upon the

    A. size of wire
    B. connected load
    C. voltage of the line
    D. rating of the switch

18. The type of lubricant commonly used for a bridge motor gear case at low temperature (below 32 degrees F) is

    A. S.A.E. 160
    B. S.A.E. 90
    C. S.A.E. 250
    D. dip-gear grease

19. When an operator of an electrically powered crane leaves the car, he *must*

    A. place all controllers in the off position
    B. place all controllers in the off position and pull the main switch
    C. test all the fuses
    D. test all the controllers

20. Variation in the size of driver wheels will cause a bridge crane to operate out of square on the runway with resulting flange wear against the side of the rail. To avoid this condition, it is necessary to keep the driver wheels paired or matched in size.
    As a general rule on cranes, the wheels should be replaced or refinished if the variation in these wheels reaches

    A. 1/16" B. 1/8" C. 5/16" D. 1/4"

21. A D.C. contactor coil has one or two turns short circuited. If the coil is kept in operation

    A. it will immediately burn out
    B. it cannot burn out due only to two shorted turns
    C. it may start to hum excessively
    D. the inducted voltage in shorted turns would cause a large current to circulate and burn out the entire cell

22. If the crane is subject to constant overloading and has been in heavy duty service for a period of ten years, the load-hook should be

    A. annealed and placed back in service
    B. scrapped
    C. tempered and placed back in service
    D. continued in use for another 10 years

23. It is NOT advisable for safety to overload bridge cranes more than _____ % of rated load.

    A. 100 B. 50 C. 25 D. 10

24. In response to a sound or audible signal system the crane engineman shall lower the load when the signal sounded is _____ bells.

    A. 2 B. 3 C. 5 D. 4

3 (#1)

25. Thermal overload protective devices for motors protect the motors against

    A. a short
    B. overload at starting
    C. temporary overloads
    D. sustained overloads

26. If the angle between the boom and the mast is decreased, the load that can be raised

    A. can be increased
    B. cannot be increased
    C. must be decreased by 10%
    D. must be decreased by 20%

27. For best results, new brushes may be fitted to commutators of D.C. machines or slip rings of A.C. machines by using

    A. sandpaper #00
    B. emery cloth
    C. a fine file
    D. sand stone

28. If a crane has a capacity of 27,500 pounds at 25 foot radius, then the load that can be raised at 40 foot radius is

    A. 50,000 pounds
    B. 27,500 pounds
    C. greater than 27,500 pounds
    D. smaller than 27,500 pounds

29. The *primary* purpose of oil in an oil-type circuit breaker is to

    A. lubricate the contents
    B. cool the breaker
    C. limit the load on the breaker
    D. quench the arc

30. A much used crane with bearings of the sleeve type should receive attention at least

    A. daily   B. weekly   C. monthly   D. yearly

31. A dash pot arrangement on a circuit breaker or motor starter provides for

    A. short-circuit protection
    B. under voltage protection
    C. delayed- time action
    D. absorbing mechanical stresses or vibration when the device is closed

32. A greatly worked crane with bearings of the ball or roller type should NOT require bearing inspection more than

    A. semi-annually
    B. weekly
    C. monthly
    D. yearly

33. Limit switches when used in connection with the operation of a hoist, serve the purpose of

    A. limiting the speed of the hoist
    B. stopping the hoist when the hoist motor controller is forced beyond a limiting point of acceleration

C. preventing the operator from raising the load above certain limits
D. preventing the operator from lowering the load

34. Crane bumpers should be

    A. fastened to the rail
    B. fastened to the girder
    C. at least 1/4 the diameter of the truck wheel in height
    D. at least 1/3 the diameter of the truck wheel in height

35. Ordinary "ring-fire," a type of sparking wholly or partially encircling the circumference of the commutator and reddish in color, is a condition *usually* brought about by

    A. incorrect brush pressure
    B. open armature coil
    C. dirty commutator
    D. shorted field coil

36. Bridge crane hoisting brakes should be able to carry

    A. double the rated load
    B. 3 times the rated load
    C. 4 times the rated load
    D. the rated load

37. Magnetic contactor tips are properly adjusted when they

    A. have a wiping or rolling motion in closing and opening
    B. make full face contact in closing and opening
    C. make line contact at the center of the face in opening and closing
    D. make line contact at top and bottom of the face in closing and opening

38. The rails of electric overhead traveling cranes should be of the correct span center throughout their entire length, with both rails level and at the same elevation. An accepted installation should have a center-to-center rail measurement deviation NOT greater than *approximately*

    A. 1 inch   B. two inches   C. 3/4 inch   D. 1/8 inch

39. The object of a rotor rheostat is to

    A. start a squirrel cage induction motor
    B. control the A.C. current of a synchronous motor
    C. start or control the speed of a wound rotor induction motor
    D. control the speed of a squirrel cage motor

40. In ordering fuses, it is necessary to specify

    A. the current capacity
    B. the voltage of the circuit
    C. current and voltage capacity
    D. voltage and length of fuse

41. Fires occurring in and around electrical apparatus are BEST extinguished by applying

    A. water
    B. sand

C. soda acid chemical solution
D. carbon dioxide or carbon tetrachloride

42. When two or more unequal resistances are connected in parallel, the equivalent or resulting resistance is

   A. *greater* than the largest resistance
   B. *smaller* than the smallest resistance
   C. *greater* than the smallest resistance
   D. *equal to* the sum of all the resistances

43. The magnetic contactors for changing direction of the rotation of motors should be

   A. electrically interlocked
   B. mechanically and electrically interlocked
   C. mechanically interlocked
   D. independently operated

44. On a crane, a squeaking noise *usually* means

   A. excessive wear on bearings and/or gear teeth
   B. a dry bearing surface
   C. a rough or dirty commutator
   D. solenoid brakes are out of adjustment

45. Energy consumption, whether A.C. or D.C. is usually measured by means of a

   A. wattmeter   B. kilowatt meter
   C. watthour meter   D. demand meter

46. A two-leg bridle sling with hooks and $\frac{1}{2}$ inch diameter ropes, has a safe load capacity of 3.2 tons with vertical legs.
    When the legs are set at 90 degrees to each other, the safe load in tons is about

    A. 3.2   B. 2.2   C. 1.2   D. 1

47. Periodical inspection should be made of secondary grid resistor connections to see that they are tight and properly made.
    A loosely stacked resistor will *most likely* cause

    A. burning, pitting and a change in resistance
    B. a greater inrush of current
    C. a decrease in current
    D. burning, pitting, and the resistance value will not change

48. The speed of a crane trolley motor is 900 r.p.m. If the motor pinion has 20 teeth and the gear has 80 teeth, the speed of the gear shaft is *most nearly* _____ r.p.m.

    A. 3600   B. 425   C. 325   D. 225

49. An electrical conductor has 19 strands, and the diameter of each strand is 114.7 mils. The size of the conductor in C.M. is about

    A. 400,000   B. 350,000   C. 300,000   D. 250,000

50. The field of a series motor should be

   A. of sufficient cross-section to carry the rated armature current
   B. connected in parallel with the armature
   C. connected across the line
   D. in series with a diver

51. A current transformer has a ratio of 20 to 1. When the ammeter connected to the transformer secondary reads 3.3 amps., the primary current is _____ amps.

   A. 11   B. 33   C. 66   D. 99

52. During manufacture of wire rope the hemp center and strands; are thoroughly impregnated with

   A. lubricant   B. red lead
   C. clear varnish   D. shellac

53. A device which may be used to ascertain whether an electric wiring system is energized with direct or alternating current is(are)

   A. test lamps in multiple   B. test lamps in series
   C. a neon tester   D. a megger

54. The characteristics of the series motor which makes its use desirable, is that a large increase in torque is obtained

   A. with a large increase in voltage
   B. with a moderate increase in current
   C. when lowering a load
   D. with a moderate decrease in current

55. To reverse the direction of rotation of a 3-phase inductions motor

   A. the three line leads are interchanged
   B. the secondary grid leads are interchanged
   C. any two line leads are interchanged
   D. only two secondary grid leads are interchanged

56. The bearings of a wound-rotor induction motor are hot, but not hotter than the other parts of the motor.
    This condition would *most likely* be caused by

   A. dirty oil in the bearings
   B. a short-circuited rotor coil
   C. an overload on the motor
   D. the rings in the bearings not rotating

57. Overload protective units of the time-limit type in circuit breakers or controllers which are used as running protection for motors should be set at NOT more than

   A. 125% of the motor full load current
   B. the maximum starting current of the motor
   C. the current carrying capacity of the wires
   D. 110% of the full load current of the motor

58. In seizing wire rope, the seizing strand should be wound around rope at LEAST _____ times, keeping wraps close together and in tension.

    A. 6   B. 7   C. 9   D. 11

59. The wires of 3-phase 208v circuit carrying 800 amps should be protected by

    A. cartridge fuses with knife blade contact
    B. a circuit breaker
    C. thermo cut-outs
    D. a cut-out switch

60. For safety, the *minimum* number of U-type clips which should be used for securing a $\frac{1}{2}$" wire rope around a thimble is

    A. 3   B. 5   C. 2   D. 4

KEY (CORRECT ANSWERS)

1. B	16. A	31. C	46. B
2. D	17. A	32. B	47. A
3. D	18. B	33. C	48. D
4. C	19. B	34. B	49. D
5. C	20. B	35. B	50. A
6. A	21. B	36. A	51. C
7. D	22. A	37. A	52. A
8. A	23. C	38. D	53. C
9. A	24. B	39. C	54. B
10. A	25. D	40. C	55. C
11. A	26. A	41. D	56. C
12. B	27. A	42. B	57. A
13. D	28. D	43. B	58. B
14. B	29. D	44. B	59. B
15. C	30. A	45. C	60. D

EXAMINATION SECTION
TEST 1

DIRECTIONS: Each question or incomplete statement is followed by several suggested answers or completions. Select the one that BEST answers the question or completes the statement. *PRINT THE LETTER OF THE CORRECT ANSWER IN THE SPACE AT THE RIGHT.*

1. Of the following lubricating greases, the one that is generally known as a heat-resisting grease is _____ grease. 1._____

   A. soda (sodium) soap
   B. lime (calcium) soap
   C. aluminum soap
   D. mixed (soda and lime)

2. The chassis grease recommended for MOST pieces of construction equipment is generally 2._____

   A. lime base-water resistant
   B. SAE-140 E.P.
   C. number 3 cup
   D. number 2 cup

3. The PRIMARY advantage that a friction clutch has over a positive clutch is that the friction clutch 3._____

   A. runs at lower speeds
   B. requires less maintenance
   C. can be engaged at either low or high speeds
   D. runs at high speeds

4. Of the following makes of power plants for cranes, the one which uses diesel fuel is the 4._____

   A. Allis-Chalmers L-525
   B. G.M. 4055-C
   C. Waukesha 140 GKU
   D. Waukesha 140 GKU (with torque converter)

5. In a 2-stroke cycle diesel engine, the cylinder is scavenged by 5._____

   A. the combustion air
   B. the exhaust gases
   C. the injected fuel oil
   D. a mixture of fuel oil and air

6. In a 6 x 19 Seale wire rope, the wires in one strand are 6._____

   A. always of the same size
   B. of different diameters
   C. meshed with soft cores
   D. of the flattened strand type

7. Of the following metals, the one that is USUALLY used for socketing wire ropes is 7._____

   A. lead
   B. tin
   C. zinc
   D. 50-50 solder

8. On the suction stroke of a four-stroke cycle full diesel engine, _____ drawn into the cylinder.

    A. fuel oil only is
    B. air and a full charge of fuel oil are
    C. air only is
    D. air and a one-half charge of fuel oil are

9. The PRIMARY purpose of crossing a belt when connecting two pulleys is to

    A. rotate the shafts in opposite directions
    B. decrease the belt friction contact
    C. be able to use a thinner belt
    D. increase the overall belt efficiency

10. Double-base safety clips having corrugated jaws when used on wire rope in making up an eye develops approximately _____ of the strength of the rope.

    A. 60%   B. 70%   C. 80%   D. 95%

11. The number of ropes usually used on the movable block of a 4 part fall is MOST NEARLY

    A. 6   B. 4   C. 3   D. 2

12.

    In the above sketch, the left P, in pounds, required to raise the 1200 pound block from the ground is MOST NEARLY

    A. 200   B. 160   C. 144   D. 96

13. In the common rail system of solid fuel injection in a diesel engine, a control wedge is generally used to

    A. control the lift of the mechanically operated spray valve
    B. meter the fuel oil at the transfer pump
    C. control the fuel oil level in the fuel tank
    D. fix the fuel oil pressure in the *common rail*

14. In the fuel system for a 4-stroke cycle full diesel engine, the oil travels in sequence from the fuel tank to the

    A. filters, transfer pump, pre-combustion chamber, injection pump, and injection valve
    B. filters, transfer pump, pre-combustion chamber, injection valve, and injection pump
    C. transfer pump, filters, injection pump, injection valve, and pre-combustion chamber
    D. filters, injection pump, transfer pump, injection valve, and pre-combustion chamber

15. The camshaft operating the valves of a 4-stroke cycle diesel engine rotates at _____ speed of the crankshaft.

    A. the same   B. half the
    C. double the   D. four times the

16. The speed of a crane trolley motor is 1200 r.p.m.
    If the motor pinion has 24 teeth and the driven gear has 92 teeth, the speed of the gear shaft is MOST NEARLY

    A. 250   B. 300   C. 350   D. 3600

17. In a 4-stroke cycle full diesel engine, the fuel is ignited by means of

    A. special spark plugs
    B. hot exhaust gases
    C. highly compressed air in the cylinder
    D. glow plugs in the cylinder heads

18. The proper gap on a spark plug can be MOST accurately set by use of a _____ gage.

    A. dial   B. conventional flat feeler
    C. square wire feeler   D. round wire feeler

19. A considerable amount of water in the crankcase of a gasoline engine would NOT be likely due to

    A. a cylinder head crack   B. cylinder head gasket leaks
    C. cylinder block cracks   D. condensation

20. A good program of preventive maintenance would NOT require

    A. having the work done in an off shift
    B. periodic inspection
    C. cleaning the equipment before servicing
    D. accurate records of the servicing done

21. The MAXIMUM ampere rating of the fuse to be used in an existing circuit depends upon the

    A. size of wire in the circuit   B. connected load
    C. voltage of the line   D. rating of the switch

22. On a truck mounted portable air compressor, the differential assembly is located in the

    A. truck transmission housing   B. air compressor crankcase
    C. truck rear housing   D. air regulating equipment

23. In operation, a gasoline driven air compressor is said to be unloaded when the

    A. air compressor is driven at low speed
    B. discharge valves on the air compressor are held in the open position
    C. safety valve on the air compressor is engaged in the open position
    D. inlet valves on the air compressor are held in the open position

24. In reference to air controlled machines operating in mid-winter, the reservoir of the anti-freezer or evaporator should be filled with

    A. methyl alcohol
    B. ethyl alcohol
    C. an alcohol containing an inhibitor
    D. prestone

25. A grade of 1 in 20 is approximately the same as a _____ rise in a _____ run.

    A. 1 foot; 200 inch   B. 1 yard; 125 yard
    C. 10 inch; 200 yard   D. 12 inch; 7 yard

26. The minimum factor of safety of a wire rope that is used for grab buckets should be NOT less than

    A. 4   B. 6   C. 8   D. 10

27. Whenever possible, it is BEST to remove a gear from a shaft by means of

    A. heating the gear with a flame
    B. heavy but uniform blows with a hammer
    C. cooling the shaft with dry ice
    D. an appropriate wheel puller

28. For digging open cuts, drainage ditches, and gravel pits, where the material is to be moved from 20 to 3000 feet before dumping, one would use a _____ Excavator.

    A. Crawler Crane   B. Gantry Crane
    C. Drag-line   D. Diesel Shovel

29. If a bucket capable of carrying 5 3/4 cubic yards is loaded to 3/4 of its capacity, it will be carrying, in cubic yards, APPROXIMATELY

    A. 3 1/2   B. 4 1/4   C. 4 7/8   D. 5 1/4

30. A guy line is generally used with a

    A. diesel driven scraper   B. stiff leg derrick
    C. truck mounted clamshell   D. gantry crane

31. The point shaft on a boom is usually located near the

    A. top of the boom   B. bottom of the boom
    C. dead end cable socket   D. hoist drum

32. Assume that a horizontal roller chain drive is used to transmit power to the jack shaft of a crane.
    For proper tension in the roller chain,

    A. there should be a small amount of sag in the chain
    B. the sag should bring the chain down to the center line of the driving sprocket
    C. there should be no sag in the chain
    D. the chain should make an angle of at least 50 when leaving the driving sprocket

33.

In reference to the above sketch, in order to balance the 100 lbs. belt pull on the 6" diameter pulley, a belt pull of approximately 67 lbs. should be attached to which one of the following pulleys?

   A. 16"   B. 12"   C. 9"   D. 8"

34. Of the following statements concerning torque converter equipped machines, the one which is MOST NEARLY CORRECT is that

    A. the torque converter is a transmission with a limited number of ratios
    B. at normal speeds, the line pulls are less than on a standard mechanical drive machine
    C. the shock loading is increased during shovel operations
    D. at stall conditions, the engine is *putting out* its maximum power

35. To transmit power between two shafts that are in the same plane but 90° to each other, it is BEST to use _____ gear(s).

    A. spur   B. worm and spur
    C. bevel   D. herringbone

36. Under normal operations, the oil pressure regulating valve piston on a torque converter should be removed and cleaned once

    A. a day   B. a week
    C. a month   D. every three months

37. The operating oil pressure in a torque converter usually has a range of approximately _____ to _____ psi.

    A. 15; 20   B. 35; 40   C. 50; 65   D. 70; 85

38. For successful operation of a machine equipped with a torque converter, the operator should

    A. watch the load or bucket
    B. listen to the engine
    C. vary the output, shaft governor setting
    D. vary the engine governor setting

39. The clutch torque delivered by a fluid coupling is APPROXIMATELY _____ the engine torque.

    A. the same as
    B. twice that of
    C. three times that of
    D. four times that of

40. The type of knot that can be used for shortening a rope which does not have free ends, without cutting the rope, is called a

    A. sheet bend
    B. hawser bend
    C. sheepshank
    D. clove hitch

KEY (CORRECT ANSWERS)

1. A	11. B	21. A	31. A
2. A	12. C	22. C	32. A
3. C	13. A	23. D	33. C
4. B	14. C	24. A	34. D
5. A	15. B	25. D	35. C
6. B	16. B	26. B	36. B
7. C	17. C	27. D	37. B
8. C	18. D	28. C	38. A
9. A	19. D	29. B	39. A
10. D	20. A	30. B	40. C

TEST 2

DIRECTIONS: Each question or incomplete statement is followed by several suggested answers or completions. Select the one that BEST answers the question or completes the statement. *PRINT THE LETTER OF THE CORRECT ANSWER IN THE SPACE AT THE RIGHT.*

1. The purpose of the hand-operated choke on a gasoline engine is to

   A. provide an excess amount of air for easy starting
   B. provide a rich mixture for starting
   C. increase the jet opening for more gasoline
   D. provide a lean mixture for starting

   1.____

2. In reference to gasoline engines, a common cause of engine back pressure is a

   A. corroded muffler   B. corroded exhaust pipe
   C. loose muffler   D. clogged muffler passage

   2.____

3. A *right* lang lay wire rope has

   A. wires and strands laid opposite to one another
   B. the wires laid left and the strands laid right
   C. both wires and strands laid to the right
   D. the wires laid right and the strands laid left

   3.____

4. An ambidextrous operator during his working hours will MOST likely

   A. handle his controls with ease
   B. handle his controls slowly
   C. be handicapped in lifting loads
   D. understand instructions easily

   4.____

5. Assume that a two leg bridle sling with hooks and 5/8 inch diameter ropes has a safe load capacity of 4.4 tons when the legs are in a vertical position.
   If the legs are set at 90% to each other, the safe load capacity, in tons, of this sling is MOST NEARLY

   A. 6.2   B. 4.4   C. 3.1   D. 2.2

   5.____

6. Fires in and around electrical equipment are BEST extinguished by using

   A. water
   B. sand
   C. carbon dioxide
   D. soda acid chemical solution

   6.____

7. A dipper trip assembly is USUALLY found on a _____ boom.

   A. shovel   B. crane
   C. drag-line   D. clamshell

   7.____

8. A convenient practical method of checking if the spark plugs in a gasoline engine are firing is to

   A. use a high tension voltmeter
   B. short them with an insulated handle screwdriver
   C. replace the spark plugs one at a time in the order of firing
   D. use a high tension ammeter across each spark plug

9. In a two-stage air compressor, if numbers are given to components as follows: 1st stage cylinder (1), 2nd stage cylinder (2), receiver tank (3), and intercooler (4); the path of the air when compressor is operating would be

   A. 1, 2, 4, 3
   B. 4, 1, 2, 3
   C. 1, 3, 2, 4
   D. 1, 4, 2, 3

10. When a lead acid type battery is fully charged, the hydrometer reading should be APPROXIMATELY

    A. 1.280
    B. 1.190
    C. 1.150
    D. 1.000

11. If battery acid comes into contact with the skin, the BEST thing to do is

    A. wipe the contact area with a piece of cloth
    B. wash away with large quantities of water
    C. wash away with a salt solution
    D. place a tourniquet above the contact area

12.

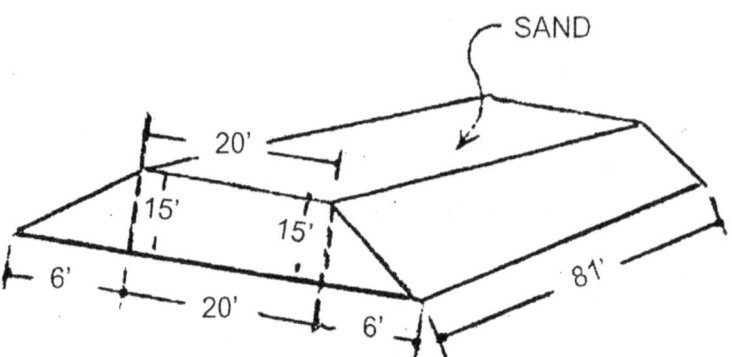

Assume that a section of a sand barge is uniformly loaded with sand as shown above.
The total number of cubic yards of sand in this section is MOST NEARLY

    A. 120
    B. 790
    C. 1170
    D. 2260

13. With reference to a gasoline-driven air compressor, the tern *CFM* refers to the

    A. gasoline consumption of the engine
    B. type of unloader used on the compressor
    C. capacity of the compressor
    D. maximum revolutions of the compressor

14. Backfiring through the carburetor of a gasoline engine may MOST likely be caused by   14.____

    A. an advanced spark
    B. a blown cylinder head gasket
    C. poor combustion
    D. a defective condenser

15. Vapor-lock in a gasoline engine is MOST likely due to   15.____

    A. fuel forming bubbles in the gas line
    B. the carburetor being clogged with dirt
    C. an over rich gas-air mixture
    D. a break in the fuel pump diaphragm

16. Of the following lubricating greases, the one that is water-resistant and can be used   16.____
    where the operating temperature does not exceed 175° F is _____ grease.

    A. lime (calcium) soap   B. soda (sodium) soap
    C. aluminum soap   D. mixed (soda and lime)

17. The speed regulation of an A.C. wound rotor induction motor is BEST obtained by   17.____

    A. using a diverter
    B. varying the resistance in the rotor circuit
    C. varying the stator voltage
    D. rotating the brushes on the slip rings

18. The type of A.C. motor commonly used for powering electric cranes is the _____ motor.   18.____

    A. slip ring type induction
    B. synchronous
    C. squirrel-cage type induction
    D. universal

19. A dash pot arrangement on a circuit breaker or motor starter USUALLY provides for   19.____

    A. under-voltage protection
    B. short-circuit protection
    C. absorbing mechanical stresses or vibration when the device is closed
    D. delayed-time action

20. The PRIMARY importance of outrigging on a truck crane is   20.____

    A. to prevent the load from swinging
    B. to operate the bucket
    C. for lateral support of truck body
    D. to hold the boom in position

21. A shovel equipped with a dual crowd will MOST likely   21.____

    A. handle more cubic yards of material per hour
    B. require superior operators
    C. stall under harder digging
    D. have less tension in the crowd cable

22. The quotation, *When an assembly is removed from a crane for replacement of a bushing, gear, or any individual part, it is an excellent practice to completely recondition the entire assembly.*
    Following the advice in this quotation, the crane engineman will MOST likely learn that

    A. it is cheaper to buy two or more different parts
    B. repetition of work on repairs can be eliminated
    C. replacement parts will wear less than original parts
    D. replacement of one part in an assembly is less costly in the long run

23. In reference to overhead traveling bucket cranes, the term dynamic braking means MOST NEARLY

    A. actuating a trustor brake
    B. energizing a magnetic type brake
    C. closing a magnetic contactor which permits the brake to close
    D. a method of reducing the speed of hoisting motors when lowering a load

24. The type of lubricant commonly used for a bridge motor gear case at low temperature (below 32° F) is

    A. S.A.E. 90
    B. S.A.E. 160
    C. S.A.E. 250
    D. dip-gear grease

25. A gear-type transfer pump is one that USUALLY contains

    A. hydraulic plungers
    B. rollers and pinions
    C. twin gear elements
    D. poppet type valves

26. On a shovel boom, the shipper shaft is USUALLY located near the

    A. top of the boom
    B. bottom of the boom
    C. jack shaft drum
    D. mid-point of the boom

27. The characteristic of a series motor which makes its use desirable for cranes is that a large increase in torque is obtained

    A. with a large increase in voltage
    B. with a moderate increase in current
    C. when lowering a load
    D. with a moderate decrease in current

28. The compression ratio of a modern diesel engine has an approximate range of (with no starting ignition device)

    A. 3-5
    B. 6-8
    C. 9-11
    D. 12-22

29. If you were to instruct an oiler to do a sequence of jobs and operations, he would MOST likely do them

    A. in any order
    B. without regards to specifications
    C. when the machine is down
    D. in the prescribed order

5 (#2)

30. The lifting ability of a crawler-mounted crane PRIMARILY depends upon the

   A. gearing
   B. engine power
   C. balance of the crane
   D. strength of the cables

31. The breaking strength of a new 1/2" diameter 6 x 19 fiber core wire rope made of plow steel is APPROXIMATELY _____ tons.

   A. 2   B. 3   C. 5   D. 10

32. Of the following tools for cutting wire rope used on construction equipment, the one that is BEST is a(n)

   A. hacksaw
   B. standard bolt cutter
   C. oxyacetylene torch
   D. cold chisel

33. The purpose of adding a jib boom to the regular boom of a crane is to

   A. act as a counterweight when lifting
   B. prevent overloading
   C. shift the center of gravity
   D. obtain greater reach

34. When a crane is equipped with a jib boom, the lifting capacity of the boom is APPROXIMATELY _____ the crane load.

   A. 1/2 of
   B. 3/4 of
   C. the same as
   D. 1 1/2 times

35. Of the following bell or whistle hoist signals, the one that is customarily used to signal the lowering of a load is _____ quick signal(s).

   A. two
   B. three
   C. one
   D. a series of

36. An authorized signalman working in conjunction with the crane operator has his arm extended, fingers clenched, and thumb upward while moving his hand up and down. The signalman is signalling the crane operator to

   A. lift the boom up
   B. lower the load
   C. hoist the load
   D. stop immediately (emergency)

Questions 37-40.

DIRECTIONS: Questions 37 through 40, inclusive, are to be answered in accordance with the paragraph below.

Operators spotting loads with long booms and working around men need the smooth, easy operation and positive control of uniform pressure swing clutches. There are no jerks or grabs with these large disc-type clutches because there is always even pressure over the entire clutch lining surface. In the conventional band-type swing clutch, the pressure varies between dead and live ends of the band. The uniform pressure swing clutch has excellent provision for heat dissipation. The driving elements, which are always rotating, have a great number of fins cast in them. This gives them an impeller or blower action for cooling, resulting in longer life and freedom from frequent adjustment.

37. According to the above paragraph, it may be said that conventional band-type swing clutches have

    A. even pressure on the clutch lining
    B. larger contact area
    C. smaller contact area
    D. uneven pressure on the clutch lining

    37.____

38. According to the above paragraph, machines equipped with uniform pressure swing clutches will

    A. give better service under all conditions
    B. require no clutch adjustment
    C. give positive control of hoist
    D. provide better control of swing

    38.____

39. According to the above paragraph, it may be said that the rotation of the driving elements of the uniform pressure swing clutch is always

    A. continuous
    B. constant
    C. varying
    D. uncertain

    39.____

40. According to the above paragraph, freedom from frequent adjustment is due to the

    A. operator's smooth, easy operation
    B. positive control of the clutch
    C. cooling effect of the rotating fins
    D. larger contact area of the bigger clutch

    40.____

KEY (CORRECT ANSWERS)

1.	B	11.	B	21.	A	31.	D
2.	D	12.	C	22.	B	32.	C
3.	C	13.	C	23.	D	33.	D
4.	A	14.	B	24.	A	34.	A
5.	C	15.	A	25.	C	35.	B
6.	C	16.	D	26.	D	36.	A
7.	A	17.	B	27.	B	37.	D
8.	B	18.	A	28.	D	38.	D
9.	D	19.	D	29.	D	39.	A
10.	A	20.	C	30.	C	40.	C

EXAMINATION SECTION
TEST 1

DIRECTIONS: Each question or incomplete statement is followed by several suggested answers or completions. Select the one that BEST answers the question or completes the statement. *PRINT THE LETTER OF THE CORRECT ANSWER IN THE SPACE AT THE RIGHT.*

Questions 1-9.

DIRECTIONS: Questions 1 through 9 refer to the figure below, a diagram of hand signals used in rigging and hoisting operations. Place the letter that corresponds to each diagrammed signal in the space at the right.

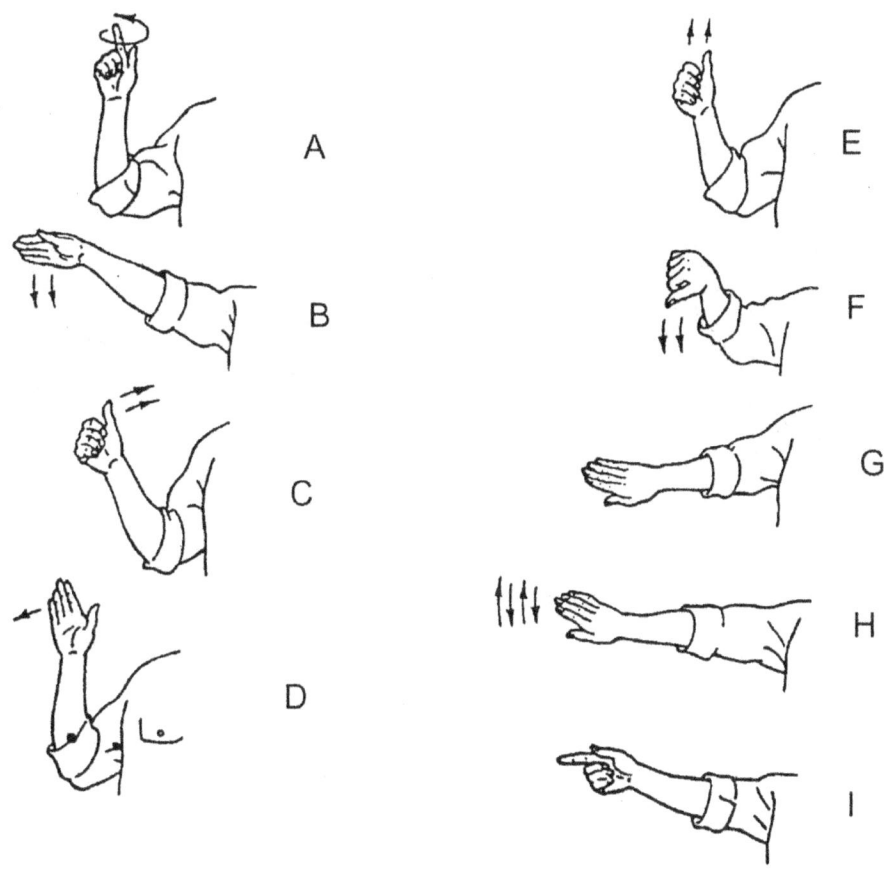

1. Boom up   1.____

2. Slew boom   2.____

3. Stop   3.____

4. Rack trolley   4.____

5. Lower load   5.____

6. Boom down 6.____

7. Emergency stop 7.____

8. Travel crane bridge or caterpillar 8.____

9. Hoist load 9.____

Questions 10-17.

DIRECTIONS: Questions 10 through 17 refer to the figure below, a diagram of a typical crane operating cycle. Place the letter that corresponds to each diagrammed component in the space at the right.

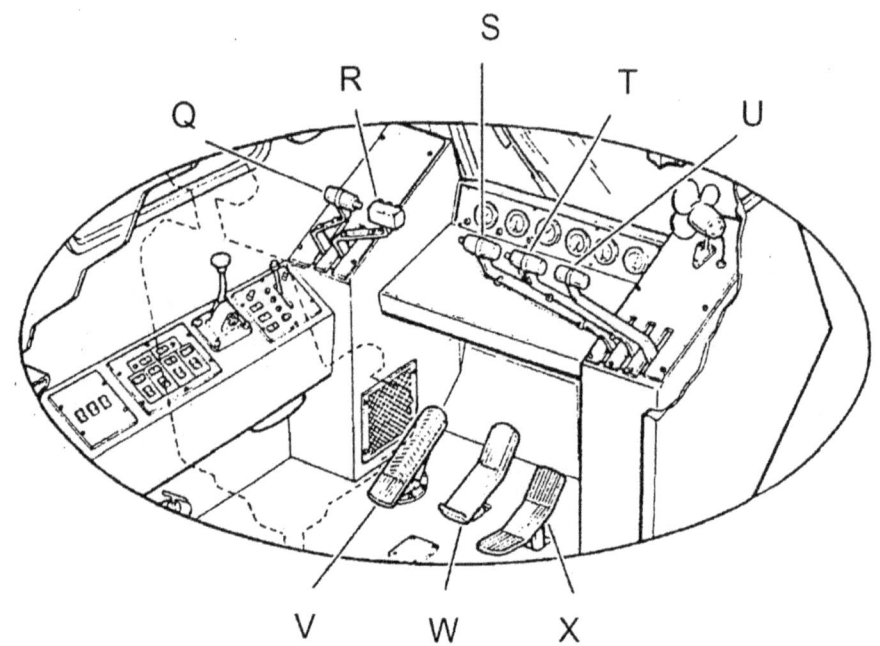

10. Main winch lever 10.____

11. Boom hoist pedal 11.____

12. Telescope lever 12.____

13. Engine throttle pedal 13.____

14. Boom hoist lever 14.____

15. Swing brake pedal 15.____

16. Swing lever 16.____

17. Auxiliary winch lever 17.____

18. A wire rope used with cranes or derricks must be removed from service when _____ the original diameter of the outside individual wires is worn. 18.____

    A. 1/8   B. 1/5   C. 1/3   D. 1/2

19. Each of the following is a type of heavy-lift attachment used with mobile cranes EXCEPT

    A. trailing counterweight B. luffing jib
    C. guy derrick D. ring system

20. A guy derrick system provides a mast with AT LEAST _____ guy lines.

    A. 6 B. 8 C. 10 D. 12

21. Truck-mounted booms are typically used for loads that do NOT exceed _____ tons.

    A. 5-10 B. 10-20 C. 15-30 D. 20-35

22. If a spur-geared hoist will not hold a load in suspension, each of the following is a possible cause EXCEPT

    A. broken or worn ratchet teeth
    B. deformed lift wheel teeth
    C. worn brake parts
    D. lower hook or load side of chain on wrong side of liftwheel

23. The MAXIMUM rate for swinging a load with a crane structure is typically set at

    A. 2 B. 4 C. 7 D. 15

24. What type of erection equipment has the LARGEST angle between its topping lift line and boom?

    A. Stiff-leg derrick B. Tower crane
    C. Truck-mounted crane D. Guy derrick

25. The telescoping boom has a load capacity of APPROXIMATELY _____ pounds.

    A. 25,000 B. 45,000 C. 70,000 D. 100,000

KEY (CORRECT ANSWERS)

1. E
2. I
3. G
4. C
5. B

6. F
7. H
8. D
9. A
10. T

11. X
12. R
13. V
14. U
15. W

16. Q
17. S
18. C
19. B
20. C

21. B
22. B
23. B
24. D
25. C

TEST 2

DIRECTIONS: Each question or incomplete statement is followed by several suggested answers or completions. Select the one that BEST answers the question or completes the statement. *PRINT THE LETTER OF THE CORRECT ANSWER IN THE SPACE AT THE RIGHT.*

1. Equipment or machines in transit, with no load and boom lowered, must maintain a minimum clearance of AT LEAST _____ feet between electric lines rated between 50 to 345 kV and any part of the crane.

    A. 4 B. 8 C. 10 D. 16

    1._____

2. According to the PCSA (Power Crane and Shovel Association), the load capacity of a mobile crane is between _____% of the crane's tipping load in the direction of least stability.

    A. 45-55 B. 55-75 C. 65-85 D. 75-90

    2._____

3. A wire running rope used with cranes or derricks must be removed from service when there are _____ randomly distributed broken wires in one lay.

    A. 1 B. 3 C. 6 D. 9

    3._____

4. Which of the following earth surfaces has a bearing capacity of about 4 tons per square foot?

    A. Loose sandy gravel B. Hardpan over rock
    C. Stiff clay D. Compact fine sand

    4._____

5. For most mobile cranes, the MINIMUM load radius is approximately _____ feet.

    A. 8 B. 12 C. 20 D. 24

    5._____

6. A configuration of two gin poles with a horizontal beam across its pole heads is known as a(n)

    A. A-frame B. guy derrick
    C. basket derrick D. gallows frame

    6._____

7. The approximate load limit, at a horizontal load radius of 30 feet, for a 12 1/2-ton crane using a 2-part hoist line is _____ pounds.

    A. 10,000 B. 17,000 C. 24,000 D. 36,000

    7._____

8. What is the term used to denote any lines that travel over drums or sheaves?

    A. Load falls B. Running lines
    C. Guy lines D. Standing lines

    8._____

9. Equipment or machines in transit, with no load and boom lowered, must maintain a minimum clearance of AT LEAST _____ feet between electric lines rated between 345 to 750 kV and any part of the crane.

    A. 4 B. 8 C. 10 D. 16

    9._____

10. Which of the following earth surfaces has a bearing capacity of about 1 ton per square foot?

    A. Soft rock
    B. Firm sandy gravel
    C. Medium sand
    D. Soft clay

11. Most gin poles should NOT typically lean to a vertical angle greater than _____°.

    A. 5   B. 10   C. 15   D. 30

12. A wire rope used with cranes or derricks with a diameter of 7/8" to 1 1/8" must be removed from service when its nominal diameter is reduced more than _____ inch.

    A. 1/64   B. 1/32   C. 3/64   D. 1/16

13. Which type of mobile crane is BEST suited for heavy lifting without much movement?

    A. Rough-terrain
    B. Truck-mounted
    C. High-lift
    D. Crawler

14. The total load capacity for MOST luffing tower cranes is _____ tons.

    A. 12   B. 24   C. 35   D. 45

15. The MOST maneuverable of all erection equipment is the _____ crane.

    A. truck-mounted
    B. crawler
    C. gantry
    D. wheeled

16. What is the lift capacity of a heavy-duty link chain air hoist?

    A. 500 pounds
    B. 1 ton
    C. 3 tons
    D. 8 tons

17. Which of the following earth surfaces has a bearing capacity of about 2 tons per square foot?

    A. Hardpan over rock
    B. Firm sandy gravel
    C. Medium clay
    D. Compact clay/sand/gravel

18. Equipment or machines in transit, with no load and boom lowered, must maintain a minimum clearance of AT LEAST _____ feet between electric lines rated less than 50 kV and any part of the crane.

    A. 4   B. 8   C. 10   D. 16

19. Generally, the maximum load for the largest tower crane unit with a horizontal jib at a 110-foot radius is considered to be _____ tons.

    A. 2   B. 12   C. 35   D. 60

20. The load-moment-indicator system of a crane is typically used to monitor each of the following functions EXCEPT

    A. drum rotation
    B. boom angle
    C. working quadrant
    D. telescoping boom length

21. According to the PCSA standard, the rated load limit of a crawler crane is _____ % of the machine's tipping load.

    A. 65 B. 75 C. 85 D. 95

22. For maximum tower crane loads, the lifting speed is GENERALLY _____ feet per minute.

    A. 10-20 B. 30-40 C. 45-55 D. 65-70

23. Which of the following types of tower crane mountings is MOST versatile?

    A. Static base
    B. Climbing base
    C. Saddle jib
    D. Traveling base

24. Mobile cranes with the shortest booms are limited in their reach for heavy loads to within a radius of approximately _____ feet.

    A. 12 B. 17 C. 24 D. 35

25. If the hook of an all-electric chain hoist will lower but not raise, each of the following is a possible cause EXCEPT

    A. phase failure
    B. excessive load
    C. wrong voltage
    D. inoperative motor reversing switch

KEY (CORRECT ANSWERS)

1.	C	11.	B
2.	C	12.	D
3.	C	13.	D
4.	A	14.	C
5.	B	15.	B
6.	D	16.	C
7.	B	17.	C
8.	B	18.	A
9.	D	19.	D
10.	D	20.	A

21. B
22. B
23. B
24. B
25. C

EXAMINATION SECTION
TEST 1

DIRECTIONS: Each question or incomplete statement is followed by several suggested answers or completions. Select the one that BEST answers the question or completes the statement. *PRINT THE LETTER OF THE CORRECT ANSWER IN THE SPACE AT THE RIGHT.*

1. To permit both vertical wheel displacement and an equalization of loading on the wheels of a crane, a rigger must assemble a

    A. barrel   B. dog   C. horse   D. bogie

2. What type of erection assembly has a vertical mast that is shorter than its boom?

    A. High lift
    C. Gantry crane
    B. Stiff-leg derrick
    D. Guy derrick

3. Typically, how many drums are required to provide power to the main hoisting cable on the upperstructure of a cable-controlled crane?

    A. 1   B. 2   C. 3   D. 4

4. The approximate load limit, at a horizontal load radius of 40 feet, for a 25-ton crane using a multi-part hoist line is _____ pounds.

    A. 10,000   B. 17,000   C. 28,000   D. 36,000

5. To reduce the unit bearing pressure on the supporting surface, _____ are typically placed beneath mobile crane tracks or outrigger floats.

    A. backstays
    C. pendants
    B. cribbing
    D. footblocks

6. Which of the following cross-sectional shapes is NOT normally used in the design of concentric sections of a telescoping boom?

    A. Triangular
    C. Rectangular
    B. Round
    D. Trapezoidal

7. What type of jib boom is used to extend the maximum height of tower cranes that are mounted on slewing platforms?

    A. Chicago   B. Saddle   C. Lift   D. Luffing

8. Generally, the MAXIMUM load for the smallest tower crane unit with a horizontal jib at a 30-foot radius is considered to be _____ tons.

    A. 2   B. 12   C. 35   D. 60

9. What is the lift capacity of a heavy-duty wire rope air hoist?

    A. 750 pounds
    C. 5 tons
    B. 1 ton
    D. 15 tons

10. According to the PCSA standard, the rated load limit of a wheel-mounted crane is _____ % of the machine's tipping load.

    A. 65   B. 75   C. 85   D. 95

11. The point of contact between the rope and drum where the rope changes layers is known as the

    A. flange point
    B. float
    C. whip
    D. fleet point

12. The line speed of cranes USUALLY ranges between _____ feet/minute.

    A. 80-125   B. 150-170   C. 150-225   D. 175-300

13. Which of the following is NOT typically carried by the counter jib on a tower crane assembly using a saddle jib?

    A. Counterweights
    B. Power plant
    C. Load winch
    D. Pendant anchors

14. Which of the following functions should typically be mechanically driven, rather than hydraulically?

    A. Load hoist
    B. Travel
    C. Boom hoist
    D. Load swing

15. The type of mobile crane that offers the GREATEST stability on natural ground is the

    A. rough-terrain
    B. truck-mounted
    C. high-lift
    D. crawler

16. The term for the angle between the centerline of a jib and the centerline of the boom on which it is mounted is _____ angle.

    A. swing   B. offset   C. topping   D. fleet

17. At a load radius of 100 feet, a gantry crane can handle up to _____ tons.

    A. 15   B. 40   C. 60   D. 80

18. To calculate the safety of total bearing for a mobile crane, each of the following factors must be known EXCEPT

    A. area of crane contacting surface
    B. load capacity of lift line
    C. bearing capacity of earth surface
    D. total loaded weight of crane

19. The lifting capacity of the largest gin poles is about _____ tons.

    A. 80   B. 150   C. 300   D. 500

20. The rope used for erection purposes is MOST commonly made from

    A. mild plow steel
    B. crucible cast steel
    C. iron
    D. improved plow steel

21. The common 6 x 19 lift line, with a diameter of 1/2 inch and a safety factor of 4.0, can safely lift APPROXIMATELY _____ ton(s).

    A. 1   B. 2.5   C. 5   D. 7.5

22. A guy derrick system uses guy lines that are USUALLY _____ inches in diameter. 22.____
    A. 1/2-1 B. 1-1 1/2 C. 1 1/2-2 D. 2-2 1/2

23. If an all-electric chain hoist will not operate at slow speed in either direction, the MOST likely cause is 23.____
    A. open circuit
    B. inoperative limit switches
    C. extreme external heat
    D. brake dragging

24. What type of crane typically uses a knuckleboom? 24.____
    A. Crawler   B. Tower
    C. Truck-mounted   D. Gantry

25. A fully extended high-lift telescoping boom, with an added jib, has a MAXIMUM reach of approximately _____ feet. 25.____
    A. 80-90 B. 90-110 C. 110-130 D. 130-140

KEY (CORRECT ANSWERS)

1. D   11. A
2. B   12. B
3. B   13. D
4. B   14. A
5. B   15. D

6. A   16. B
7. D   17. B
8. A   18. B
9. D   19. C
10. B   20. D

21. B
22. C
23. A
24. C
25. D

TEST 2

DIRECTIONS: Each question or incomplete statement is followed by several suggested answers or completions. Select the one that BEST answers the question or completes the statement. *PRINT THE LETTER OF THE CORRECT ANSWER IN THE SPACE AT THE RIGHT.*

1. Guy ropes attach to a fitting mounted at the top of a derrick mast known as a(n)   1.____

    A. spider   B. topping   C. tackle   D. rooster

2. Which of the following types of cranes is mounted on a single-engine, self-propelled wheel mounting?   2.____

    A. Rough-terrain   B. Crawler
    C. High-lift   D. Truck-mounted

3. The _____ sheave is used to prevent excessive fleet angle during crane operation.   3.____

    A. drum   B. plain bore
    C. self-lubricating   D. fleeting

4. Which of the following earth surfaces has a bearing capacity of about 12 tons per square foot?   4.____

    A. Hard, sound rock   B. Hardpan over rock
    C. Soft rock   D. Compact clay/sand/gravel

5. The telescoping boom typically has a MAXIMUM working radius of _____ feet.   5.____

    A. 17   B. 24   C. 45   D. 72

6. What type of erection equipment is considered to be MOST economical in terms of cost per pound hoisted?   6.____

    A. Stiff-leg derrick   B. Tower crane
    C. Truck-mounted crane   D. Guy derrick

7. According to SAE standards, the load hoist drums of a cable-controlled crane must have a diameter of AT LEAST _____ times the nominal diameter of the rope line used with them.   7.____

    A. 12   B. 15   C. 18   D. 21

8. A fully extended high-lift telescoping boom has a maximum reach of approximately _____ feet.   8.____

    A. 80-90   B. 90-110   C. 110-130   D. 130-140

9. Which of the following is NOT a factor used to determine the stability of a loaded crawler crane?   9.____

    A. Boom weight   B. Load carrying capacity
    C. Lift angle   D. Load radius

10. A _____ is mounted to the base of a derrick mast to receive and guide the ropes used for swinging.

    A. butt section
    B. foot mast
    C. footblock
    D. bull wheel

11. What is the typical lift capacity of a hand-chain hoist?

    A. 800 pounds
    B. 5 tons
    C. 25 tons
    D. 50 tons

12. When outriggers are used on a mobile crane, the wheels or crawler tracks within the smallest radius containing the outriggers must be relieved of _____ % of the weight by outrigger jacks or blocking.

    A. 50 B. 70 C. 85 D. 100

13. What type of tower crane mounting, consisting of a steel-legged structure that adds little support weight, is used when passage beneath the crane is necessary, or when the crane travels on rails?

    A. Portal B. Gantry C. Revolver D. Overhead

14. _____ stability is NOT one of the stability factors that must be checked before placing a tower crane into service.

    A. Basic
    B. Rated
    C. Dynamic
    D. Extreme load

15. If the hook of an all-electric chain hoist fails to stop at either or both ends of travel, each of the following is a possible cause EXCEPT

    A. shaft not rotating
    B. open circuit
    C. limit switch failure
    D. loose guide plate

16. The PCSA requires that for mobile cranes, the weight bearing down on all wheels, outriggers, crawler tracks or idlers on the side or end of the undercarriage supporting the least load shall NOT be less than _____% of the total weight of the crane.

    A. 5 B. 10 C. 15 D. 20

17. The measure for stability against backward tipping of a truck- or wheel-mounted crane is based on all wheels on the side of the carrier under the loaded side/end of the crane taking AT LEAST _____ % of the weight of the equipment.

    A. 5 B. 15 C. 25 D. 35

18. Where space between buildings does not allow the back projecting part of a tower crane jib to extend, the lift-loading jib can be balanced by

    A. gantry-type backstay
    B. free-hanging counterweight
    C. outriggers
    D. luffing jib

19. A two-part line allows approximately _____ the lifting speed of a single line.   19.____

    A. the same as   B. one-half
    C. twice   D. three times

20. Which special tower crane mounting is a fixed structure to which the crane's slewing ring is attached?   20.____

    A. Portal   B. Pedestal   C. Overhead   D. Gantry

21. According to the PCSA standard, the rated load limit of a crane using outriggers is _____ % of the machine's tipping load.   21.____

    A. 65   B. 75   C. 85   D. 95

22. Derrick booms are swung by _____ lines reeved to the boom.   22.____

    A. winch   B. sill   C. tag   D. vang

23. The highest working vertical angle of a telescoping boom is APPROXIMATELY _____.   23.____

    A. 30   B. 45   C. 60   D. 80

24. The approximate load limit, at a horizontal load radius of 20 feet, for a 60-ton crane using a multi-part hoist line is _____ pounds.   24.____

    A. 15,000   B. 25,000   C. 40,000   D. 55,000

25. For a cable-controlled crane with a latticed boom that requires an additional drum for raising and lowering the boom, the boom hoist diameter must be AT LEAST _____ times the nominal diameter of the rope line used with it.   25.____

    A. 12   B. 15   C. 18   D. 21

EXAMINATION SECTION
TEST 1

DIRECTIONS: Each question or incomplete statement is followed by several suggested answers or completions. Select the one that BEST answers the question or completes the statement. *PRINT THE LETTER OF THE CORRECT ANSWER IN THE SPACE AT THE RIGHT.*

Questions 1-15.

DIRECTIONS: Questions 1 through 15 are to be answered on the basis of the figure below, a diagram of the machinery typically found in a mobile crane upperstructure. Place the letter that corresponds to each diagrammed component in the space at the right.

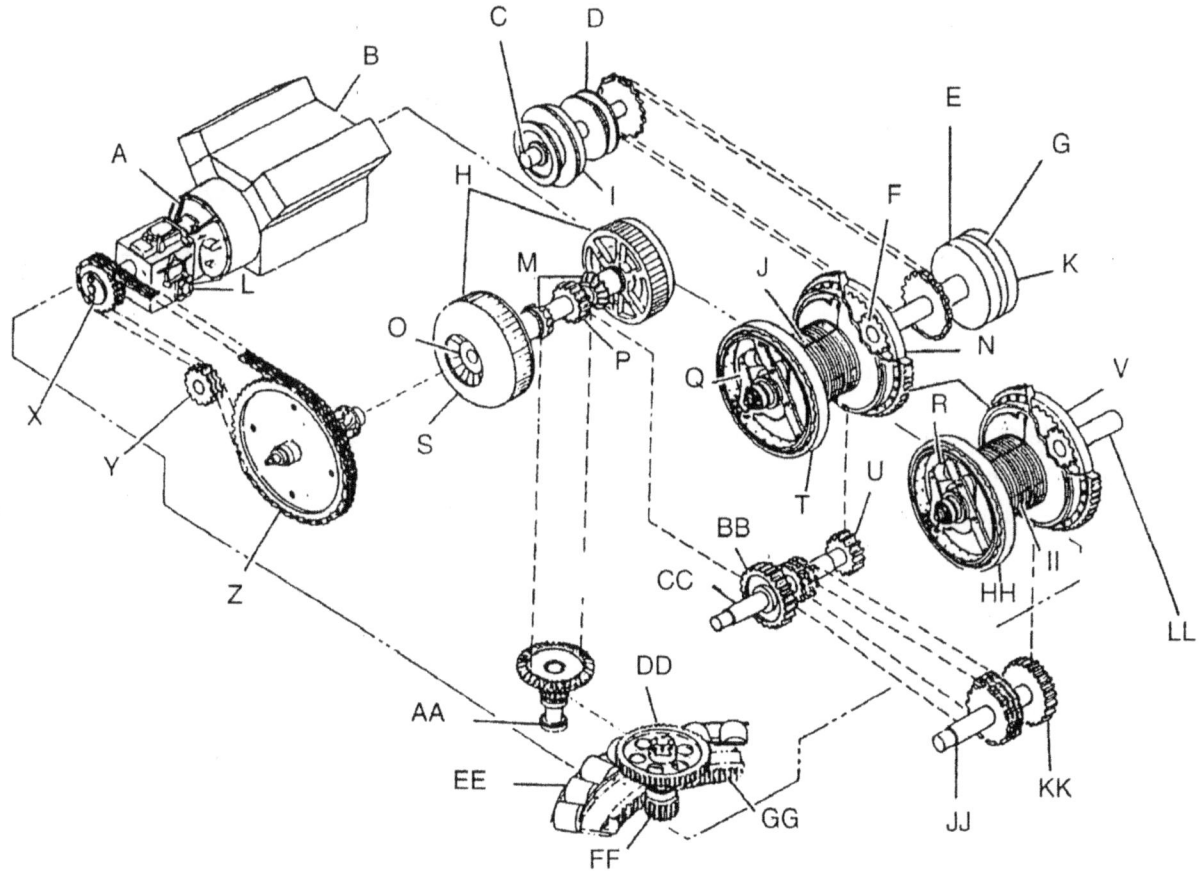

1. Planetary gear 1.____

2. Brake band surface 2.____

3. Magnetorque sprocket 3.____

4. Swing shaft pinion 4.____

5. Jack shaft 5.____

6. Engine clutch 6.____

7. Boon hoist clutch   7._____

8. Swing gear   8._____

9. Engine transmission or torque converter   9._____

10. Planetary pinion   10._____

11. Front drum   11._____

12. Outer drum drive pinion   12._____

13. Engine sprocket   13._____

14. Rear drum clutch   14._____

15. Intermediate reduction shaft   15._____

16. To ensure that all sections of a telescoping boom are thoroughly lubricated, the boom should be extended and brushed with _____-type lubricant.   16._____

   A. CG   B. EP   C. WGL   D. OG

17. If the hook of an all-electric chain hoist lowers when the hoisting control is operated, the probable cause is   17._____

   A. low voltage   B. brake dragging
   C. open control circuit   D. phase failure

18. Records are required of visual inspections made of hoists operating under _____ service conditions.   18._____

   A. infrequent   B. normal
   C. heavy   D. severe

19. The rated load of a rope used with an electric hoist, divided by the parts of the rope used in the hoist, should NOT exceed _____% of the nominal breaking strength of the rope.   19._____

   A. 20   B. 40   C. 55   D. 75

20. An electric hoist's brakes should be able to slow the load descent by AT LEAST _____% of the rated lowering speed for the load.   20._____

   A. 30   B. 75   C. 100   D. 120

21. How often should the bolts used to attach boom mountings be inspected, regardless of use?   21._____

   A. Daily   B. Weekly   C. Monthly   D. Bimonthly

22. Normal operation of a chain hoist is defined as operation with uniform loads up to _____% of capacity during a single work shift.   22._____

   A. 25   B. 45   C. 65   D. 85

23. Inspection of hoists under severe operation should occur   23._____

   A. daily   B. daily to weekly
   C. weekly to monthly D. monthly

24. If the jack cylinder of a hydraulic outrigger retracts under a load, each of the following is a possible remedy EXCEPT

    A. replace cylinder seals
    B. replace valve assembly
    C. add hydraulic oil to reservoir
    D. replace cylinder

25. Which of the following operations involved in aligning and servicing a telescoping boom would occur FIRST?

    A. Turn adjusting screws snug against boom section
    B. Adjust side wear pads snug against boom section
    C. Retract boom sections to align high point on boom section
    D. Lubricate boom completely

KEY (CORRECT ANSWERS)

1. N
2. HH
3. Z
4. FF
5. JJ

6. A
7. K
8. GG
9. L
10. F

11. II
12. P
13. X
14. Q
15. CC

16. B
17. D
18. A
19. A
20. D

21. A
22. C
23. B
24. C
25. D

TEST 2

DIRECTIONS: Each question or incomplete statement is followed by several suggested answers or completions. Select the one that BEST answers the question or completes the statement. *PRINT THE LETTER OF THE CORRECT ANSWER IN THE SPACE AT THE RIGHT.*

Questions 1-14.

DIRECTIONS: Questions 1 through 14 are to be answered on the basis of the figure below, a diagram of a typical control valve assembly for a hydraulic crane. Place the letter that corresponds to each diagrammed component in the space at the right.

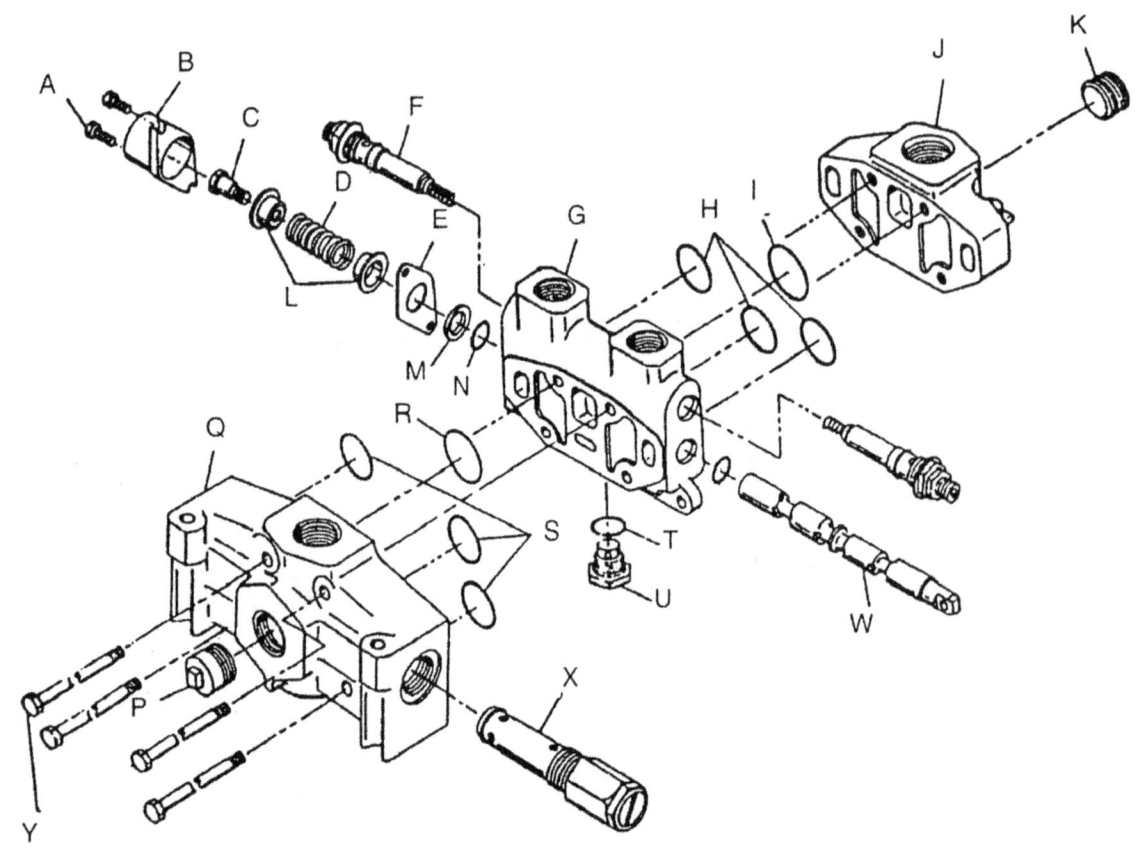

1. Spring guide   1.____

2. Inlet section   2.____

3. Spring   3.____

4. Circuit relief valve   4.____

5. Housing   5.____

6. Backup ring   6.____

7. Tie bolt   7.____

50

8. Ring seal

9. Outlet relief

10. Spool

11. Cap screw

12. Load check valve

13. Main relief valve

14. Retaining plate

15. Which of the following operations involved in flushing a crane's hydraulic circulatory system would occur LAST?
    A. Fill reservoir with fuel oil/hydraulic oil solution
    B. Return crane to stowed-boom position
    C. Flush
    D. Cycle crane through all hydraulic functions

16. Inspection of hoists under normal operation should occur
    A. daily
    B. daily to weekly
    C. weekly to monthly
    D. monthly

17. If the spool of a hydraulic crane's control valve is sticking, each of the following is a possible remedy EXCEPT
    A. retorque
    B. replace pump
    C. clear pipe line
    D. flush system

18. Which of the following conditions could cause a failure of hydraulic outriggers to set?
    A. Cracked piston
    B. Low hydraulic oil
    C. Improper activation sequence
    D. Damaged hydraulic cylinder

19. If a crane's hydraulic pump is not delivering fluid, each of the following is a possible cause EXCEPT
    A. sheared coupling
    B. internal contamination
    C. system relief valve set too high
    D. air entering at suction manifold

20. The voltage at an electric hoist's pendant push buttons should NOT exceed _____ V for a unit using alternating current.
    A. 75
    B. 150
    C. 225
    D. 300

21. Which of the following conditions could cause a crane load to drop when the hydraulic control valve spool is moved from neutral?

    A. Excessive back pressure
    B. Valve cap binding
    C. Dirt in relief valve
    D. Dirt in check valve

22. If a hydraulic crane's boom swing is erratic in either direction, which of the following is NOT a possible remedy?

    A. Level machine
    B. Replace relief valve
    C. Replace swing motor
    D. Retorque turntable bolts

23. Electric hoists should be clearly marked with each of the following power supply quantities EXCEPT

    A. resistance
    B. phase
    C. frequency
    D. voltage

24. If a hydraulic crane's solenoid valve shows external leakage, which of the following is NOT a likely cause?

    A. Damaged quad rings
    B. Pressure in excess of valve rating
    C. Loose tie bolts
    D. Damaged solenoid

25. Inspection of hoists under heavy operation should occur

    A. daily
    B. daily to weekly
    C. weekly to monthly
    D. monthly

KEY (CORRECT ANSWERS)

1.	L	11.	A
2.	Q	12.	U
3.	D	13.	X
4.	F	14.	E
5.	G	15.	C
6.	M	16.	D
7.	Y	17.	B
8.	V	18.	C
9.	J	19.	C
10.	W	20.	B

21. D
22. A
23. A
24. B
25. C

EXAMINATION SECTION
TEST 1

DIRECTIONS: Each question or incomplete statement is followed by several suggested answers or completions. Select the one that BEST answers the question or completes the statement. *PRINT THE LETTER OF THE CORRECT ANSWER IN THE SPACE AT THE RIGHT.*

Questions 1-17.

DIRECTIONS: Questions 1 through 17 are to be answered on the basis of the figure below, a diagram of typical lubrication points on a wheel-mounted hydraulic crane. Place the letter that corresponds to each diagrammed lubrication point in the space at the right.

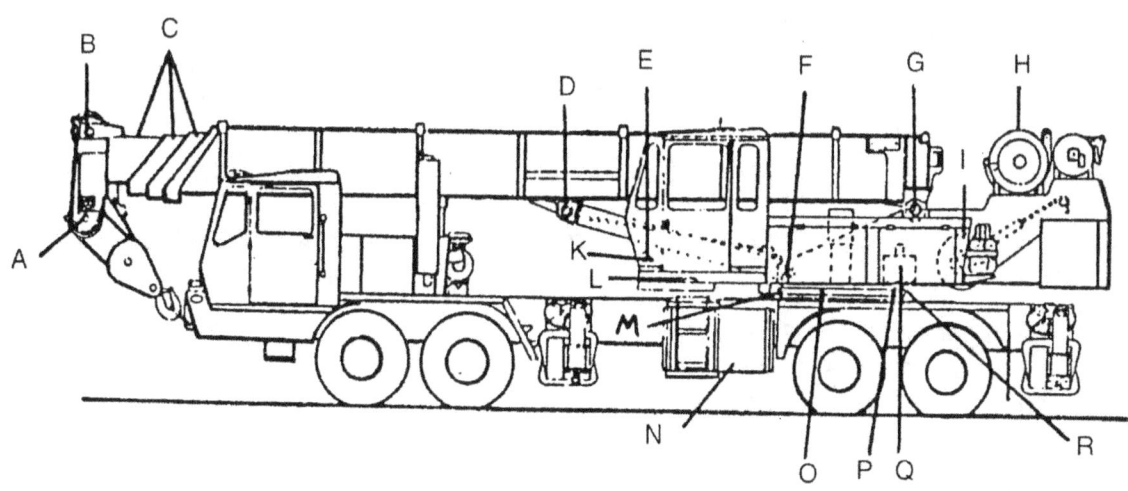

1.	Hoist final drive assembly	1._____
2.	Swing box bearing	2._____
3.	Boom sections	3._____
4.	Pinion	4._____
5.	Hose reel	5._____
6.	Turntable bearing	6._____
7.	Swing brake pedal	7._____
8.	Base lift cylinders	8._____
9.	Swing box gear case	9._____
10.	Hydraulic oil reservoir	10._____
11.	Turntable pinion gear	11._____
12.	Top lift cylinders	12._____

13. Brake master cylinder   13.____

14. Boom nose idler sheave   14.____

15. Throttle pedal   15.____

16. Boom nose sheaves   16.____

17. Boom pivot   17.____

18. If oil foams in the reservoir of a crane's hydraulic pump, the MOST likely remedy is to   18.____

    A. fill reservoir to adequate level
    B. clean pump-to-control valve supply line
    C. adjust system relief valve
    D. clear reservoir-to-pump supply line

19. The original filter for a crane's hydraulic system should be replaced after the crane's first   19.____
    _____ hours of operation.

    A. 24   B. 50   C. 100   D. 200

20. If the swing motor of a hydraulic crane is turning in the wrong direction, the MOST likely   20.____
    cause is

    A. damaged output shaft bearing
    B. sticking control valve spool
    C. improper swing brake release
    D. improper port connections

21. What is the ratio of fuel oil to hydraulic oil used in flushing crane systems?   21.____

    A. 1:1   B. 1:3   C. 1:5   D. 2:1

22. If a spur-geared chain hoist will not operate in the hoisting direction, the MOST probable   22.____
    cause is

    A. overload
    B. chain binding
    C. lower load side of chain on wrong side of liftwheel
    D. pawl not engaging with ratchet

23. What is represented by the hydraulic system symbol shown at the right?   23.____
    A. Push-button operation
    B. Connector
    C. Mechanical operation
    D. Check valve

24. What is represented by the hydraulic system symbol shown at the right?   24.____
    A. Pressure relief valve
    B. Fixed restriction
    C. Line to vented manifold
    D. Variable restriction

25. What is represented by the hydraulic system symbol shown at the right? 25.____
    A. Single motor, fixed displacement
    B. Reversible motor, variable displacement, reversible
    C. Rotating shaft
    D. Variable displacement pump

KEY (CORRECT ANSWERS)

1.	H	11.	O
2.	R	12.	D
3.	C	13.	M
4.	P	14.	B
5.	J	15.	K
6.	M	16.	A
7.	E	17.	G
8.	F	18.	A
9.	Q	19.	B
10.	N	20.	D

21. A
22. B
23. A
24. B
25. C

TEST 2

DIRECTIONS: Each question or incomplete statement is followed by several suggested answers or completions. Select the one that BEST answers the question or completes the statement. *PRINT THE LETTER OF THE CORRECT ANSWER IN THE SPACE AT THE RIGHT.*

Questions 1-25.

DIRECTIONS: In Questions 1 through 25, what is represented by each of the hydraulic system symbols shown?

1.
   A. Flow control valve, adjustable, non-compensated
   B. Manual operation
   C. Pressure gauge
   D. Check valve

1._____

2.
   A. Differential double-acting cylinder
   B. Non-differential double-acting cylinder
   C. Detent operation
   D. Single-acting cylinder

2._____

3.
   A. Push-button operation
   B. Internal supply pilot pressure
   C. Manual operation
   D. Pressure reducing valve

3._____

4.
   A. Differential double-acting cylinder
   B. Manual shut-off valve
   C. Lines passing
   D. Flow direction

4._____

5.
   A. Variable restriction
   B. Flexible line
   C. Plugged connection
   D. Lines passing

5._____

6.
   A. Drain line
   B. Flow direction
   C. Pilot line
   D. Working line

6._____

2 (#2)

7.

A. Heater
B. Gas-charged accumulator
C. Vented reservoir
D. Connector

7.____

8.

A. Cooler
B. Fixed-displacement pump
C. Detent operation
D. Remote supply pilot pressure

8.____

9.

A. Filter
B. Temperature control
C. Manual shut-off valve
D. Pressure gauge

9.____

10.

A. Lines passing
B. Lines joining
C. Line to reservoir
D. Adjustable flow-control valve, non-compensated

10.____

11.

A. Cooler
B. Single-winding solenoid
C. Heater
D. Filter

11.____

12.

A. Electric motor
B. Pressure gauge
C. Rotating shaft
D. Reversing motor

12.____

13.

A. Nonreversible fixed displacement motor
B. Pressure gauge
C. Pressure relief valve
D. Fixed displacement pump

13.____

57

14.

A. Variable line restriction
B. Line to vented manifold
C. Plug or plugged connection
D. Passing lines

15.

A. Adjustable flow control valve
B. Double-acting non-reversible cylinder
C. Two-position, two-connection valve
D. Valve capable of infinite positioning

16.

A. Pressure compensated operation
B. Spring-loaded accumulator
C. Single-winding solenoid
D. Remote supply pilot pressure

17.

A. Lever operation
B. Manual operation
C. Pressure compensated operation
D. Pedal or treadle operation

18.

A. Single-acting cylinder
B. Temperature controller
C. Non-differential double-acting cylinder
D. Internal supply pilot pressure

19.

A. Plugged connection B. Line to vented manifold
C. Line to reservoir D. Vented reservoir

4 (#2)

20.
- A. Two-position, two-connection valve
- B. Two-position, three-connection valve
- C. Lines passing
- D. Two-position, four-connection valve

21.
- A. Electric motor
- B. Heater
- C. Reversing motor
- D. Filter

22.
- A. Mechanical operation
- B. Enclosure
- C. Pressure-compensated operation
- D. Detent operation

23.
- A. Fixed displacement, non-reversible motor
- B. Check valve
- C. Fixed displacement pump
- D. Variable replacement, reversible motor

24.
- A. Vented reservoir
- B. Gas-loaded accumulator
- C. Enclosure
- D. Drain line

25.
- A. Plug or plugged connection
- B. Direction of flow
- C. Connector
- D. Line to vented manifold

KEY (CORRECT ANSWERS)

1.	D	11.	A
2.	A	12.	B
3.	C	13.	D
4.	B	14.	A
5.	B	15.	C
6.	D	16.	C
7.	B	17.	D
8.	C	18.	A
9.	A	19.	B
10.	A	20.	D

21. B
22. C
23. A
24. C
25. A

EQUIPMENT OPERATION

TABLE OF CONTENTS

	Page
ASPHALT AND CONCRETE	1
TEST 1	1
TEST 2	3
CABLE DRILLING	5
TEST 1	5
TEST 2	7
CRANES AND DERRICKS	9
TEST 1	9
TEST 2	11
TEST 3	13
TEST 4	15
TEST 5	17
PILE DRIVER AND POWER SHOVEL	19
TEST 1	19
TEST 2	21
TEST 3	23
TEST 4	25
TEST 5	27
WELL DRILLING	29
TEST 1	29
TEST 2	31
TEST 3	33

EQUIPMENT OPERATION EXAMINATION SECTION

ASPHALT AND CONCRETE TEST 1

DIRECTIONS: Answer the following questions directly, briefly, and succinctly.

1. What does the screed ride on?

2. How long may concrete, poured from a mixer, stand before the finishing machines goes to work?

3. How many trips does the finishing machine make over a plain concrete job?

4. What is the purpose of the screed on a finishing machine?

5. What type of wheels are used on the machine to keep it from running off the forms?

6. What happens if the front screed is NOT kept full?

7. With what do you raise and lower the screeds?

8. What are three methods of curing a concrete pavement?

9. On what trip is the belt used?

10. Name two makes of finishing machines.

11. What are the leveling plates called that smooth the concrete?

2 (#1)

KEY (CORRECT ANSWERS)

1. Road forms (rails) (header boards)

2. Not more than one hour

3. Two to four

4. Level concrete

5. Flanged (grooved)
   Track (car) wheels

6. Low spots

7. Levers

8. Wet burlap
   Ponds of water
   Wet hay or straw
   Calcium chloride
   Cotton sheet
   Curcrete
   Silica
   Paper
   Salt

9. Last (finish) (second)

10. Lakewood
    Ord
    Comet
    French
    Jaeger
    Cleveland
    Heltzel
    Blaw-Knox
    Woodhall

11. Screeds (blades)

TEST 2

DIRECTIONS: Answer the following questions directly, briefly, and succinctly.

1. Where does one begin rolling a dirt road?
2. Where does one start to roll a curved surface?
3. What is the center of the roadway called?
4. What is the average working pressure of the boiler on a steam roller?
5. How many clutches are there on a roll-a-plane?
6. What is done to the rollers to keep the asphalt from sticking to them?
7. What is the device called that feeds water into the boiler of a steam roller?
8. What is used to brake the roller on a downgrade?
9. What type of roller is used first in rolling asphalt?
10. Where on the surface does the rolling start?
11. How often is the machine greased?
12. What speed is used for rolling?
13. When is the water sprinkler used?
14. When the boiler is in first-class condition, at what pressure is the pop-off valve set on the ordinary asphalt roller?
15. At about what pressure is the roller operated on asphalt road work?

KEY (CORRECT ANSWERS)

1. On the side (shoulder) (curb)

2. Start on low side and work to high side
   Follow the curve

3. Crown (center line)

4. 125 pounds per square inch

5. Two

6. Wet them
   Oil them

7. Injector (pump)

8. Reverse

9. Tandem

10. At curbs (gutters) (shoulders)

11. Every day

12. Low
    1 to 4 miles per hour

13. Rolling hot asphalt
    Rolling bituminous concrete

14. 100 to 120 pounds

15. 60 to 120 pounds

CABLE DRILLING
TEST 1

DIRECTIONS: Answer the following questions directly, briefly, and succinctly.

1. What tool would be used to recover a tool that unscrewed from the stem?
2. What fishing tool can be used to recover a bailer?
3. What are two types of rope sockets?
4. When is a swivel wrench used?
5. How do fishing jars differ from drilling jars?
6. Why is the heel sheave designed to move along the shaft?
7. The *stinger* is part of what mechanism?
8. If tools are heavy, what can be done to get more leverage or power on the walking beam?
9. What is the pole called that is used to reinforce the mast pole while handling heavy casting?
10. What fishing tool is used to recover tools that have rope?

KEY (CORRECT ANSWERS)

1. Slip (horn) socket
   Friction (corrugated) socket
   Combination socket
   Pin socket
   Collar socket

2. Latch jack (spear)
   Bell socket

3. Swivel (Prosser) (loose)
   Stiff (Babcock) (straight)
   Woodpecker (wing) (manila line)

4. Making up tools (put on bits)
   Breaking down tools (taking off bits)
   Changing bits

5. Longer (longer stroke)

6. To spool the line
   Keep line straight

7. Swivel socket (swivel)
   Wire line (rope socket) (socket)

8. Shorten stroke (set hole back in crank) (set pitman back)
   Weight the beam
   Counter-balance (add balance to engine)

9. Shear (gin) (sub) pole

10. Spear (tool with points)
    Grab

TEST 2

DIRECTIONS: Answer the following questions directly, briefly, and succinctly.

1. What part of the rig determines the length of the stroke?
2. How many strands are there in a bailing line?
3. After the casing has been tightened by hand with chain tongs, what is used to tighten the casing further?
4. In what order, starting from the top, can a string of fishing tools be made up?
5. What is the arm called that connects the walking-beam to the crank arm?
6. What is old rope called that will NOT stretch?
7. What do you call the process of drilling below the casing, in order that the casing may be lowered?
8. What mechanism releases the line as the hole gets deeper?

KEY (CORRECT ANSWERS)

1. Hole in crank (crank) (arm)
   Hole wrist pin is in

2. 6

3. Dunn (bull) tongs
   Wilson tongs
   Cathead
   Casing pole
   Jerk line (crank arm)

4. Socket
   Stem (sinker bar) (drill bar)
   Jars
   Tool (spear)

5. Pitman

6. Dead (no life)
   Soft
   Junk
   Worn out

7. Under reaming (reaming)
   Under rimming
   Under digging

8. Brake
   Temper screw (screw) (clamp)

CRANES AND DERRICKS
TEST 1

DIRECTIONS: Answer the following questions directly, briefly, and succinctly.

1. With what part of the crane would you lower the hoist if the brake failed?
2. What applies power to the drums?
3. What is the purpose of the eccentric on a steam crane?
4. What is called the steel wheel at the bottom of the derrick that rotates the derrick?
5. What is the cable called that runs from the boom to the clamshell to keep the clamshell from spinning?
6. What is injected into the steam line to maintain the proper operation of the hammer?
7. By what means is the speed of a gasoline crane motor regulated?
8. What is the cable called that holds the bucket open when lowering to dig?
9. What are the two controls on each drum?
10. What is the lower sheave pulley called that guides the cable?

2 (#1)

KEY (CORRECT ANSWERS)

1. Friction clutch
2. Friction clutch
3. Operate slide valve
4. Bull wheel
5. Tag line (monkey line) (guy line) (dolly line)
6. Oil (cylinder oil)
7. Hand throttle
   Governor
8. Holding cable
9. Clutch
   Brake
10. Lead block (fair lead) (lead sheave)

TEST 2

DIRECTIONS: Answer the following questions directly, briefly, and succinctly.

1. What is the MAIN advantage of the revolving type over the boom-swinging type of crane?
2. On what part of the crane are counterweights placed?
3. What is the purpose of the counterweight on a clamshell bucket?
4. What is the cable called that closes the clamshell bucket?
5. What is used to prevent a truck crane from overturning?
6. What is used on the butt end of a pile in order to sink or drive it below the surface of the ground?
7. On what part of the lead do you put the hammer when lifting heavy pontoons?
8. To what part of the bucket is the lifting line attached?
9. Where is the lubricator located in the steam engine?
10. What is the device called that uses the steam in the boiler to force feed water into it?

KEY (CORRECT ANSWERS)

1. Greater working area (increased working radius)

2. Back of crane

3. Open the bucket
   Weight for digging
   Prevent turning

4. Closing cable

5. Outriggers Jack

6. Follower (dummy)

7. Bottom

8. Head (top)

9. In steam line
   Above throttle

10. Injector
    Force pump

TEST 3

DIRECTIONS: Answer the following questions directly, briefly, and succinctly.

1. What is used to fasten the bottom of the boom to the crane?
2. Where is the head sheave located?
3. How many sheaves does a clamshell have at the boom point?
4. What part shows undue wear on a machine operated with low boom?
5. Name three things which might cause a clutch to slip.
6. What is the proper angle to set the boom for MOST loads?
7. What is done to stop lowering a load?
8. What is another name for the single line hoisting cable that runs over the sheave at the end of the boom?
9. What is the temporary boom called that is attached to the main boom?
10. What can be done to increase the lifting speed of the hoist?

KEY (CORRECT ANSWERS)

1. Steel pin

2. Top end (head end) of boom

3. Two

4. Center pin
   Front rollers

5. Heat
   Grease
   Worn
   Wet
   Oil
   Loose

6. 45 degrees
   20-foot radius

7. Apply brakes on drum

8. Whip (hoisting line) (runner line)

9. Gib boom
   Extension boom

10. Leg the drum
    Increase size of drum

TEST 4

DIRECTIONS: Answer the following questions directly, briefly, and succinctly.

1. What part of the crane operates when it is only necessary to lift the load?
2. How many control levers are there on an electric traveling crane?
3. What is the part of the crane called that travels over the crane bridge?
4. What is the part of the crane called that is found across the tram?
5. What device is used to prevent overtravel of the lifting block?
6. What switch is turned on first when starting operation?
7. In how many directions can the hook of a crane move at one time?
8. Why is the motor to the bridge located in the center of the crane?
9. What is the operation called when the carriage moves away from the operator?
10. What stops the motors of an electric-powered hoist?
11. What is checked when you leave the crane?

2 (#4)

KEY (CORRECT ANSWERS)

1. Hoist
2. Three
3. Carriage
   Trolley
4. Bridge
5. Safety switch (limit switch)
6. Master (main)
7. Three (up and down, back and forth, sideways)
8. To give an even pull
   To keep from twisting
9. Racking out
10. Switches off (power off)
11. Brake

TEST 5

DIRECTIONS: Answer the following questions directly, briefly, and succinctly.

1. What holds the boom or hoisting cable in position?
2. On what part of the machine do the boom and hoisting cables wind and unwind?
3. What part of the machine is adjusted if the operating lever pulls out?
4. With what is the side arm connected to the cross head?
5. What collects all the mud and silt in the boiler water?
6. How far should the eccentric be set ahead of the pin?
7. What is the small plate called that is in the boiler that is removable for inspection purposes?
8. What is the small steam winch called that is used to rotate the bull wheel?
9. What is the large wheel called that is attached to the mast that is turned to rotate the derrick?
10. What safety device should always be used if the cage is to remain stationary for any length of time?

2 (#5)

KEY (CORRECT ANSWERS)

1. Dog
   Drums
   Sheaves
   Friction clutch

2. Drums

3. Clutch (friction)

4. Wrist (cross-head) pin

5. Mud ring (drum) (pan)

6. 1/4 turn
   90 degrees

7. Hand-hole plate

8. Swing

9. Bull wheel

10. Dog

PILE DRIVER AND POWER SHOVEL
TEST 1

DIRECTIONS: Answer the following questions directly, briefly, and succinctly.

1. What is a whip line used for?
2. What is the spool on a drum of an engine called?
3. What are the two upright timbers between which the hammer operates?
4. Name two different methods of driving piles.
5. Why is a follower used?
6. What power is used to operate a sheet-pile hammer?
7. In large pile hammers, where is the lubricator usually connected?
8. By what means can a steam hammer be used to pull piles?
9. What are used to anchor sheet piles to wooden piles?
10. What is a timber foundation called that is built on uneven ground?
11. What is the pile line or runner used for?

2 (#1)

KEY (CORRECT ANSWERS)

1. Dragging (or hoisting) piles

2. Winch (gypsy)

3. Leads (guides)

4. Gravity (drop) hammer
   Steam hammer
   Water jetting

5. Drive piles below leads
   Drive piles below ground
   When hammer is too short

6. Steam
   Air

7. In steam line
   On top of cylinder

8. Invert (reverse) (turn upside down)

9. Bolts (spikes)

10. Cribbing (falsework)

11. Raise (snake) and lower piles

TEST 2

DIRECTIONS: Answer the following questions directly, briefly, and succinctly.

1. What is the hammer called whose ram is raised by steam and falls by gravity?
2. What is the line called that is used to snake piles in?
3. What process is used in driving a pile when the driving becomes difficult?
4. What is a single sheave block called that opens at the hook?
5. What are the two uprights called that guide the hammer as it falls?
6. What is put on the points of piles when driving into hard soil?
7. By what means are the hammer cylinders oiled?
8. Name two kinds of knots used to tie the ends of lines together to make a safe hitch?
9. Why is a follower used?
10. Name two different methods of driving piles?
11. What is the short auxiliary pile called that is put on top of the main pile to drive it farther into the ground?
12. What kind of knot do pile drivers most often use in tying ropes and cables?
13. What is the worker called who works in the leads at a pile-driving rig?
14. What makes the hammer hit the bottom of the cylinder on the upswing?
15. What is meant by the brooming of a pile?

2 (#2)

KEY (CORRECT ANSWERS)

1. Single action (drop)

2. Whip (runner) (pile line)

3. Water jetting (jet)

4. Snatch (gate) (foot) block

5. Leads (guides) (gins)

6. Metal shoes (points) (noses)

7. Lubricator (oil cups) in steam line

8. Two bowlines
   Bowline and two half hitches
   Square (hard) (flat) Reef
   Fisherman's bend

9. Drive piles below leads (surface of ground)

10. Gravity (drop) hammer
    Steam hammer
    Water jetting

11. Follower (dummy)

12. Bowline

13. Leadsman (loftman) (monkey) (tripper)

14. Too much steam (pressure)

15. Spreading (splitting)

TEST 3

DIRECTIONS: Answer the following questions directly, briefly, and succinctly.

1. What is the arm called that is connected to the dipper?
2. What is done to turn the shovel around?
3. What are the three main digging motions?
4. On what is the booster mounted?
5. What do the two foot pedals on the machine control?
6. About how much yardage of dirt can usually be moved in 10 hours, in easy digging, using a half-yard bucket?
7. What dumps the dirt from the dipper?
8. What adjusts the chain tension?
9. What adjusts the chain tension?
10. What holds the dipper handle and racks up to the shipper-shaft pinions?

2 (#3)

KEY (CORRECT ANSWERS)

1. Dipper stick

2. Cut out one cat
   Swing lever (gear)

3. Hoist
   Swing
   Crowd (dig)

4. Drum shaft (drum)
   A-frame

5. Hoisting brake
   Crowding action (closing line)

6. 300 to 500 yards

7. Power trip (dump line)
   Latch bar

8. Take-up
   Adjustment screws
   Links
   Idlers

9. Idle sprocket wheels (idlers)
   Adjustment screws

10. Saddle block

———

TEST 4

DIRECTIONS: Answer the following questions directly, briefly, and succinctly.

1. What should be done if the rollers on the turntable circle slide?
2. Where is the shipper-shaft drum located?
3. How many hand levers are there on the shovel of the Lorrain 75.4?
4. What does the shipper-shaft drum do?
5. If a long trench was being dug with a power hoe, in what direction would you move the dipper to dig the earth?
6. Where are the fair leads mounted?
7. What does the hoist cable run through?
8. What are most of the bushings on a shovel made of?
9. What cable runs through the fair leads on a dragline?
10. What are three of the most common causes of clutch slipping?

KEY (CORRECT ANSWERS)

1. Use sand
   Use ashes

2. On boom

3. Three

4. Controls length of dipper stick
   Crowds bucket (dipper stick)

5. Backward (toward the machine) (to you)

6. Foot of the boom (boom)

7. Sheave (padlock)

8. Bronze
   Brass
   Babbitt

9. Drag cable

10. Oil (grease)
    Hard
    Worn
    Wet
    Out of adjustment

TEST 5

DIRECTIONS: Answer the following questions directly, briefly, and succinctly.

1. With what type of clutch are most gas shovels equipped?
2. On what do the rollers on the bottom of the cab move?
3. What can be done to change the direction of the machine on the cat base while it is being moved forward?
4. How many load lines control the stick on a hoe machine?
5. Into what types of machines may a shovel be changed?
6. What is meant by an *orange peel*?
7. What pressure should the oil gauge on a gas shovel show at full speed?
8. What is the position of the cable drums inside the cab?
9. Where is the latch plate of the shovel?
10. What keeps the shovel from traveling forward or backward when working?

KEY (CORRECT ANSWERS)

1. Multiple disc (disc)

2. Tracks
   Turntable (circle)
   Ring gear

3. Cut out one cat
   Swing lever
   Reverse

4. Two

5. Crane
   Dragline
   Pullshovel
   Skimmer

6. Type of bucket
   3- or 4-part bucket

7. 20 to 50 pounds

8. Tandem
   Horizontal

9. On dipper (bucket)

10. Locking pawl (dog)
    Block

WELL DRILLING
TEST 1

DIRECTIONS: Answer the following questions directly, briefly, and succinctly.

1. How can the driller tell whether or not the valve in a mud scow is working?
2. What does rough, angular gravel indicate?
3. What equipment is used to install stovepipe casing in the well?
4. What is done after the joints have been slipped into place in order to hold them?
5. What type of perforator is used in the majority of wells?
6. What will happen if the casing is shoved onto any type of a bottom other than gravel?
7. If there is a low standing water level in the well, what should be done to help prevent the gravel from heaving?
8. What is the MOST important part of well-drilling in relation to locating strata, determining formation structures, and perforating the correct stratum?
9. For what reason is the casing starter fabricated with three-ply?
10. State the size and number of jacks you would recommend if you were drilling a twenty-inch well, fifteen hundred feet in depth, through average alluvium.

2 (#1)

KEY (CORRECT ANSWERS)

1. Feeling cable (feel on line) (feel it)
   Look at cable (look at line)

2. Dry (not washed) (no water)
   Not much water

3. Jacks (hydraulic jacks)

4. Pick (dent with pick)
   Welded

5. Mills
   Hydraulic

6. Stick (freeze) (sticks casing) (sets casing)

7. Add water (put more water in)

8. Correct log (log)

9. Make stronger
   Stiffen (won't bend)
   Protection from wear

10. 4 (4 jacks)
    8 inch (8)

———

TEST 2

DIRECTIONS: Answer the following questions directly, briefly, and succinctly.

1. What will happen if the main sill under the rig has NOT been sturdied when drilling a well?

2. What would be the FIRST thing to be done if while drilling through conglomerate you found hydraulic jacks would not move the casing?

3. For what reason should very little material be removed when drilling through gravel strata that heave up in the well?

4. What is the danger, using a mud scow, of drilling an open hole so far below the casing that the tools are outside the casing?

5. When a casing has been dented in or has collapsed, what is done to force it back to its original diameter?

6. For what reason is it better to use a long scow when drilling a hole?

7. How can clay cause a *tight hole*?

2 (#2)

KEY (CORRECT ANSWERS)

1. Out of line (out of level)
   Crooked hole
   Rig will shift (rig settles to one side)

2. Underream (underreamer)
   Ream
   Drive under it (ream under shoe)

3. Prevent cavity
   Keep from making pockets
   Liable to cause cave-in

4. Get caught under shoe
   Scow (tool) gets hung up on shoe (hung up) (caught) (stuck)
   Cave-in on them (hard to pull up when formation caves)

5. Swedge

6. Straighter hole (prevent crooked hole)

7. Swells
   Expands (water-soaked and expands)

———

TEST 3

DIRECTIONS: Answer the following questions directly, briefly, and succinctly.

1. What is meant by a *dead* drilling line?
2. What fishing tool can be used to straighten leaning tools you can't land on top of?
3. What is the purpose of the holes on the side of a swivel or Prosser socket?
4. How do fishing jars differ from drilling jars?
5. How many strands are there in a drilling line?
6. What is the smaller perforated pipe called that sets on the bottom of the well?
7. What is the joint called that is used to connect different-sized tools?
8. What other terms are used for the male and female ends of a drill stem?
9. What is used on the walking-beam at the header block or spudding sheave to absorb shock?
10. What is the difference between the two wrenches you use to tighten tool joints?

2 (#3)

KEY (CORRECT ANSWERS)

1. No life (no stretch) (no spring) (no twist) (not elastic) Worn out (old)

2. Spud
   Hook (wall hook)
   Hollow reamer (hollow rimmer)

3. Let mud (sand) (sediment) out
   Let water (fluid) out
   Let cuttings (drillings) out
   Keep it clean (wash it out)
   Circulation

4. Longer (longer stroke)

5. 6

6. Liner
   Screen (strainer)

7. Sub (substitute)

8. Pin
   Box

9. Spring
   Rubber (rubber cushions)

10. Right and left (left and right)

BASIC FUNDAMENTALS OF POWER CRANES AND ATTACHMENTS

CONTENTS

I.	Types and Uses of Power Cranes	1
II.	Crane Attachments	7
III.	Operations of Cranes and Attachments	14
IV.	Operator's Maintenance	28
V.	Changing Crane Attachments	28
VI.	Crane and Attachment Safety	31
VII.	Wire Rope	32

BASIC FUNDAMENTALS OF POWER CRANES AND ATTACHMENTS

Cranes, one of the basic tools of earthmoving, first made their appearance about 1835 in the form of a part swing dipper shovel, mounted on flat cars and moved over railroad tracks. Although the crane, powered by steam, was slow and clumsy, it did work. Over the years, cranes gradually acquired a variety of attachments and left the rails to appear on crawler tracks and rubber tires.

The modern crane and attachments constitute a versatile and important piece of equipment which can be used on most types of building, road, and airstrip construction under varying conditions.

General information on the operation, maintenance capabilities and utilization of cranes is presented in this chapter. Step-by-step procedures are given for changing and adapting cable/hydraulic assemblies on crawler-, truck-, and wheel-mounted cranes. The characteristics, construction, and usage of wire are discussed, as well as the use of slings, spreaders, pallets, cargo nets, and hooks. In addition, safety precautions to be observed when operating or working near power cranes are noted throughout the chapter.

I. TYPES AND USES OF POWER CRANES

Cranes and attachments are designed primarily to ensure the performance of weight-lifting and excavating operations under varied conditions. To make the most efficient use of cranes and attachments, it is important that the EO recognize their capabilities and limitations.

Although the superstructure is about the same on all makes and models of power cranes, the carrier or mounting may be one of three types: crawler, truck, or wheel (fig. 1). In order to make the basic unit complete and operable, any one of six attachments may be installed: hookblock, clamshell, dragline, shovel, backhoe, or piledriver (fig. 2). Once an attachment is installed, the entire unit acquires the name of that attachment.

CRAWLER-MOUNTED POWER CRANES

The crawler-mounted power (gas or diesel) crane is perhaps the most basic of the power

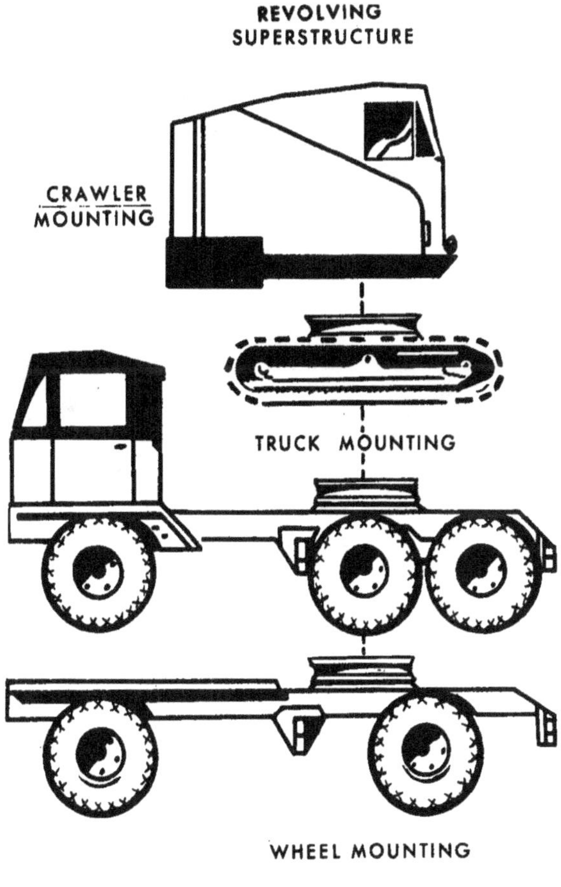

Figure 1.—Mounting for the power crane.

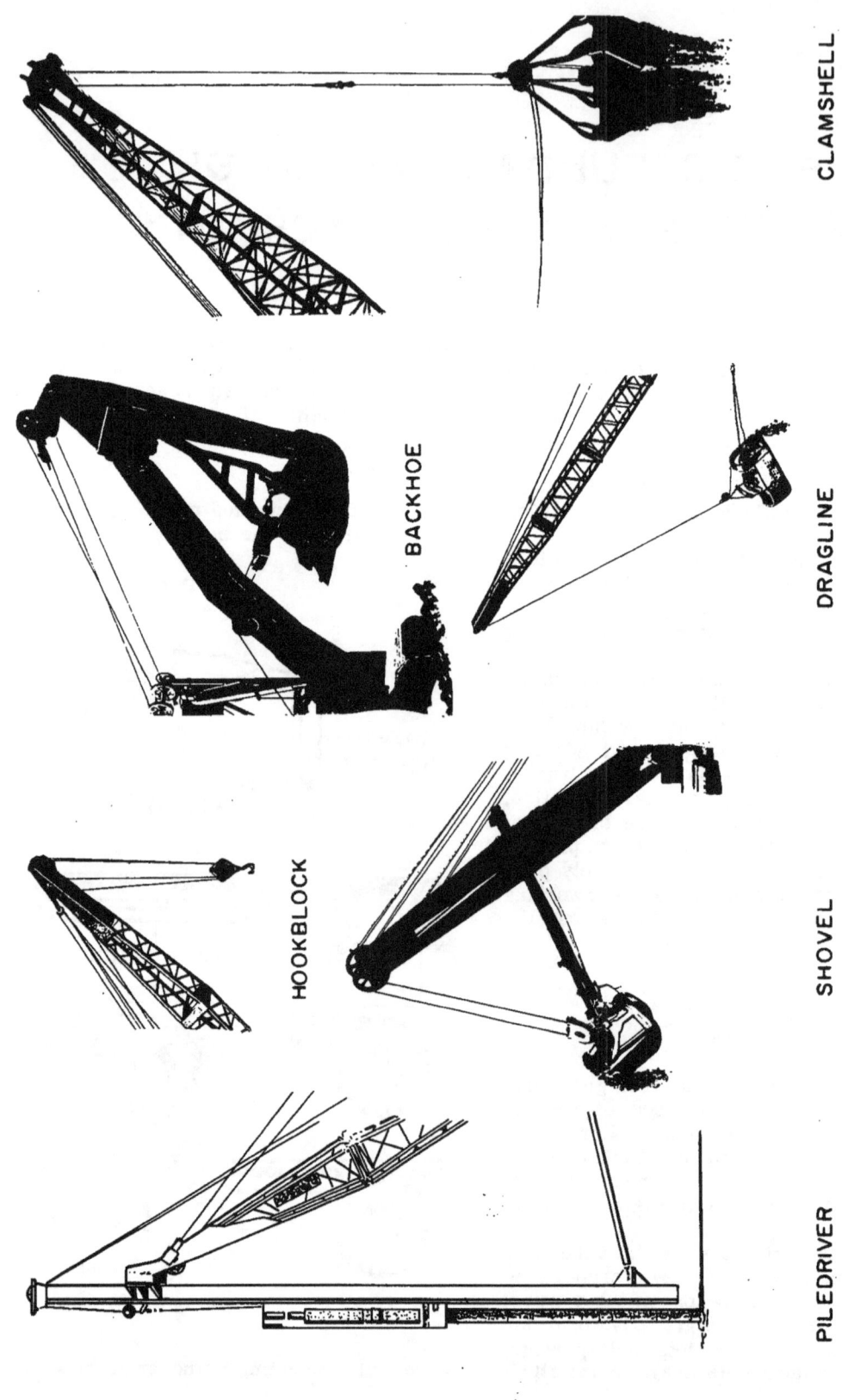

Figure 2.—Power crane attachments.

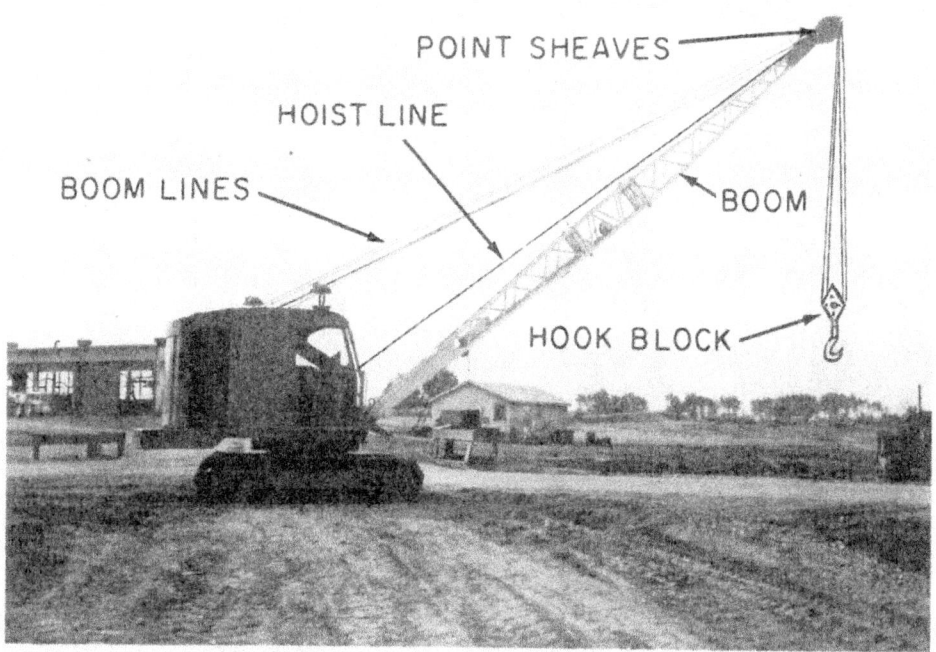

Figure 3. — Crawler power crane.

cranes (see fig. 3.) While slow and cumbersome in comparison to the truck-mounted power crane, the crawler crane is an easy machine to operate. The crawler crane provides a stable base for operation of the revolving superstructure.

The travel unit of the crawler crane is shown in figure 4. The unit includes the base, travel gears, clutches, travel brakes, sprockets, rollers, roller chains, and crawler treads.

The upper revolving unit of the crawler crane (fig. 5) consists of the engine, controls,

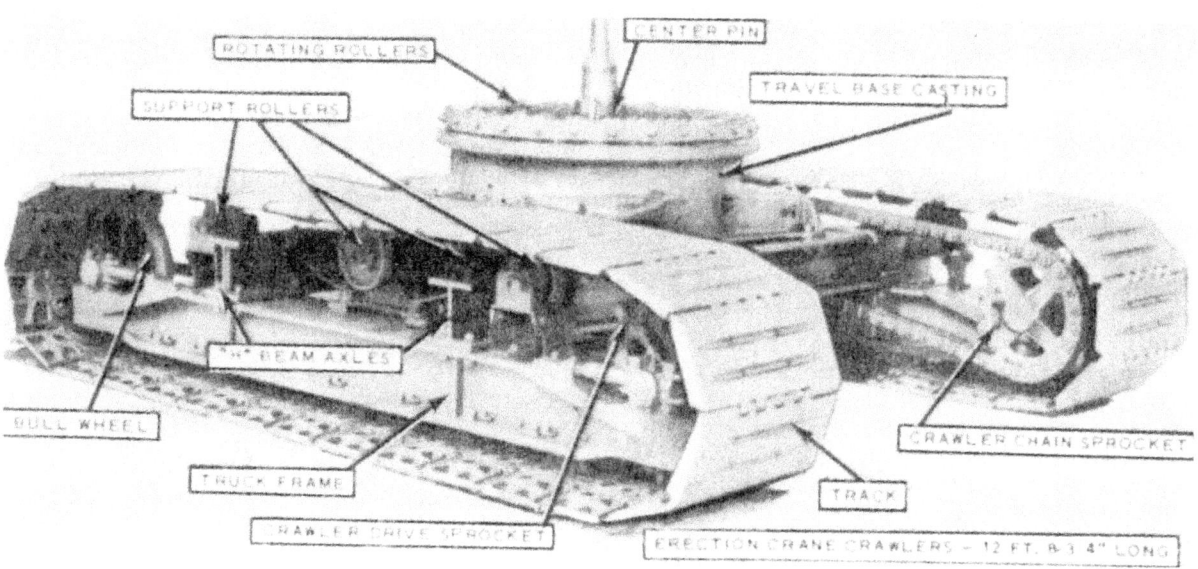

Figure 4. — Crawler crane travel unit.

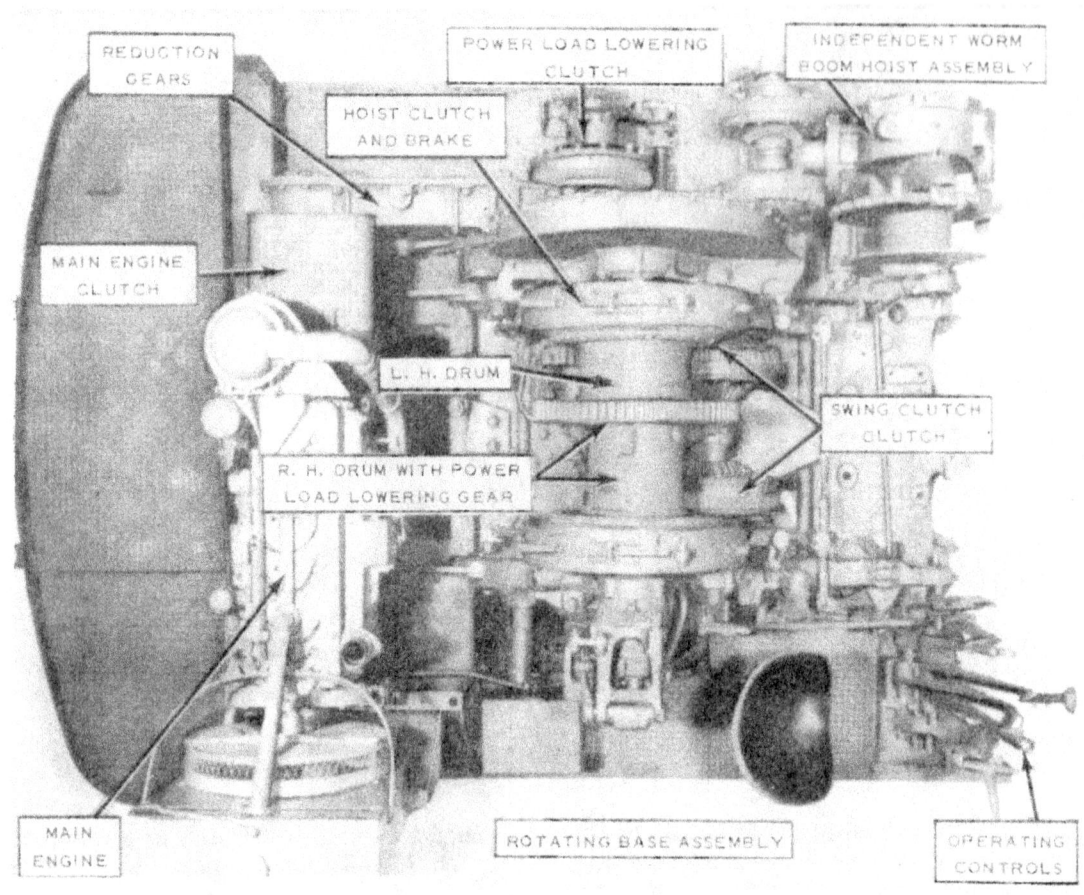

Figure 5. — Crawler crane upper revolving unit.

cable drums, operator's cab, and counterweights. The basic upper revolving unit is supported by rollers running in a circular track or turntable. The turntable (fig. 6) is rotated by the vertical shaft and gear.

The crawler crane has a decided advantage over the truck-mounted crane, especially on continuous work in remote areas which are not readily accessible to truck-mounted cranes due to terrain conditions. Crawler steering with positive traction permits travel and turn without cutting up the work area or roadways.

The weight of the machine is spread over a large area due to the size of the crawler treads. This feature gives the crawler crane a ground bearing pressure of 5 to 12 psi, which enables it to travel over soft terrain. However, when climbing grades, the maximum grade capability is 30 percent on firm dry material. Crawler cranes have a radius of approximately the length of the tracks and speeds ranging from 1/2 to 2 miles per hour. The speed is one factor that limits the crawler crane's travel range, and it is recommended that the travel distance not exceed 1 mile. When the travel distance exceeds 1 mile, the crawler crane should be loaded on an equipment trailer for transportation.

Figure 6. — Crawler crane turntable assembly.

POWER CRANES AND ATTACHMENTS

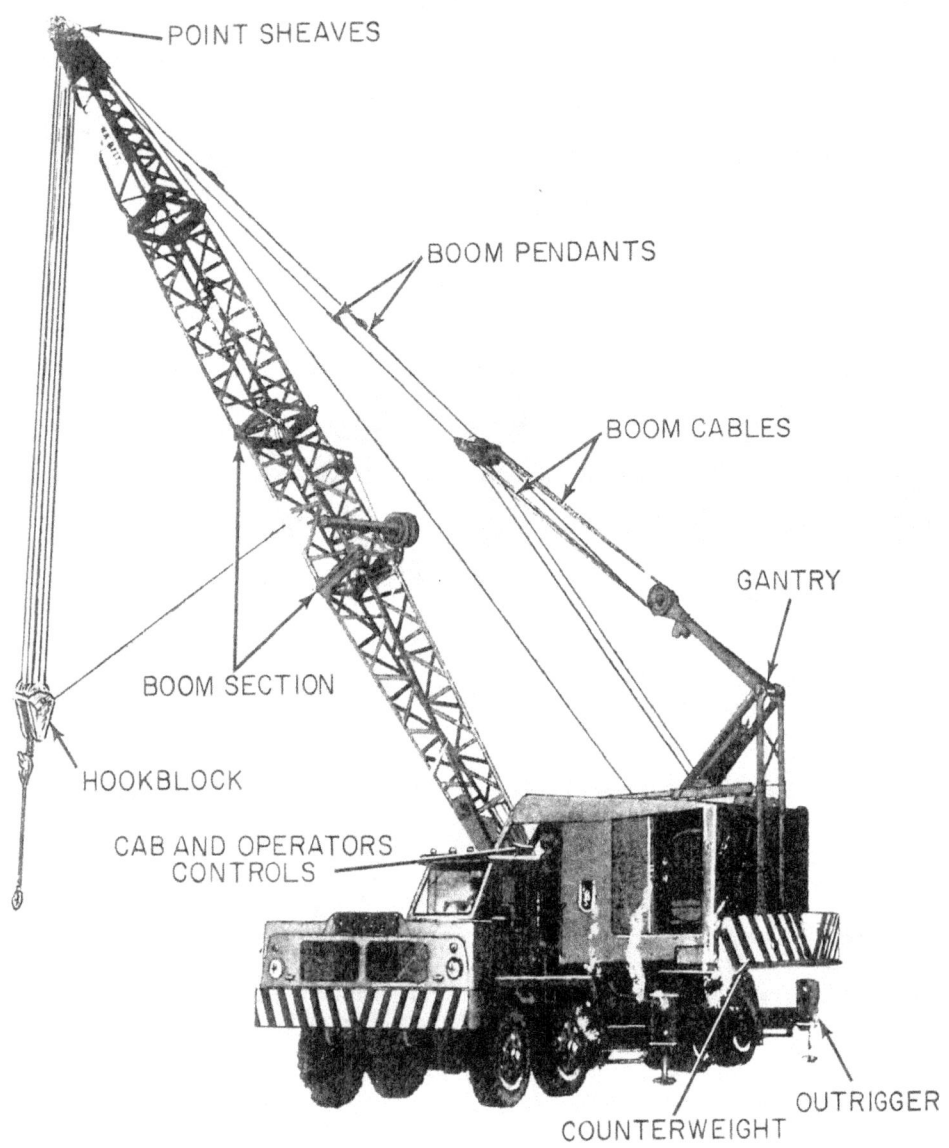

Figure 7.—Truck-mounted power crane.

In soft terrain, the large bearing area of the crawler tracks ensures proper movement and stability. When working on hard footing such as that found in quarry operations, the crawler crane shows great stability. The crawler crane is better suited to quarry operations than truck-mounted cranes since the sharp rock fragments present in quarries would be detrimental to the truck's rubber tires.

On-the-job moves can be made with ease as long as they are relatively short. Job maneuverability is increased further by the crane's small turning radius. Cleats or grousers may be fabricated to increase traction in extremely soft or slippery material.

TRUCK-MOUNTED POWER CRANES

The truck-mounted crane (fig. 7) consists of a truck carrier and upper revolving unit. The truck crane's upper revolving unit can be locked in traveling position and moved along the highway at 20 to 35 miles per hour. This is a pleasant contrast to the slow and laborious job

Figure 8. — Wheel-mounted power crane.

of loading and securing a crawler-mounted crane on a low-bed trailer to move it from one jobsite to another and then having to unload it.

The truck crane has a high ground bearing pressure, which ranges from 75 to 100 psi, due to the pneumatic tires on which the machine travels. On firm dry earth, the truck crane can negotiate a 40 percent grade, whereas, the turning radius is in excess of 50 feet; for some models, the turning radius may be as high as 89 feet. The large turning radius greatly limits its maneuverability. The travel range of the truck crane is approximately 250 miles.

To prevent damage to the truck frame and tires, the use of the truck crane should be limited to firm, level terrain, or footings. Under normal operations, the truck crane is used on jobs of short duration; this is a rule because one does not tie up a highly mobile crane on jobs of long duration.

The truck crane requires two operations, one to move the machine and the other to operate the upper revolving unit with its attachment. By towing a trailer, the truck crane can carry all the basic attachments needed to the jobsite.

WHEEL-MOUNTED POWER CRANES

The wheel-mounted power crane (fig. 8) is a hydraulically operated crane consisting essentially of a 4-wheel-drive, 4-wheel-steering, pneumatic-tired, diesel-engine-powered carrier, with a center-mounted telescopic boom.

The major superstructure of the wheel-mounted crane consists of the following components: a telescoping boom, a single-acting hydraulic lift cylinder, a hydraulically operated cable winch, hydraulic outriggers, and a hook-block attachment.

The wheel-mounted crane has a ground bearing pressure of approximately 35 psi. The machine can travel at speeds ranging from 2 to 30 mph. The wheel-mounted crane can turn in a 30-foot radius using two-wheel steering, and a 17-foot radius using four-wheel steering. It can also negotiate a grade of 40 percent on firm, dry terrain.

Factors involving the use of the wheel-mounted crane are similar to those of the truck-mounted crane. The wheel-mounted crane is well adapted for delivery to job locations. The crane can be driven on roads or off roads over rough terrain.

The wheel-mounted crane is a highly mobile and very flexible machine. This makes its use

POWER CRANES AND ATTACHMENTS

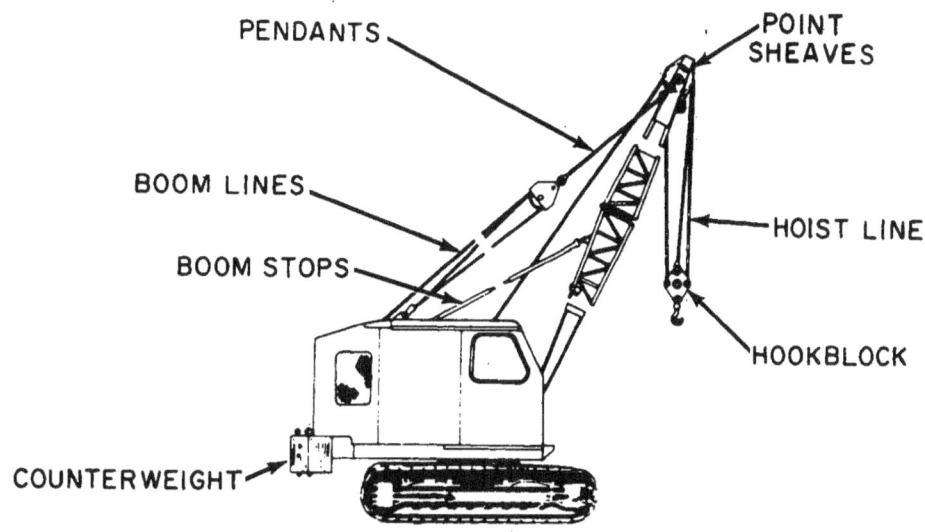

Figure 9. — Crane with hookblock attachment.

desirable for a wide range of operations regardless of location—on or off the road. These operations include lifting and carrying loads of every shape and size; positioning heavy components; installing pipes, tanks, etc., below grade; reaching inside trucks and boxcars; handling, stacking, and stockpiling materials.

CRANE RATINGS

Crawler-mounted cranes are rated at not more than 75 percent of the minimum load which causes tipping at any specified radius with the standard boom in the least stable position. Thus, the 10- and 40-ton crawler-mounted cranes are capable of lifting a "maximum safe" load of 10 and 40 tons, respectively, at a "minimum safe" operating radius of approximately 12 feet.

Truck- and wheel-mounted cranes are rated at not more than 85 percent of the load which will cause tipping at a 10-foot operating radius with outriggers employed over the rear or front of the mount. Therefore, a truck- or wheel-mounted crane rated at 20-ton capacity is capable of lifting a "maximum safe" load at a "minimum safe" operating radius of 10 feet with the standard boom length.

Before making a lift, consult the tables furnished with the machine concerning the recommeded radii and boom lengths required when handling specific weights of materials.

II. CRANE ATTACHMENTS

A variety of front-end attachments and mountings are required for cranes because no one type of boom, size of machine, or mounting is suitable for every type of job. The advantages and usual limits of application for each type of crane front-end attachment are described in the following sections.

HOOKBLOCK (CRANE)

A crane equipped with a hookblock (fig. 9) is used for lifting an object or load, transferring it to a new location by swinging or traveling, and then placing it. Incidentally, a crane with a hookblock is commonly referred to simply as a crane.

The basic crane equipment consists of a crane (lattice type) boom, hoisting drums or lagging for desired line pulls and speeds, hookblock to provide the required parts of line reeving), and the boom suspension and hoist wire ropes.

The crane boom is usually made in two sections, fastened approximately in the center by one of two methods: bolted butt plate (flange) connections or pin and clevis connections. The upper section with the boom head and a system of sheaves (usually two or more) is not necessarily the same length as the lower section.

Boom Length In Feet	Load Radius In Feet	Boom Angle In Degrees	Boom Point Pin Height	With Outriggers Set†		Without Outriggers		
						Over Side		Over Rear
				Over Side	Over Rear**	8'-0" Wide	9'-0" Wide	8' or 9' Wide
30	10	78	35'6"	*50,000	*50,000	28,800	32,200	39,300
	12	74	35'0"	*50,000	*50,000	22,500	24,900	30,800
	15	68	34'0"	*50,000	*50,000	16,800	18,500	23,200
	20	57	31'3"	36,800	*43,700	11,700	12,800	16,200
	25	44	27'3"	26,000	31,100	8,800	9,700	12,400
40	12	78	45'3"	*50,000	*50,000	22,200	24,600	30,600
	15	74	44'6"	*50,000	*50,000	16,500	18,200	22,900
	20	66	42'9"	36,600	*41,300	11,400	12,500	16,000
	25	58	40'0"	25,800	30,900	8,600	9,400	12,200
	30	49	36'3"	19,800	23,700	6,800	7,400	9,700
	35	38	30'9"	15,900	19,100	5,500	6,050	8,000
50	15	77	55'0"	*50,000	*50,000	16,400	18,000	22,700
	20	71	53'6"	36,500	*40,000	11,300	12,300	15,800
	25	65	51'6"	25,700	*30,400	8,450	9,250	12,000
	30	58	48'9"	19,600	23,600	6,650	7,250	9,500
	35	51	45'0"	15,800	19,000	5,400	5,900	7,800
	40	43	40'6"	13,100	16,800	4,500	4,900	6,600
	45	34	34'0"	11,200	13,500	3,800	4,150	5,650
60	15	79	65'3"	*48,800	*48,800	16,100	17,600	22,500
	20	74	64'0"	36,400	*39,100	11,000	12,100	15,600
	25	69	62'3"	25,500	*29,600	8,150	8,950	11,800
	30	64	60'0"	19,500	23,400	6,350	7,000	9,300
	35	59	57'3"	15,600	18,800	5,100	5,650	7,600
	40	53	53'9"	13,000	15,700	4,200	4,650	6,400
	45	46	49'6"	11,000	13,300	3,500	3,900	5,350
	50	39	44'3"	9,500	11,600	2,950	3,300	4,700
	55	32	37'9"	8,400	10,200	2,500	2,800	4,000
70	20	77	74'3"	36,200	*37,300	10,700	11,800	15,400
	25	72	73'0"	25,300	*28,800	7,850	8,700	11,600
	30	68	71'0"	19,300	*23,100	6,100	6,700	9,100
	40	59	66'0"	12,800	15,500	3,900	4,350	6,200
	50	49	58'6"	9,350	11,400	2,700	3,000	4,500
	60	36	47'6"	7,200	8,850	1,850	2,150	3,350
80	20	78	84'6"	*32,800	*32,800			
	25	75	83'3"	25,200	*28,400			
	30	71	81'9"	19,100	*22,600			
	40	63	77'6"	12,600	15,300			
	50	55	71'3"	9,200	11,200			
	60	45	62'9"	7,050	8,700			
	70	34	50'9"	5,600	6,950			
90	20	80	94'9"	*29,000	*29,000			
	25	77	93'9"	25,100	*26,000			
	30	73	92'3"	19,000	*22,200			
	40	66	86'6"	12,500	15,200			
	50	59	83'3"	9,050	11,000			
	60	51	76'3"	6,900	8,550			
	70	43	66'9"	5,450	6,800			
	80	32	53'6"	4,400	5,600			
100	20	81	105'0"	*25,300	*25,300			
	30	75	102'9"	18,800	*20,500			
	40	69	99'3"	12,300	15,000			
	50	63	94'9"	8,850	10,800			
	60	56	88'9"	6,700	8,400			
	70	49	81'0"	5,250	6,600			
	80	40	70'6"	4,200	5,350			
	90	30	56'3"	3,350	4,400			
110	20	81	115'0"	*22,000	*22,000			
	30	76	113'0"	*17,700	*17,700			
	40	71	110'0"	12,100	*14,000			
	50	65	106'0"	8,650	10,700			
	60	59	100'6"	6,500	8,200			
	70	53	93'9"	5,050	6,450			
	80	46	85'3"	4,000	5,200			
	90	38	74'3"	3,200	4,250			
	100	29	59'0"	2,600	3,500			

Figure 10.—Typical crane capacity chart.

POWER CRANES AND ATTACHMENTS

Incidentally, when the boom length exceeds the normal or standard length, as shown in figure 10, the crane's lifting capacity is reduced.

The crane boom can be increased by two methods. The most common method is by inserting intermediate center sections. The second method is by adding a boom tip extension, called a jib (fig. 11).

In general, when crane booms are lengthened, the gantry, or "A" frame, must be extended so that a sufficient lifting angle for the boom lines can be provided. Some cranes used by the SEABEES are equipped with stationary or non-adjustable gantries.

Special devices are available to prevent crane booms from going over backwards. Such devices consist of telescopic boom stops, cable anchor stops, or fixed stops to limit the backward free travel of the boom, boom hoist clutch, or engine clutch and throw-out linkage which permits the operator from accidentally pulling the boom over backwards by power.

The hookblock used on the crane should be of ample capacity to handle the maximum safe load. The safe working capacity (SWC) of a hook can be approximately by using the following rule of thumb: SWC (in tons) = D^2. The diameter (D) in inches of the hook is where the inside of the hook starts its arc. Thus, the safe working capacity of a hook with a diameter of 2 inches is as follows: SWC = D^2 = $(2)^2$ = 4 tons, or 8,000 pounds.

Tables of lifting capacities, posted inside the crane, usually do not include allowances for the weight of the hookblock being used. Therefore, the hookblock weight must be added into the overall weight being lifted.

CLAMSHELL

Like the crane, the clamshell (fig. 12) is a vertically operated attachment capable of working in three zones: at, above, and below ground level. Clamshell equipment consists of a crane-type boom, hoist drum laggings, clamshell bucket, tagline, and necessary wire ropes. The clamshell is capable of digging loose to medium type soils in all three zones, as well as dumping in any of the three zones. The height that can be reached by the clamshell is dependent on the length of the boom used, and the depth reached depends upon the length of the wire rope employed. The amount of wire rope that can be put on the cable drums is limited by the size of the drums and laggings.

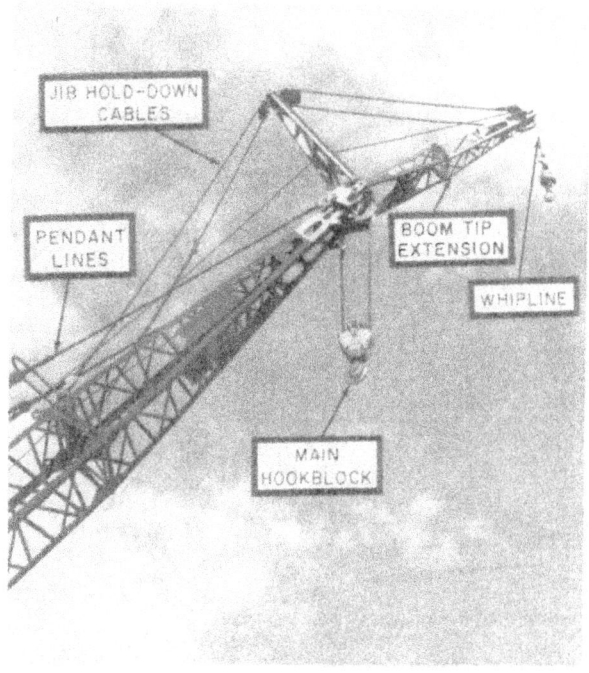

Figure 11.—Boom tip extension (jib).

The clamshell bucket (fig. 13) consists of two scoops hinged together. Each scoop includes a back bottom plate, side plates, lip, teeth, hinge, and arm brackets. One scoop is equipped with tagline attachments. Counterweights are bolted around the hinge. The bucket is controlled by the holding line, closing line, and tag line. There are three types of buckets, classified as Type I (light duty rehandling), Type II (general purpose), and Type III (heavy duty excavation). On most projects, the Type II bucket, in sizes from 1/2-cubic yard to 2 1/2 cubic yard capacity, is generally used. Buckets with a capacity of 3 1/2 cubic yards are available for special units.

The tagline winder is a device used to control the tension on the tag line to prevent the clamshell bucket from twisting during operation. Some older machines use various devices, such as a heavy weight which slides or rolls up and down the boom, to control this twisting motion. The winder type of tagline shown in figure 14, however, is commonly used today. This type of tagline winder is interchangeable with any make or model of crane.

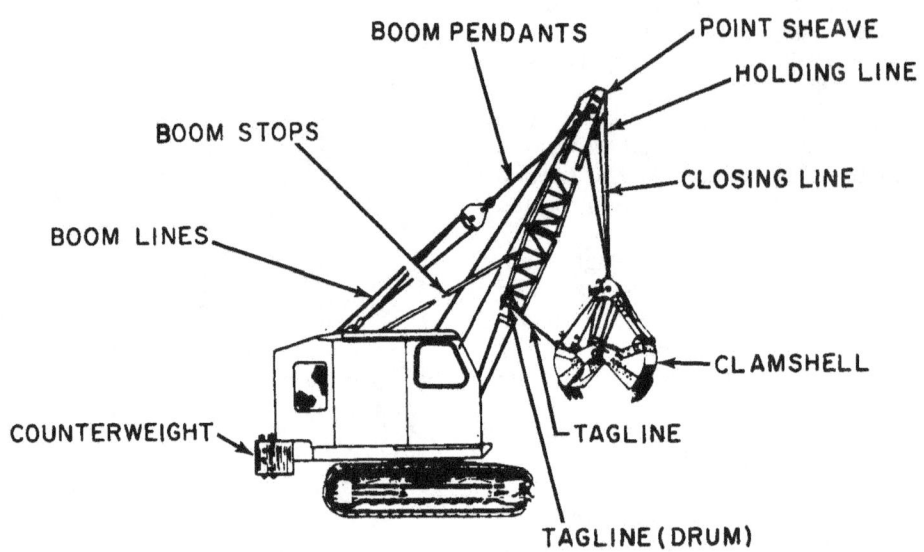

Figure 12.—Crane with clamshell attachment.

To obtain the safe working capacity for the clamshell, refer to the appropriate crane capacity table for the boom length and operating radius, then multiply the allowable load listed by 0.88. This reduces the allowable load to 2/3 of the tipping load for an additional safety factor.

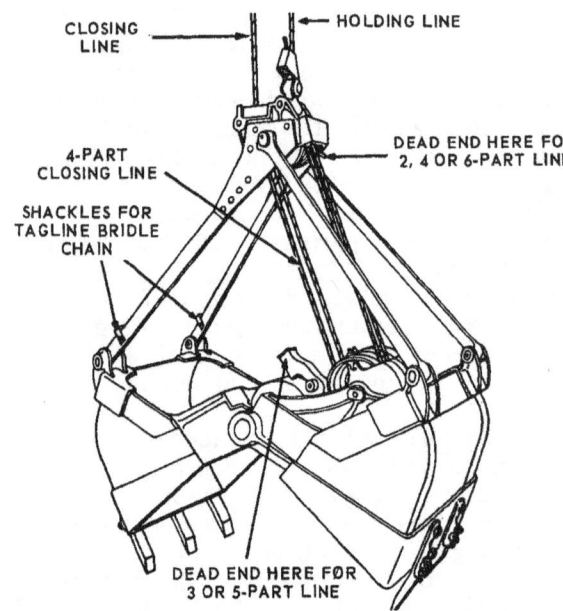

Figure 13.— Clamshell bucket.

The drum laggings used on the clamshell may be the same type as those used for the crane or may be changed to meet the speed and pull required for effective operation. This requirement depends upon the design of the equipment, so the manufacturer's technical manual on the machine should be consulted.

DRAGLINE

Draglines are best used for excavating loose materials below the working level of the machine. They are also used in underwater excavation. In digging operations, the dragline is used to dig dirt, shale, and well blasted rock. Such jobs include stripping overburden, digging borrow pits, and digging and cleaning drainage ditches. The dragline is capable of digging well below the ground level.

The dragline (fig. 15) consists of a crane-type boom, dragline bucket, fairlead assembly, and the necessary wire ropes. The fairlead accomplishes what its name implies — it "fairleads" the drag rope when it is wound in on the drum during loading operations of the dragline bucket.

In dumping operations, the dragline disposes of the excavated materials either by loading into haul units or by casting onto a spoil bank. (Either of these operations must be done by an experienced operator.) The casting method is used to build a levee or dike.

POWER CRANES AND ATTACHMENTS

Casting and dumping material as far as possible from the unit is accomplished by the dragline because of its long, low boom. When ditching in swampy areas (as may be required in malaria control ditching), large, rigid, timber mats are fabricated and fitted with lifting slings so that the operator can lift one mat and place it ahead of the crane when movement is necessary.

BACKHOE

The backhoe (fig. 16) is a positive digging tool and incorporates some of the characteristics of both the shovel and the dragline. It is used primarily to dig below ground level. It will dig harder material than the dragline or clamshell, because the weight of the boom is used to force the dipper into the material. The backhoe is limited in digging depth by the length of the boom, the length of the stick, and the bucket size. The backhoe dipper can be controlled more accurately than the dragline bucket; therefore, it is better suited to close-limit work.

The attachment consists of five major components: dipper, dipper handle, box type boom, auxiliary A-frame, and a grooved drum lagging that is installed on the front drum for the dipper pull rope. Used with these components are the dipper pitch braces, dipper padlock, sheave, dipper teeth and side plates, dipper hinge pin, dipper hoist sheave, boom foot pins, wire rope for the A-frame suspension boom hoist, and dipper pull rope.

The backhoe is used to dig trenches, footings, and basements. It is excellent for this type work because it digs straight, vertical sidewalls; cuts a level floor; trims corners neatly and squarely; works from the top on dry safe ground; and reduces hand trim to a minimum.

The backhoe disposes of material either by loading into hauling units or by dumping on a spoil bank. Its dumping range is not as far as that of the dragline unit because of the fixed dimensions of the boom stick.

The following factors have a major effect upon the capacity of a backhoe: width of excavation desired, depth to be worked, type of material to be handled, and method of disposal of material. All of these factors affect the cycle of operation which directly affects the output capacity of the backhoe. Therefore, for planning purposes or as a guide, the selection of the right size dipper bucket for the backhoe is a critical element of backhoe production. The effect of this selection can best be described by the following

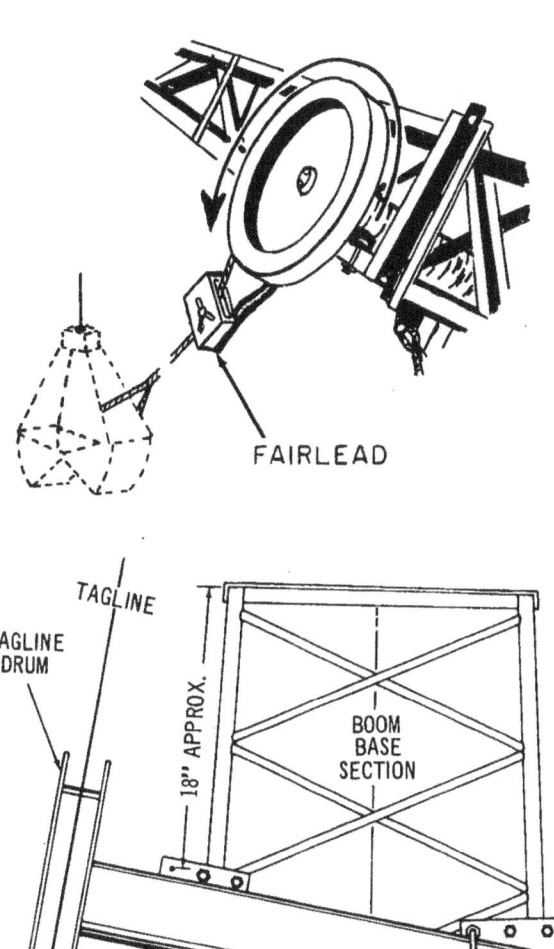

Figure 14.— Typical tagline winder.

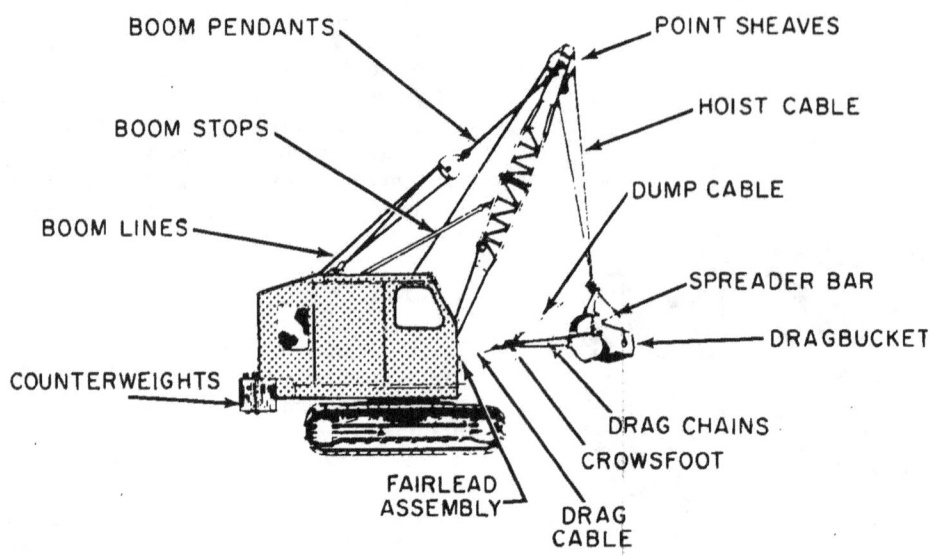

Figure 15.—Crane with dragline attachment.

examples: a typical backhoe equipped with a 1/2-yard bucket will only have a rated digging depth of about 17 feet; using a 3/4-yard bucket will give a 20-foot rated digging depth; and a machine equipped with a 1-1/2-yard bucket will have a rated digging depth of 26 feet.

It should be noted that the cycle of operation of the backhoe is somewhat less than that of the clamshell and closer to that of the shovel—allow 20 to 35 seconds per pass.

POWER SHOVEL

The shovel attachment (fig. 17) is composed of four major components: a heavy-duty box type boom, saddle block, dipper-stick, and dipper.

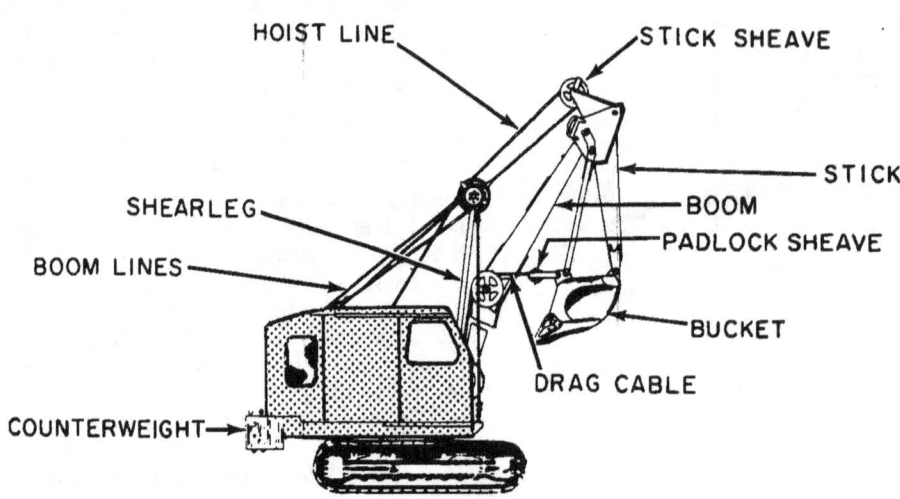

Figure 16.—Crane with backhoe attachment.

POWER CRANES AND ATTACHMENTS

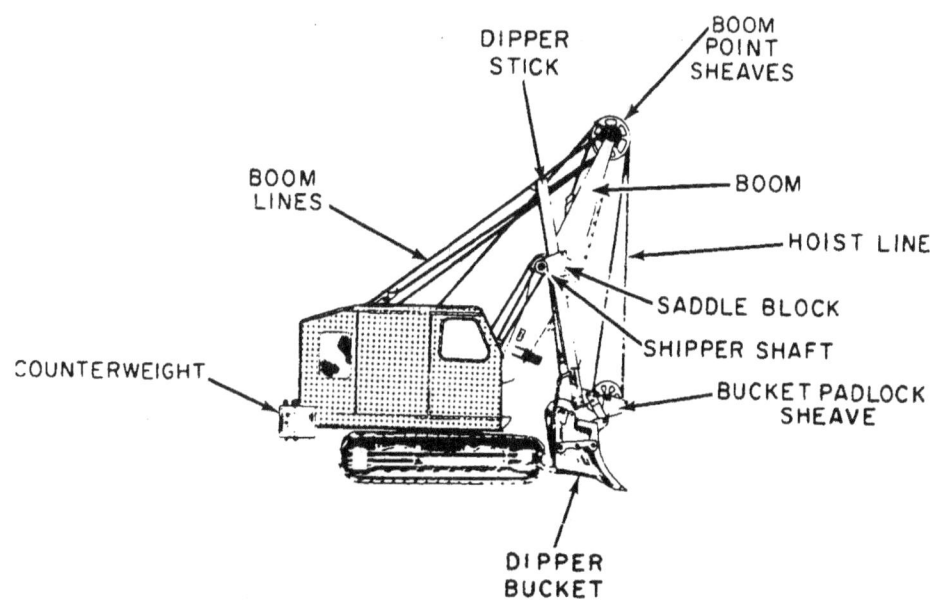

Figure 17.—Crane with shovel attachment.

Used with these components are wire ropes for boom suspension, for dipper hoist, and for crowd and retract action. Some shovels have a roller chain and wire rope combination crowd and retract, or all chain crowd and retract.

The shovel will dig at, above, and below ground level. It is capable of digging and loading material that is loose to hard, such as bank gravel. The shovel can load trucks that are spotted on the bank above ground level of the machine. When digging below ground level, the shovel is limited to depth by the length of the dipper-stick. When the shovel is used to excavate below ground level, the machine must straddle the trench as it is being dug. Caution must be exercised when excavating a ditch in soft soil, to ensure that the excavation does not cave in and the machine tip over.

The shovel is the most effective attachment to use for the excavation of hard, compact material at the face of an embankment and for loading the material onto haul units.

The shovel can be used for stripping of overburden with the material being dumped onto spoil banks. On hillside or mountainside road construction, material can be dumped over the embankment. In sand or gravel pits, material can be dumped onto a belt conveyor or grizzly.

The nature of the excavation requires a sufficient depth of cut for maximum effect. The height of the embankment should not exceed the height of the boom tip. With the top of the embankment higher than the boom tip, the dipper will undercut because it cannot reach high enough to cut the material down due to the shipper shaft height. This situation can cause the embankment to break off in large chunks which can severely damage the machine.

In hard digging, with the shovel boom set at an angle of approximately 50 degrees, the radius between the center pin and the dipper is shorter. This makes the counterweight more effective in preventing tipping of the machine.

Excavating too far beyond the boom point is never practical because the power available diminishes rapidly as the dipper-stick is extended beyond the imaginary line plumbed from the boom point to the ground.

PILEDRIVER

The piledriver is used to drive various types of wood, steel, and concrete piling for foundations, bridge bents, piers, and wharves.

The piledriver shown in figure 18 consists of a crane boom, adapter plates, leads, catwalk (lead braces), hammer, and necessary wire ropes.

EQUIPMENT OPERATOR 3 & 2

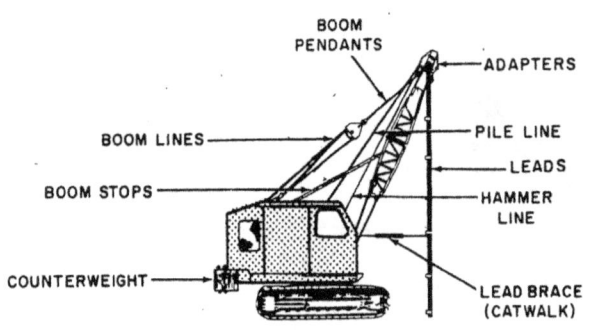

Figure 18.—Crane with piledriver attachment.

The adapter plates are bolted to the top section of the leads and fastened to the boom tip shaft. The leads are fastened to the foot of the boom by the telescopic braces that make up the catwalk. The hammer may be air-, steam-, diesel-, or gravity-operated.

To help ensure maximum production, the piledriver should be placed so that a minimum amount of time is lost due to moving. This placement is generally parallel to the long axis of the pile group. The piles should be close enough to the site that the operator need only swing to pick up the next pile. The piledriver should be placed on level, stable soil while driving. When driving from a barge, the barge should be anchored tightly and remain stationary. Piles are preferably driven off the end of the barge. Light continuous blows by the pilehammer are perferable to heavy frequent blows, which cause more pile failure.

III. OPERATION OF CRANES AND ATTACHMENTS

Information on prestart checks, during operation checks, operating procedures, and securing methods typical of cranes and attachments used by industry is given in the following sections. Bear in mind, however, that this chapter does not attempt to tell you all you need to know about the operation of cranes and attachments. The sole source of complete and authentic information on crane and attachment operations is the operator's manual provided by the manufacturer of the crane or attachment concerned.

PRESTART CHECKS

Prestart checks and operator services made on cranes and attachments are similar to those described for equipment in previous chapters of this manual. However, the location of items to be checked differs from one type of crane and attachment to another.

Make sure the hydraulic boom is cradled and all hydraulic control valves are in the hold position. Remove the hydraulic tank screen and breather from the hydraulic reservoir located on the left side of the operator's compartment. Check the level of the hydraulic oil in the reservoir. When necessary, add the specified type of hydraulic oil to bring the level within 6 inches below the top of the tank.

STARTING CHECKS

After starting the engine, and before putting a crane into operation, a few checks are necessary. These checks are basically the same which have been covered in previous chapters. Only additional checks peculiar to the hydraulic type of crane will be given below.

The hydraulic system pressure gage will show the safe and log ranges of the hydraulic system pressure. When the pressure reaches approximately 1550 psi, the system has attained safe operating pressure. As the controls are operated, the constant use of hydraulic oil will eventually cause the accumulator pressure to drop to the low end of the operating range, at approximately 1400 psi.

Check the rear steering indicator light. When the RED light is on, it indicates that the rear wheels are not straight ahead. When the RED light is off, it indicates the rear wheels are straight.

DURING OPERATION CHECKS

Malfunctions may be present even though all indicators on the crane register within the specified range during operation. There are various symptoms by which common types of malfunctions can be identified. These symptoms are the same as described in previous portions of this manual for automotive vehicles and tractors and attachments; therefore, the symptoms need not be repeated here.

POWER CRANES AND ATTACHMENTS

OPERATING CRAWLER-
MOUNTED CRANE

A variety of front-end attachments are used on crawler-mounted cranes because no one type of boom or mounting is suitable for every job. Therefore, the safe and efficient use of a crawler-mounted crane requires skill and alertness on the part of the operator.

Before operating the crawler-mounted crane, you should first become familiar with its different indicators and controls. Figure 19 shows the indicators and controls of the P & H model 640 crawler-mounted crane. The purpose of the various indicators and controls is explained below; the numbers in parentheses correspond to those used in figure 19 to indicate the location of indicators and controls.

The ENGINE STARTING SWITCH (1) is an automotive type switch which closes the circuit that energizes the engine starting motor.

The GLOW PLUG SWITCH (2) is provided to turn on the engine heating device, called a glow plug, for cold weather starting. A light will indicate when the glow plug is energized.

The PRIMING PUMP PRESSURE GAGE (3) indicates fuel pressure under starting conditions only.

The ENGINE HOUR METER (4) records the actual hours of engine operation. It eliminates guesswork when determining proper lubrication and maintenance periods.

Before starting in cold weather, the ENGINE PRIMING PUMP LEVER (5) is used to prime the engine.

To engage or disengage the locking device within the cooling fins of the crane's REAR drum, the MANUAL LOCK LEVER (6) is used.

To engage or disengage the locking device within the cooling fins of the crane's FRONT drum, the MANUAL LOCK LEVER (7) is used.

By mechanically applying the SWING BRAKE LOCK LEVER (8) in the forward position, the swing brake is applied, locking the crane's upper revolving unit over the front of the crawler assembly.

The HYDRAULIC SYSTEM PRESSURE GAGE (9) shows the safe and low ranges of the hydraulic system pressure.

The CRAWLER STEERING LEVER (10) controls the crane steering operations. Push the control lever away from you and the machine turns left; pull the control lever towards you and the machine turns right; release the lever and it returns to the "hold" position.

To engage the REAR (HOIST) DRUM BRAKE LOCK LEVER (11), pull it towards you to retain the pressure applied to the rear drum brake. To release the pressure, first apply a small amount of pressure to the rear drum brake pedal. Then, gradually push the lever away from you to release the pressure on the brake.

To engage the FRONT (DIGGING) DRUM BRAKE LOCK LEVER (12), pull it towards you to retain pressure applied to the front drum brake. To release the pressure, first apply a small amount of pressure to the front drum brake pedal. Then, gradually push the lever away from you to release the pressure on the brake.

The engine fuel tank gage, engine oil pressure gage, engine temperature gage, and the ammeter gage are contained in the GAGE GROUP (13).

The TRANSMISSION SHIFT LEVER (14) is used to select and position the crane transmission for slow line speed, normal service, or light crane application or service.

The ENGINE CLUTCH LEVER (15) is used to engage or disengage the engine clutch. By pushing the lever forward, the engine clutch is engaged. By pulling back on the lever, the engine clutch is disengaged.

When the SWING LEVER (16) is pushed forward, the upper revolving unit swings to the left. When you pull back on the lever, the upper revolving unit swings to the right.

By depressing the FRONT DRUM BRAKE PEDAL (17), the front drum brake is applied.

When the FRONT DRUM LEVER (18) is pulled toward you, the front drum rotates in the direction that will wrap wire rope on the drum. When you push the lever forward, the wire rope will pay off the drum.

By pulling the REAR DRUM LEVER (19) toward you, the rear drum rotates in the direction that will wrap wire rope on the drum. When you push the lever forward, the wire rope will pay off the drum.

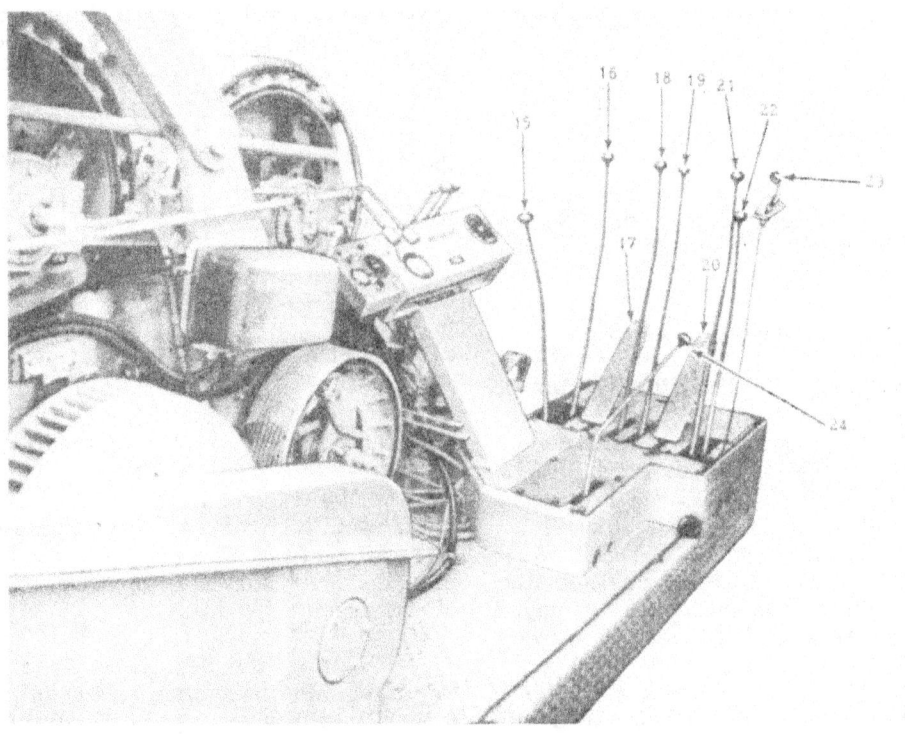

Figure 19.—Indicators and controls, P & H model 640, crawler crane.

POWER CRANES AND ATTACHMENTS

By depressing the REAR DRUM BRAKE PEDAL (20), the rear drum brake is applied.

When the BOOM HOIST BRAKE AND CLUTCH LEVER (21) is pulled towards you, the boom will raise. When you push the lever forward, the boom will lower. It may be necessary to raise the boom slightly before it can be lowered in order to disengage the boom hoist pawl.

When you pull the SWING BRAKE LEVER (22), hydraulic pressure is supplied, allowing release of the swing brake. However, you must pull the SWING BRAKE LOCK LEVER (8) towards you to retain this pressure as the swing brake is released.

The ENGINE THROTTLE CONTROL (23) is used to control engine speed and to shut down the engine by cutting off the fuel.

By pushing forward on the PROPEL CONTROL LEVER (24) the propel clutch is engaged and the machine is propelled forward. When you pull backwards on the lever, the machine is propelled to the rear.

NOTE: All propel and steering directions mentioned above are based on the assumption that you have positioned the upper revolving unit over the front of the crawler assembly, traveling forward.

Starting The Engine

In starting the P & H model 640 crawler-mounted crane engine under normal conditions, follow the step-by-step procedure given below.

(1) Disengage the engine clutch and place the transmission in neutral.
(2) Place the ignition switch in the START position to start the engine. Do not hold the starting motor ON for more than 30 seconds at a time. If the engine does not start in this period of time, wait until the starting motor stops before trying again.

When the engine starts, allow it to run at part throttle, no load, for about 5 minutes to warm up. Observe the gages on the instrument panel for proper readings.

Steps For Operating

To place the P & H model 640 crawler-mounted crane in motion after the engine has started, follow this procedure:

(1) Set the crane engine throttle at load speed.
(2) Check all controls and brakes for proper operating position.
(3) Engage the engine clutch lever.
(4) Position the transmission shift lever in the desired speed of operation.
(5) Engage the propel control lever in the desired position and move the crane to the operating area.

Stopping The Crawler-Mounted Crane

To bring the crane to a stop, proceed as follows:

(1) Disengage the propel control lever.
(2) Lower the crane load or attachment to the ground.
(3) Set all brakes and safety pawls.
(4) Position the transmission shift lever to neutral.
(5) Disengage the engine clutch.

Stopping The Engine

To stop the crane engine, follow this procedure:

(1) With no load on the engine, decrease engine speed and allow the engine to run at half speed or less for a few minutes before closing the throttle and stopping the engine. This will allow the engine to cool down and permit gradual and uniform cooling.
(2) Place the engine throttle control in the fuel shut-off position.
(3) Turn the key switch counterclockwise to the OFF position.

Hookblock Operations

In operating a crane equipped with basic attachments, start all jobs, when possible, from relatively level ground. If necessary, level and area large enough to provide sufficient working space for the crane. When using the crane with the HOOKBLOCK attachment (fig. 9), follow the procedure below for efficient operation.

1. Be sure the footing is adequate.
2. Where repetitive lifting is involved, position the crane for the shortest possible swing.
3. Level the crane to avoid swinging "uphill" or "downhill." Level footing requires less power and is faster and safer.

4. Use taglines to avoid excessive swinging of bulky loads.

5. Use adequate lengths of hoist line to assure full travel of the hookblock to the lowest point required.

6. Organize the work for minimum travel time. All lifts required in one area should be completed before moving to a new location.

7. Use power down equipment where precise load handling is required.

8. Do not use excessive counterweight or tiedown devices to increase stability. Their use will cause additional stress and equipment failures.

The crane operating cycle includes the following steps: setting the boom angle (boom hoist operations), lifting the load, swinging, spotting, and lowering the load.

To set the boom angle, position the crane boom at the proper angle for the load and working conditions. Find the correct angle from the load rating data plate mounted in the cab. On some cranes, the boom is raised by engaging a boom hoist clutch. Lower the boom by first releasing the boom gear locks and then moving the boom lever in the opposite direction. Lowering is usually controlled by a boom brake. However, the booms on most makes of cranes used by the industry are lowered under power. In this case, the boom is lowered through the gears.

To lift the load, attach the crane hook securely to the load. Engage the hoist clutch and release the hoist drum brake to take up on the hoist cable. Hoist the load to the desired height. To stop hoisting, apply the hoist drum brake and disengage the hoist drum clutch.

To swing the load, engage the swing clutch for a right or left swing. This should be done slowly so that the swing motion will start and stop smoothly. When the swing has been completed, engage the opposite swing clutch lightly to stop the motion.

Spotting and lowering the load requires accurate control of the hoist and swing movements in order to locate the load at the exact spot without hunting or overshooting. The load can be lowered by partially releasing the hoist brake or by power.

Clamshell Operations

When using the crane with the CLAMSHELL attachment (fig. 12), the following procedure applies:

1. Level ground is preferred for positioning the unit.

2. Position the unit so that the clamming or digging operation is the same radius as the dumping operation; this is to avoid excessive wear on the boom mechanism and the wasting of production time by moving the boom.

3. Select the correct bucket size for the machine.

4. When lowering the clamshell bucket, if too much pressure is applied to the closing line brake, the bucket will close and excess line will unwind off the holding drum. To avoid this, release the holding line and closing line brakes to lower the open clamshell into the material for the initial bite. Engage the closing line clutch and release the brake. Control the digging depth by using the holding line clutch and brake.

5. During hoisting, if the hoist line gets ahead of the closing line—the bucket will open and spill the material. (This could be caused by too much wire rope on the hoist drum). In this event, when the bucket is at the desired height, apply both holding and closing line brakes and disengage both clutches.

The clamshell operating cycle includes the following four steps: filling (closing) the bucket, raising the loaded bucket, swinging and dumping. The boom position is set before beginning the digging operations.

Filling (closing) the bucket is accomplished by lowering the open clamshell until it is about a foot above the material to be worked.

As soon as the bucket is almost closed and loaded, keep the closing line clutch engaged and engage the holding line clutch so that both cables are taken up at the same time.

When the clamshell is raised enough to clear all obstacles, start the swing by engaging one of the swing clutches. Hoisting the bucket can be continued as it is swung to the dumping site. The spring-loaded tagline will retard the twisting motion of the bucket if the swing is done smoothly.

Dumping or unloading the clamshell is accomplished by keeping the holding line brake applied while the closing line brake is released. Apply the closing line brake quickly after the load is dumped to prevent the closing line from unwinding more wire than is needed to drop the material. After the bucket is emptied, swing the open clamshell back to the digging site. Then lower the open bucket and repeat the cycle.

POWER CRANES AND ATTACHMENTS

Dragline Operations

When using the crane with a DRAGLINE attachment (fig. 15), follow the operational procedures below.

1. The dragline bucket teeth should be kept sharp and built up to proper size.
2. The dump rope should be kept short so the load can be picked up well out from the machine.
3. The working area should be excavated in layers, not in trenches, and kept sloped upward toward the machine.
4. The bucket should not be dragged in so close to the machine that it will build up piles and ridges of material in front of the machine.
5. The bucket should never be guided by swinging the machinery deck frame while digging. This puts side stress on the boom which can cause failure. The swing should not be started until the bucket has been raised clear of the ground.
6. A pair of drag chains are attached to the front of the bucket through brackets by which the pull point may be moved up or down. The upper position is used for deep or hard digging as it pulls the teeth into a steeper angle.
7. The dragline cable can be end-for-end to prolong cable life, reduce early cable replacement, and keep cable replacement costs to a minimum.

The dragline operating steps can be worked in a smooth, even order. These steps include: filling the bucket, lifting the bucket, swinging the load, and dumping the load. The boom angle is usually set before beginning the digging operation.

In lowering the dragline bucket into the area to be worked, release the drag brake to tip the cutting edge down and then release the hoist brake. It is not necessary to drop the bucket to force the teeth into the material. The bucket is filled as it is dragged toward the machine by engaging the drag drum clutch and releasing the drag brake. The cutting depth is controlled by slacking off on the hoist brake.

When lifting the dragline bucket, raise the load by engaging the hoist clutch and releasing the hoist brake. At the same time, slip the drag brake to allow the bucket to carry toward the boom point. To hold the bucket at the desired height, apply both footbrakes and disengage the hoist clutch.

When swinging as the bucket is raised, engage the swing clutch to swing toward the dump site. The hoisting and swinging operations can be done at the same time.

For dumping the load when approaching the dump site, release the drag brake to unreel enough cable for the bucket to dump completely. Apply the drag brake to keep from unwinding excess cable. Swing the boom back to the digging area and repeat the steps of the operating cycle.

Backhoe Operations

When using the crane with the BACKHOE attachment (fig. 16), here is the operational procedure to follow.

1. The backhoe dipper teeth should be kept sharp and built up to proper size.
2. The most convenient position for a truck to be loaded by a backhoe is as close to the machine as possible in order to reduce spillage. Back the haul unit toward the backhoe to allow dumping in the full length of the truck body. The danger in this position is the possibility of the drag rope breaking which may permit the dipper to swing outward, taking the truck cab with it. For this reason, trucks are often loaded from the side. The dipper should be guided by swinging the machinery deck frame only before the digging begins. Never swing the machinery deck frame during the time of digging, otherwise undue side stress on the boom results.

The backhoe operating cycle, which is basically the same as the dragline, includes the following steps: filling the bucket during its digging motion, dragging, hoisting, swinging, dumping, and return to the digging position. The backhoe main boom angle, being flexible, allows the operator to change the digging depth and the hoisting height.

Filling the backhoe bucket requires coordination in hoisting and dragging (pulling). The bucket can be moved out horizontally from any raised position by releasing or slipping the drag brake so that the bucket swings out, engaging the hoist clutch enough to prevent hitting the ground. When it is almost fully extended or is at the desired distance, the drag clutch is applied and the hoist drum released. The boom, stick, and bucket will fall together, striking the teeth on the ground with a pickaxe effect. Engage the drag clutch, release the hoist, and the bucket will move toward the basic crane. The drag clutch is partially or intermittently engaged. As soon as the bucket is filled, the hoist clutch is engaged, the drag clutch is released, and the drag brake applied with the hoist continuing.

The swing clutch is engaged to swing to the left or right. All models require the use of the opposite swing clutch to slow the swing to a stop. During the swinging of the bucket, hoisting continues until you reach the dumping position, and finish dumping.

When the bucket reaches the dumping position, the drag brake is released and the bucket swings outward, dumping the material. As it reaches its outward swing, release the hoist clutch and apply the hoist brake. Start swinging the empty bucket back toward the cut being worked. Lower the bucket by releasing the hoist brake to allow the boom and stick to lower to the digging position and start the cycle once again.

Shovel Operations

When using the crane with the SHOVEL attachment (fig. 17) for shovel operation, the following procedure applies.

1. The shovel should be positioned on ground that is as level as possible. When used in areas where material is soft, the shovel should be supported on construction mats. Only material that is broken up small enough to pass through the dipper should be handled.

2. At the start of digging, the dipper should be at crawler (or wheel) level and two or three feet in front of the crawlers (or wheels).

3. The shovel should travel on ground that is free of holes and large boulders so that the tracks will have bearing for their full length. A rocking shovel is difficult to operate and may cause damage to the track frames.

4. For best results, the shovel should be kept moved up to the working face. After each move up, the proper digging sequence is to start at the center of the face and make alternate passes on each side of the center until all of the face within reach is cut back evenly. The dipper should be filled by a straight forward pass against a working face at optimum bank height. When the excavation is deep, the working face is terraced.

5. When excavating hard material with the shovel, lifts that raise the tracks off the ground should be avoided because of possible damage to the track frames.

The shovel operating cycle includes the following steps: filling the dipper, swinging, dumping and return to the digging position. The shovel boom angle is usually set before beginning shovel operation. The boom angle for shovel operation is approximately 45 degrees.

Filling the dipper requires the coordination of two movements: hoisting and crowding (shoveling). Hoisting the bucket is done first by engaging the bucket hoist clutch and releasing the bucket hoist brake. As the dipper begins its lift, the digging depth is controlled by engaging the crowd clutch and releasing the crowd brake; this allows the dipper to crowd into the bank. As soon as the dipper is filled, both brakes are applied and the hoist and crowd clutches are released.

Before swinging the extended dipper, make sure that it will clear the bank by rehauling the dipper, if necessary. After this is done, the swing clutch is engaged to swing either left or right. All models require the use of the opposite swing clutch to slow the swing to a stop. As the shovel is swinging, adjust the length of the dipper-stick by crowding or retracting so that the dipper door will be directly over the dumping point when the swing is completed.

When the dipper is over the dumping point, raise or lower the dipper, if necessary, to the proper height for dumping. Then engage the dipper trip clutch to open the dipper door. Hoist the dipper enough to allow the open door to clear all obstructions.

Start swinging the empty dipper back toward the cut being worked. Retract the dipper as necessary to clear the bank. Lower the dipper by releasing the hoist brake to allow the dipper to swing back under the boom. Also, release the crowd brake to drop the dipper to the ground. Do not let the dipper strike the boom or the carrier.

Piledriver Operations

The crane with a PILEDRIVER attachment is shown in figure 18. The type of piledriving hammer used in piledriving operations may be a drophammer, a diesel-driven hammer, or a pneumatic/steam hammer. Assume for the purposes of this discussion that you are using the drophammer. The piledriving operational procedure to follow when using this type equipment is given below.

POWER CRANES AND ATTACHMENTS

1. The piledriver should be placed on level, stable soil while driving.
2. The piledriver should be placed so that only a minimum amount of time will be lost in moving.
3. The piledriver placement is generally parallel to the long axis of the pile group.
4. The piles should be close enough to the site that you need only to swing the crane to pick up the next pile.

The piledriving operating cycle includes the following steps: positioning the hammer and pile cap, raising the pile from the horizontal to the vertical, lowering the hammer and cap onto the top of the pile, removing the pile hoist line hitch from the pile and the cap sling from the hammer, and driving the pile. The piledriving lead's position is set before beginning the driving operation.

Hoist the hammer and cap by engaging the rear drum hoist clutch lever (hammer and cap line) and releasing the rear drum hoist brake. As the hammer and cap begin to lift, the height of the lift is controlled by applying the brake and releasing the hoist clutch.

Hoist the pile into the desired position by engaging the front drum hoist clutch lever (pile line) and releasing the front drum hoist brake. As the pile reaches the desired position, apply the brake and release the hoist clutch.

Lower the hammer and cap by releasing the hammer line brake until the hammer and cap are positioned over the pile.

Remove the pile hoist line hitch from the pile and the cap sling from the hammer before driving.

Engage the rear drum hoist clutch lever and release the rear drum hoist brake, raising the hammer about 10 feet. Control the lift by applying the brake and releasing the hoist clutch.

Lower the hammer by releasing the hoist brake to allow the hammer to drive the pile, and start the cycle once again, remembering to keep a steady rate of speed on the hammer while raising and lowering it.

OPERATING TRUCK-MOUNTED CRANES

Before operating a truck-mounted crane, you should first become familiar with its different indicators and controls. Figure 20 shows the indicators and controls of the upper revolving unit of the P & H model 325TC truck-mounted crane. The purpose of various indicators and controls is described below; the numbers in parentheses correspond to those used in figure 20 to indicate the location of individual indicators and controls.

By pushing forward on the SWING CLUTCH LEVER (1), the upper revolving unit swings to the left. When you pull back on the lever, the upper revolving unit swings to the right.

When the LEFT MAIN DRUM CLUTCH LEVER (2) is pulled towards you, the left main drum rotates in the direction that will wrap wire rope on the drum. When you push the lever forward, the wire rope will pay off the drum.

By pulling the RIGHT MAIN DRUM CLUTCH LEVER (3) towards you, the right main drum rotates in the direction that will wrap wire rope on the drum. When you push the lever forward, the wire rope will pay off the drum.

When the BOOM HOIST CLUTCH LEVER (4) is pulled towards you, the boom raises. When you push the lever forward, the boom hoist brake will release and the boom will lower under power through the planetary gear system. Returning the lever to the neutral position will set this boom hoist brake and hold the boom in the new position. With the boom hoist drum stopped, pull the BOOM HOIST DRUM PAWL CONTROL (17) to engage the safety pawl in the drum ratchet. The pawl should be engaged at all times except when lowering the boom.

The ENGINE HAND THROTTLE (5) is used to control engine speed and to shut down the engine by cutting off the fuel.

The LEFT (6) and RIGHT (7) MAIN DRUM BRAKE PEDALS are pushed down to apply the left and right main drum brakes. The ratchet-type foot pedal lock is engaged by pressing down on the toe of the pedal before releasing the brake. To disengage the brake lock, press down on the pedal and tip the pedal back, using the heel of the pedal. When the optional planetary lowering is not supplied for the left and right main drums, loads on the drum lines are lowered by gravity under control of the brake.

The TRANSMISSION SHIFT LEVER (8) is used to select and position the upper revolving unit engine transmission for slow line speed for fine line control, normal service for all types of operation, light service where speedy operation is desired, or light service for maximum line speed.

When the SWING BRAKE LEVER (9) is pulled towards you the swing brake is applied. When the pushbutton on the lever handle is depressed and the lever is pushed forward, the swing

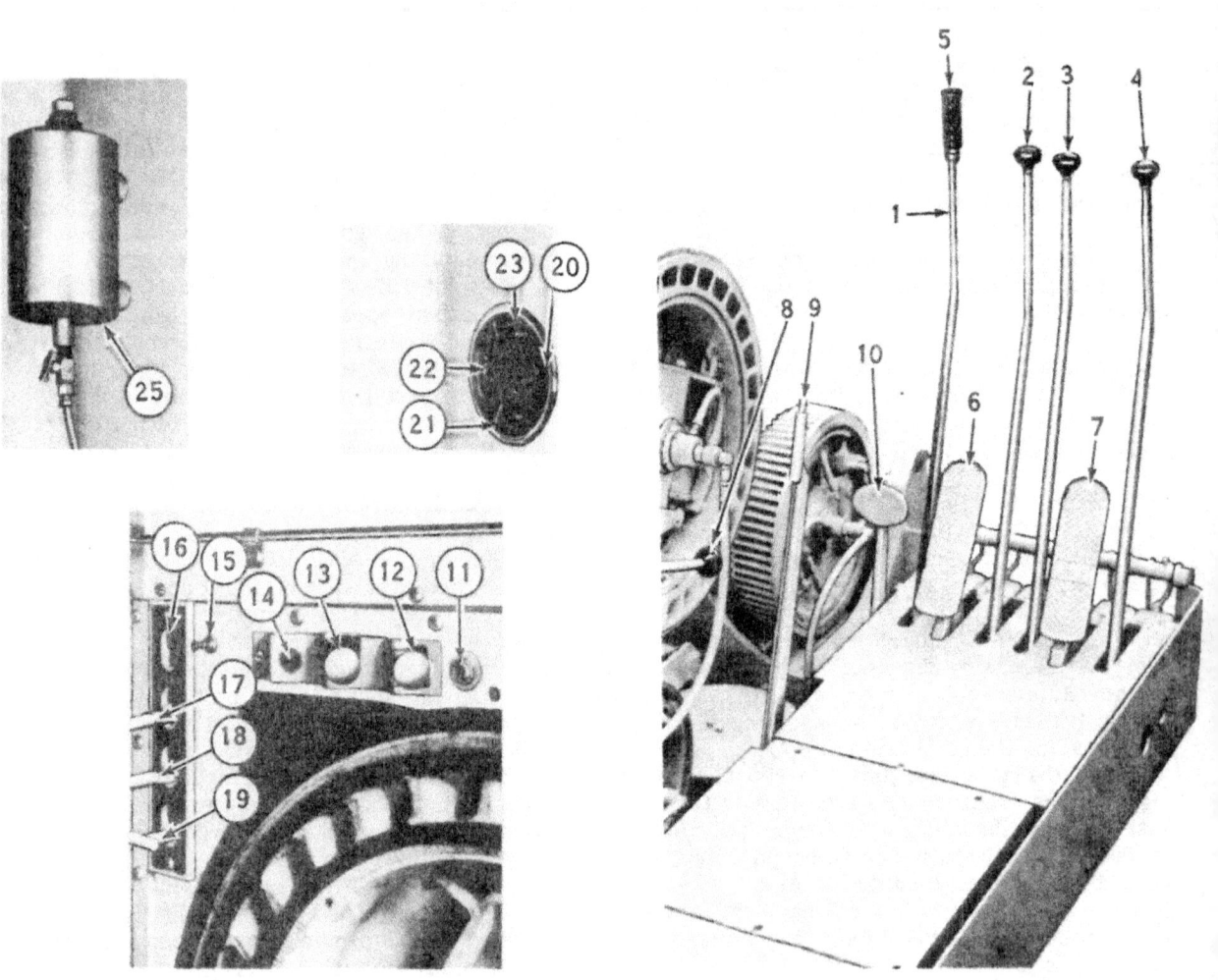

Figure 20.—Indicators and controls, P & H model 325TC, truck-mounted crane upper revolving superstructure.

brake is released, allowing you to swing the upper revolving unit in the desired direction.

The ENGINE CLUTCH PEDAL (10) is depressed to disengage the engine clutch before shifting the TRANSMISSION SHIFT LEVER (8) into the desired operating speed. When shifting is completed, release the clutch pedal.

The STOP KNOB (13), when pushed in, stops the gasoline engine. This knob is used as an emergency stop with diesel engines.

The IGNITION SWITCH (15) is pulled out to turn on the engine ignition.

The RIGHT (18) and LEFT (19) MAIN DRUM PAWL CONTROL LEVERS are pulled out to engage the safety pawl in the right and left drum ratches when the right and left main drums are stopped. This pawl should alway be engaged when suspending a load aloft.

The ENGINE OIL PRESSURE GAGE (20 registers the pressure at which lubricating o is circulating through the engine.

The ENGINE WATER TEMPERATURE GAG (21) registers the temperature of the coolar circulating through the engine.

The ENGINE FUEL GAGE (22) indicates th level of fuel within the fuel tank.

The ENGINE AMMETER (23) indicates the rat at which the battery is being charged or dis charged.

The HYDRAULIC OIL RESERVOIR (25) con tains the proper amount of hydraulic brake flui to supply the individual compensators (or maste

POWER CRANES AND ATTACHMENTS

cylinders) for each clutch and brake operated by the various controls and pedals.

Starting The Upper
Revolving Unit Engine

In starting the P & H model 325TC upper revolving unit engine under normal conditions, follow the step-by-step procedure given below.

(1) Disengage the engine clutch, place the transmission in neutral, and open the throttle slightly.

(2) Place the ignition switch in the START position to start the engine. Do not hold the starting motor ON for more than 30 seconds at a time. If the engine does not start in this period of time, release the starting switch and wait until the starting motor stops before trying again.

After the engine starts, allow it to run idle, at part throttle, for about 5 minutes to warm up. Observe the gages on the instrument panel for proper readings.

Steps For Operating

Observe the following operating steps for placing the P & H model 325TC upper revolving unit in motion after the engine has been started:

(1) Set the engine hand throttle control at load speed.
(2) Check all controls and brakes for proper operating position.
(3) Disengage the engine foot clutch pedal.
(4) Position the engine transmission shift lever in the desired speed of operation.
(5) Release the engine foot clutch pedal.
(6) Depress the pushbutton on the swing brake lever and place the lever in the forward position; this allows the crane to be swung in either direction.
(7) To perform the various functions desired, actuate the necessary control levers and drum brake pedals.

Stopping The Upper
Revolving Unit

To bring the upper revolving unit to a stop, proceed as follows:

(1) Swing the upper revolving unit in proper position over the truck carrier.

(2) Engage the swing brake lever.
(3) Position the load or attachment for travel.
(4) Set all control levers and drum brakes.
(5) Disengage the engine foot clutch pedal.
(6) Place the transmission shift lever in neutral.
(7) Release the engine foot clutch pedal.

Stopping The Upper
Revolving Unit Engine

To stop the upper revolving unit engine, the following steps must be taken:

(1) With no load on the engine, decrease engine speed and let the engine run at half speed or less for a few minutes before closing the throttle and stopping the engine. This will allow the engine to cool down and permit gradual and uniform cooling of engine parts.
(2) Place the engine throttle in the FUEL SHUT OFF position.
(3) Turn the key switch counterclockwise to the OFF position.

OPERATION OF TRUCK CARRIER

Before operating the truck carrier of the truck-mounted crane, you should first become familiar with its different indicators and controls. Figure 21 shows the indicators and controls of the truck carrier for the P & H model 325TC truck-mounted crane. The purpose of various indicators and controls is described below; the numbers in parentheses correspond to those used in figure 21 to indicate the location of individual indicators and controls.

When shifting the main transmission from one speed to another when moving the truck crane, the ENGINE TACHOMETER (1) allows the operator to read and maintain proper engine rpm.

The MAXIBRAKE CONTROL KNOB and EMERGENCY RELEASE VALVE (16) are used in the application and release of the truck carrier parking brakes. By depressing the control knob the truck carrier brakes are applied. When you depress the emergency release valve, the truck carrier parking brakes are released.

Low brake system air pressure is indicated by the LOW AIR PRESSURE GAGE (17).

The AIR PRESSURE GAGE (18) registers the air pressure within the airtank reservoirs (60 lbs pressure is required).

Before shifting the TRANSMISSION SHIFT LEVER and AUXILIARY TRANSMISSION SHIFT LEVER (25) into the desired operating speed,

24

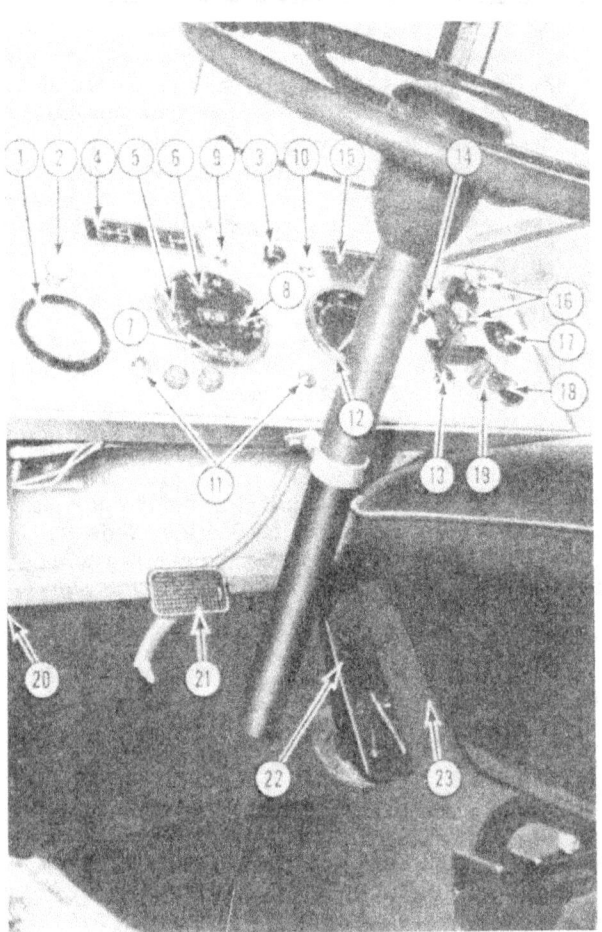

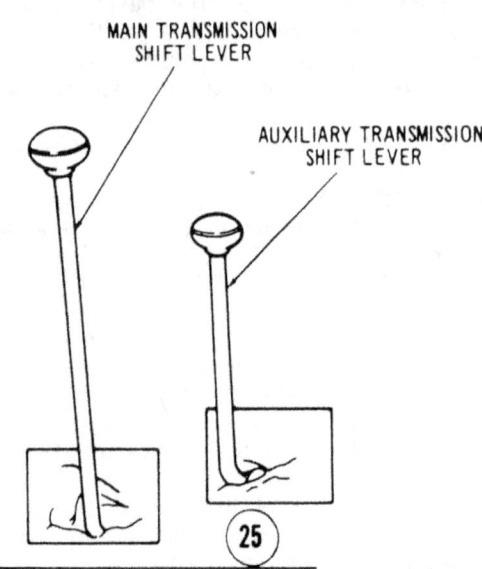

Figure 21.—Indicators and controls, P & H model 325TC, truck-mounted crane truck carrier.

the CLUTCH PEDAL (21) is depressed to disengage the truck carrier engine clutch. When shifting is completed, release the clutch pedal.

The TREADLE BRAKE PEDAL (22) provides you with a graduated means of applying and releasing the truck carrier brakes.

Starting The Truck
Carrier Engine

In starting the P & H model 325TC truck carrier engine under normal conditions, follow this step-by-step procedure:

(1) Disengage the engine clutch and place the transmission in neutral.
(2) Place the engine ignition switch in the ON position and depress the starter button. After the engine starts, allow it to run idle, at part throttle, for about 5 minutes to warm up. Observe the gages on the instrument panel for proper readings.

Steps For Operating

Observe the following steps for placing the truck carrier in motion after the carrier engine has been started:

(1) Disengage the engine clutch pedal.
(2) Position the transmission shift lever and auxiliary transmission shift lever in the desired speed range.
(3) Release the parking brake.
(4) Engage the engine clutch by releasing the clutch pedal and depress the foot accelerator pedal, thus increasing the speed of the engine.
(5) Shift the main transmission lever into the proper speed ranges as the crane moves to the operating area.

Stopping The Truck Carrier of
The Truck-Mounted Crane

To bring the truck crane to a stop, proceed as follows:

(1) Decrease the engine speed by releasing the foot pressure on the accelerator.
(2) Apply pressure to the treadle brake pedal.
(3) Disengage the engine clutch.
(4) Shift the transmission shift lever and the auxiliary transmission shift lever to neutral.
(5) Engage the truck crane parking brake

122

POWER CRANES AND ATTACHMENTS

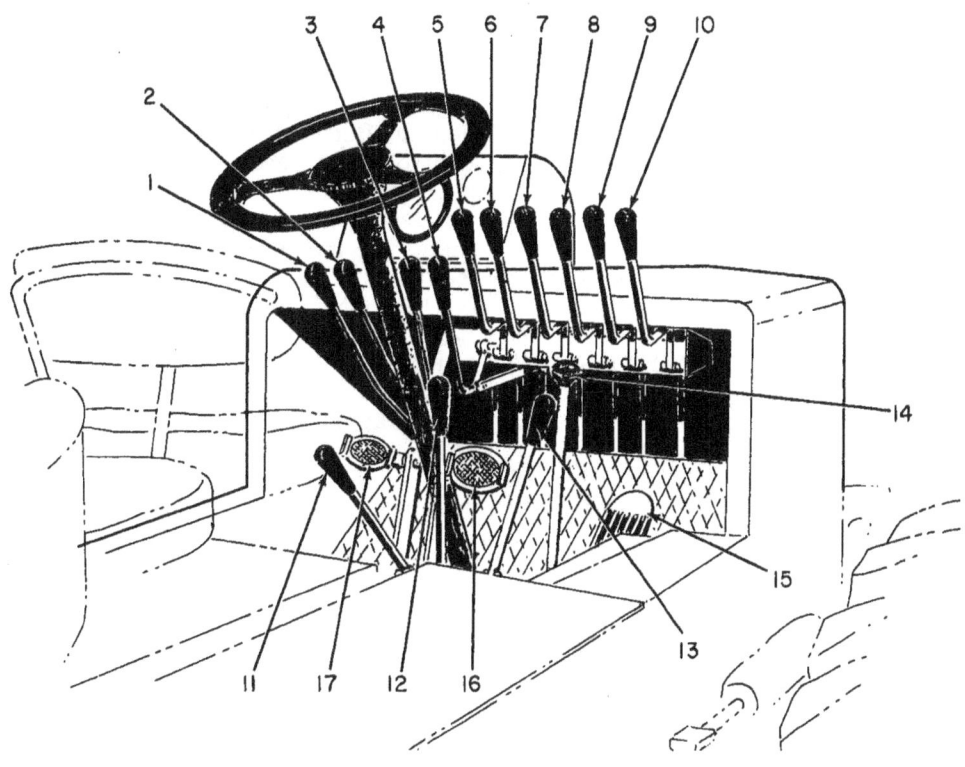

Figure 22. — Controls, Galion model 125, wheel-mounted crane.

Stopping the Truck Carrier Engine

To stop the truck carrier engine, take the following steps:

(1) With no load on the engine, allow it to idle before turning the ignition switch to the OFF position. This allows the engine to cool down and permits gradual and uniform cooling of engine parts.

(2) Turn the ignition switch to the OFF position.

Operation Techniques

Operating techniques which were described in previous sections of this chapter on the operation of the crawler-mounted crane also apply basically to the truck-mounted crane. Therefore, these operating techniques need not be repeated here.

OPERATING WHEEL-MOUNTED CRANE

In previous sections, we discussed the crawler-mounted crane and the truck-mounted crane. Now let's turn our attention to the wheel-mounted crane. The following information will acquaint you with the instruments, controls, and operational capabilities of the Galion model 125 wheel-mounted crane. The purpose of this crane's various controls is explained below; the numbers in parentheses correspond to those used in figure 22 to indicate the location of the controls.

When the LEFT REAR (1), LEFT FRONT (2), RIGHT FRONT (3), and RIGHT REAR (4) OUTRIGGER CONTROL LEVERS are pushed forward, this will cause the left rear, left front, right front, and right rear outriggers to be lowered; when these levers are pulled backwards, the left rear, left front, right front, and right rear outriggers are raised.

By pushing forward on the REAR STEERING CONTROL LEVER (5), the rear wheels on the crane will turn left; when you pull this lever backwards, the rear wheels will turn right.

By pushing forward on the BOOM ROTATION CONTROL LEVER (6), the boom will rotate counterclockwise. Pull the lever backwards and the boom will rotate clockwise.

When the LOW LINE SPEED CONTROL LEVER (7) is pushed forward, the hook will lower; when this lever is pulled backwards, the hook will raise.

When the INTERMEDIATE LINE SPEED CONTROL LEVER (8) is pushed forward, the hook will lower. When this lever is pulled backwards, the hook will raise.

> NOTE: When both control levers are operated together, a HIGH LINE SPEED is obtained.

By pushing forward on the BOOM-EXTEND RETRACT CONTROL LEVER (9), the boom sliding section will extend; when you pull this lever backwards, the boom sliding section will retract.

The boom will lower when the BOOM-RAISE /LOWER CONTROL LEVER (10) is pushed forward; the boom will raise when this lever is pulled backwards.

When the REAR WHEEL DRIVE SELECTOR CONTROL LEVER (11) is pushed fully forward and held in this position, the rear wheel drive is engaged and the control lever will remain in approximate forward position. When the rear wheel drive selector control lever is pulled backwards, the rear wheel drive is disengaged and the control lever will remain in approximate rearward position.

The FORWARD and REVERSE CONTROL LEVER (12) is used to engage the powershift forward-reverse gear box when you move the control lever in the direction of desired travel. The center position is neutral.

Pull the ENGINE SPEED CONTROL LEVER (13) backwards to increase engine speed and push the lever forward to decrease engine speed. Twist the control lever clockwise to lock it in the desired position when working the crane during lifting operations.

When traveling with the crane from one jobsite to the next, the ENGINE ACCELERATOR PEDAL (15) is used to control engine speed.

The TRANSMISSION GEAR SELECTOR LEVER (14) is used to select the desired transmission gear ratio to provide 5 speeds forward or reverse.

The hydraulically operated SERVICE BRAKE PEDAL (16) is depressed to stop the crane.

When applied, the INCHING VALVE PEDAL (17) controls the engagement of the power forward-reverse gear box. It is used in the same manner as an engine clutch to control movement of the crane whether forward or reverse.

The PARKING BRAKE LEVER (not shown) is located to the left of the operator's seat. When the lever is pulled up the parking brakes are applied; when the lever is pushed down to the horizontal position, the brakes are released.

The purpose of the various instruments is explained in the remaining part of this section; the numbers or letters in parentheses correspond to those used in figure 23 to indicate the location of individual instruments.

To close the circuit and energize the engine starting motor, the KEY SWITCH (1) is used.

The HOURMETER (3) records the actual hours of engine operation. It eliminates guesswork when determining proper lubrication and maintenance periods.

The COMBINATION GAGE GROUP (4) contains the engine oil pressure gage (A), the voltmeter (B), the engine temperature gage (C), and the fuel supply gage (D).

When lit, the REAR STEER INDICATOR LIGHT (5) indicates that the crane rear wheels are not

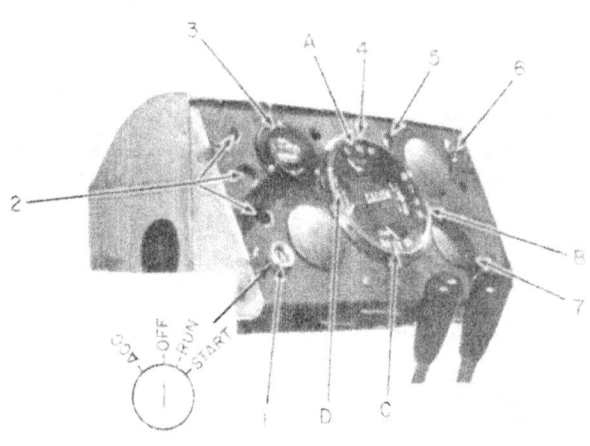

Figure 23.—Instruments, Galion model 125, wheel-mounted crane.

POWER CRANES AND ATTACHMENTS

in the straight-ahead position. When the light goes out, it indicates that the crane rear wheels are in the straight-ahead position.

Starting The Wheel-
Mounted Crane Engine

In starting the Galion model 125 wheel-mounted crane engine under normal conditions, the following procedure applies:

(1) Set the parking brake.
(2) Depress the inching valve control pedal. Keep the pedal depressed when starting to reduce load on the starting motor.
(3) Move the forward-reverse control lever to the neutral position.
(4) Move the engine speed control lever to the rear about 1/3 distance and twist clockwise to lock.
(5) Turn the key switch clockwise to engage the starting motor. When the engine starts, release the key switch and the engine will run. Allow the engine to warm up, and observe the gages on the instrument panel for proper readings.

Steps For Operating

Observe the following steps to place the Galion model 125 wheel-mounted crane in motion after the engine has been started:

(1) Disengage the inching valve control panel.
(2) Position the transmission shift lever in the desired speed range.
(3) Place the forward-reverse control lever in the desired position.
(4) Release the engine speed control lever lock and move the control lever forward to idle position.
(5) Release the parking brake.
(6) Engage the inching valve control pedal by releasing the control pedal; then depress the foot accelerator pedal, which increases the speed of the engine and thus allows the crane to move to the operating area.

Stopping The Wheel-
Mounted Crane

To bring the crane to a stop, proceed as follows:

(1) Decrease the engine speed by releasing foot pressure on the accelerator.
(2) Apply pressure to the footbrake pedal.
(3) Disengage the inching valve control pedal.
(4) Shift the forward-reverse control lever to neutral.
(5) Shift the transmission shift lever to neutral.
(6) Engage the crane parking brake.

Stopping The Crane Engine

To stop the crane engine, follow the procedure below.

(1) With no load on the engine, let it idle 3 to 5 minutes before shutting down. This allows the engine to cool down and permits gradual and uniform cooling of engine parts.
(2) Turn the key switch counterclockwise to the OFF position.

Operation Techniques

In operating the wheel-mounted crane, start all jobs, when possible, from relatively level ground. Avoid holes, rocks, extremely soft ground, slopes, and any other obstacle which might subject the crane to undue stress or possible overturn.

When operating on level terrain in a fixed position, the crane may be supported either on its pneumatic rubber tires or on outriggers only (outriggers set with all four wheels off the ground). Either of these positions assures firm, four-point stability during crane operations.

To pick up a load, maneuver the crane into position. Stop the crane by depressing the brake pedal. Then disengage the inching valve control pedal, place the forward-reverse shift lever in the neutral position, shift the transmission lever in the neutral position, and increase engine speed by pulling the engine speed control lever rearward and locking in the desired position. Now position the outriggers by pushing the control levers forward to the down position. Position the boom with the boom raise/lower, extend/retract, or rotation control lever. Lower the hookblock over the material to be moved by pushing the desired line speed control lever forward. In order to save undue wear on the boom and for stability, the load should be lifted with the boom in the highest position possible. When the load is attached, the rigger will signal you to raise the load. Raise the load by pulling back on the desired line speed control lever which will swing the load clear. When desirable, or necessary, you may raise the boom. If the boom is raised before the hookblock, the load will be dragged along the ground. The hookblock should not be raised so high that it becomes blocked or comes in contact with the boom head. Maximum height and rotation of the boom are controlled by you. Be aware, at all times, of the position of the boom and load.

If the load must be carried further than the boom can reach, it will be necessary to move the crane. The crane should not be moved until the load and the boom are in the proper position for travel. Remember to raise the crane outriggers if in use. In order to reduce the swing of the load, you should move the crane slowly and smoothly, avoiding sudden stops and turns.

After rigging the load for travel, place the transmission in the desired speed range, place the forward-reverse control lever in the desired position, engage the inching valve control pedal, release the footbrake pedal, release the engine speed control lever lock, move the control lever forward to the idle position, and accelerate to desired speed.

While the crane is traveling, you must not allow the load to swing to far. A swinging load causes severe strain on all parts of the crane. When there is danger of the load swinging, have a rigger attach a tag line to the load. The purpose of the tag line is to steer the load and control its swing. Normally, the rigger will walk ahead of the loaded crane with the tag line guiding the load while giving necessary signals concerning travel. When you have maneuvered the crane into position for placing the load, use the boom rotation and extend/retract controls to center the load over the spot where it is to be placed. Then lower the load by moving the desired line speed control lever to the forward position. The rigger should guide the load into position as it is lowered and unhook the load. After the load is unhooked by the rigger, operations can be resumed.

SECURING

When securing a crawler-mounted crane, position the upper revolving superstructure and attachment for traveling, walk the crane to the designated securing area, and position the crane in a safe manner. After the machine has stopped, lower the attachment to the ground, set all brakes and safety pawls, position the transmission shift lever in neutral, disengage the engine clutch, place the engine throttle control in the fuel shut-off position, and turn the key switch counterclockwise to the OFF position. Secure all doors and windows before dismounting the machine.

When securing a truck-mounted crane, position and secure the upper revolving superstructure and attachment for traveling, drive the crane to the designated securing area, and position the crane in a safe manner. After the machine has stopped, disengage the engine clutch, position the main transmission and auxiliary transmission shaft levers in neutral, engage the truck carrier parking brake, and turn the key switch counterclockwise to the OFF position. Secure all doors and windows before dismounting the machine.

When securing the wheel-mounted crane, position the outriggers (if used), hookblock, and boom for traveling; drive the crane to the designated securing area; and position the crane in a safe manner. After the machine has stopped, disengage the inching valve control pedal, move the forward-reverse shift control lever to the neutral position, shift the transmission lever to the neutral position, apply the parking handbrake, allow the engine to idle, check accessories, and stop the engine by turning the key switch counterclockwise to the OFF position.

IV. OPERATOR'S MAINTENANCE

Every equipment operator is required to perform certain daily maintenance services on the crane and attachments he operates. This maintenance includes the required inspection services, lubrication, and adjustments which will maintain the crane and attachments in a safe operating condition, prevent malfunctions, and delay or avoid the need for major repairs.

General procedures used in an operator's maintenance inspection of the various components of cranes and attachments are similar to those described in previous portions of this manual for vehicles, materials-handling equipment, and tractors, and therefore need not be repeated here.

For specific instructions on the maintenance of cranes and attachments, follow the guidelines set forth in the manufacturer's lubrication charts and service manuals.

V. CHANGING CRANE ATTACHMENTS

The crane is a versatile piece of equipment in that it can be equipped with various attachments so that it can be used to perform a number of different operations involving construction work. The attachments include a shovel,

POWER CRANES AND ATTACHMENTS

dragline, clamshell, backhoe, piledriver, and hookblock. This section provides information that will aid you in changing attachments on cranes.

Various makes and models of cranes and attachments are available, so the procedures for changing an attachment made by one manufacturer may not be the same as for the same type of attachment furnished by another manufacturer. In that case, you can understand why only general information on changing attachments is given here. For specific instructions in changing a particular attachment, follow the procedures recommended in the operator's manual supplied by the manufacturer of the attachment concerned.

POWER SHOVEL CONVERSION

A power shovel is most widely used in quarries where digging is too hard for front-end loaders and it is not feasible to blast. Power shovel equipment includes the shovel boom proper, the dipperstick, the bucket, and the bucket trip mechanism.

There are various procedures to use when removing the shovel. These procedures are outlined in step-by-step sequence in the appropriate manufacturer's manual. A general summary is as follows:

The entire front-end assembly should be removed as a unit when changing to another attachment. The revolving superstructure should be in line with the carrier. A substantial crib should be placed under the boom near the foot end. Timbers are used to support the tip end of the boom and the dipper. After the boom foot pins have been removed, the suspension hoist and dipper trip ropes are removed. The machine can then be moved away and another attachment mounted. The time required to make the conversion from shovel to another attachment is about 6 to 8 hours.

DRAGLINE CONVERSION

Dragline buckets, attached to crane booms, are generally used for operations where extended reach is an important factor — for example, in excavating irrigation and drainage canals, in strip mining, and in gravel production. The basic machine remains on firm or undisturbed ground and is capable of digging below its own level, backing away from the excavation as the material is displaced. It is unexcelled for casting and is used extensively as a loading tool because of its large capacity and area coverage.

There are various procedures to use when removing the dragline. The procedures are outlined in step-by-step sequence in the applicable manufacturer's manual.

When converting to an attachment that does not require a boom change, such as the crane hookblock or clamshell attachment, the time required is 2 to 3 hours. When converting to the shovel or backhoe attachment the time required is 6 to 8 hours because the entire attachment must be changed.

To convert from the dragline to the shovel or backhoe, the lattice boom must be lowered onto a substantial timber crib placed to support the tip end of the boom. Another timber crib is placed to support the foot end of the boom. Depending upon the length of the boom, it may be necessary to support the boom in the center on a third timber crib.

The boom foot pins can easily be removed if they are first loosened by driving wedges between the underside of the boom foot and top of the cribbing. After removal of the pins, the suspension and hoist ropes can be removed and the dragline cable can be wound on the secondary drum for storage. The machine can now be backed away and moved to another attachment for mounting.

CLAMSHELL CONVERSION

The clamshell bucket is used as an attachment with a crane boom for vertical digging below ground level; for placement of materials at considerable height, depth, or distance; and for moving bulk materials from stockpiles to plant bins, loading hoppers, and conveyors.

There are various procedures to use when removing the clamshell. The procedures are outlined in step-by-step sequence in the applicable manufacturer's manual.

When converting to an attachment that does not require a boom change, such as the crane hookblock or dragline attachment, the time required is 2 to 3 hours. The basic components such as the tagline winder, cable drum laggings, wire ropes, and clamshell bucket may be installed on a machine already equipped with a crane boom.

To convert from the clamshell to the shovel or backhoe, the procedure is the same as described earlier for the dragline.

BACKHOE CONVERSION

The backhoe incorporates some of the characteristics of both the shovel and the dragline. Its primary function is to dig below ground level. It is capable of digging into harder material than either the dragline or the clamshell, because the weight of the boom can be used to force or crowd the bucket into the material. The digging depth of the backhoe, however, is limited by the length of the boom and stick.

The backhoe is used to dig trenches, footings, and basements. It excels in this type of work because it digs straight, vertical walls; cuts a level floor; trims corners neatly and squarely; and works from the top on dry, safe ground.

The procedure for removing the backhoe attachment is quite similar to that used in removing the shovel front-end assembly. It requires the same type of cribbing built up from timbers so that the boom foot will rest at the same height as the boom foot pins — about 4 feet high.

> NOTE: Do not release any cables or pins until the front end is securely blocked, otherwise the boom or dipper handle may drop and damage the attachment. After the backhoe attachment is removed, lubricate all cables and secure with seizing.

PILEDRIVER CONVERSION

A piledriver is a machine that hammers piles made of timber, steel, concrete, or a combination of these materials into the ground. In construction work, piles are used to support buildings, retaining walls, waterfront structures, and so forth.

In removing the piledriver attachment the hammer is first removed from the leads. If a hammer with a separate pile cap is used, it is removed with the hammer and they are stored together on the attachment rack. In the case of a diesel hammer, follow the manufacturer's recommendations regarding its removal and storage.

In removing the leads the telescopic braces are removed and the foot-ends of the leads brought to rest on the ground. The boom is then lowered and, at the same time, the machine is backed away a sufficient distance to permit placing the leads horizontally on the ground. Wood blocks are placed under the boom near the tip and the weight of the boom is allowed to bear on the blocking.

Only one of the lead adapter plates need be unbolted from the top section of the leads. When this is done the boom suspension sheaves on the boom tip shaft are removed. The leads then are slid over to allow the lead adapter plate, still bolted to the top section of the leads, to slide off the end of the boom tip shaft.

The boom suspension sheaves are then replaced, the boom is raised to lifting position and the leads are picked up with the machine and placed on the attachment rack for storage.

Other attachments such as the dragline or clamshell can be installed without a boom change. With attachments such as the shovel or backhoe the boom must be changed.

HOOKBLOCK CONVERSION

A crane rigged with a hookblock attachment is a primary unit for lifting an object or load, transferring it to a new location by swinging or traveling, and then placing the load. All cranes, regardless of size, are rated on their maximum safe lifting capacity, which is based on such factors as boom length, operating radius or boom angle, type of footing, use of outriggers, amount of counterweight, size of hookblock, and position of the lift.

The procedure used to remove a hookblock attachment is generally listed step-by-step in the operator's manual supplied by the manufacturer of the attachment concerned. In most cases, the procedure will be similar to that given below.

Position the boom on cribbing which is high enough to take the "bind" from the foot pins. The boom foot pins can easily be removed if they are first loosened by driving wedges between the underside of the boom foot and top of the cribbing.

Remove the hoist line and the hookblock. If the hoist line can be used on the attachment that will replace the hookblock, then spool the line on the hoist drum; otherwise remove the line.

Next remove the boom hoist pendant cables and allow the bridle sheave system to rest on the boom. Then remove the boom suspension cable by loosening the outside anchor point and use the engine power to unreeve the line from the sheaves. If the suspension line cannot be used on the attachment that will replace the hookblock, then it should be removed, tagged, and stored with the boom.

The boom stops should be removed from the superstructure and also stored with the boom.

In some cases, the hoist drum laggings may have to be removed and replaced with other types. If so, those which are removed should be tagged and stored with the crane boom.

POWER CRANES AND ATTACHMENTS

The total time required to remove a complete attachment will vary, depending upon the size of the equipment being worked on, but will usually take three men approximately 2 to 3 hours.

VI. CRANE AND ATTACHMENT SAFETY

Statistics on accidents show that a free moving power crane is one of the most destructive machines used in **public** as well as in private industry. Over one-third of all crane accidents result in fractured, broken, or amputated limbs. Over one-third of those injured are crane operators; more than one-fourth are crewmembers other than operators. This means, ironically enough, that the people who sustain the majority of the injuries inflicted by cranes are the very ones who can do the most to prevent them.

Most crane accidents are preventable simply because they are caused by situations, conditions, or actions which are under control of the operating crew. The term "preventable accident" is illogical, however, for if an accident is preventable it is not, in fact, an accident, but results from an act of omission or commission on somebody's part.

Most crane work is, or should be, a coordinated activity of a team of skilled technicians and workers. The lives and well being of the whole team are in the hands of each member of the team during a continually shifting scene requiring constant judgment and responsibility. The operator, oiler, rigger, signalman, flagman, and anyone else working on the rig, all assume and transfer back and forth to each other control of lifts, movements, and other activities.

It is, therefore, vitally important that these control responsibilities be clearly defined, and that the procedure for assuming and transferring them be laid out in advance and thoroughly understood by all hands. While the authority for giving signals must be assigned to only one person under normal working conditions, the responsibility for giving an emergency signal belongs to anyone in the vicinity who believes such a signal is necessary. Hand signals used during crane operations are depicted in appendix I.

Some of the hazardous conditions and practices encountered in the operation and maintenance of cranes and attachments are listed below. Make sure you study this list carefully, noting particularly the hazards connected with your type of work. Heed seriously the instructions and warnings of your project petty officer regarding safe practices to be followed during operation and maintenance, and make every effort to avoid accidents from any of the major causes listed:

1. Backing and turning machines, swinging booms, lowering buckets, and performing similar operations without looking, warning, or signaling.
2. Getting on and off equipment carelessly while it is in operation, or riding equipment when not authorized to do so.
3. Operating equipment with defective brakes, clutches, cables, or other improperly functioning parts.
4. Working or walking under lifts, buckets, or loads.
5. Failure to adjust controls properly before attempting to crank an engine.
6. Oiling, adjusting, or repairing equipment while it is in operation.
7. Using equipment with unguarded or inadequately guarded engine fans and other dangerous moving parts.
8. Failing to use protective devices or clothing such as goggles, safety shoes, gloves, and hard hats.
9. Failing to properly block equipment or heavy parts while repairing equipment.
10. Operating equipment in a thoughtless or unsafe manner, such as moving too fast over rough ground or working too near the edge of a soft fill.
11. Operating cranes too close to powerlines without adequate watches and supervision.
12. Failing to secure equipment, brakes, booms, and movable parts before repairing, leaving, or moving the machine
13. Poor housekeeping either on equipment itself or in the operating area.
14. Overloading equipment.
15. Obstruction to the free passage of boom or the load of the crane.
16. Operators not familiar with equipment.
17. Operating on uneven ground.
18. Lifting load to an unknown greater radius.
19. Boom contacting high tension wires.
20. Using weight indicators without checking recommended usage data.
21. Not changing capacity charts on cranes when different boom lengths are used.
22. Use of boom with bent or dented chord member.

23. Use of weight indicators as weighing devices.
24. Use of frame for towing.

Some major hazards due to UNSAFE EQUIPMENT that you may encounter in the operation of cranes used as a shovel, dragline, clamshell, backhoe, and piledriver are:

1. Dropping or slipping of load.
2. Breaking of cables.
3. Non-use of outriggers.
4. Faulty or poorly adjusted brakes and clutches.
5. Clutch or brake slipping and allowing boom radius to increase.
6. Job exceeding safe boom radius.
7. Job exceeding capacity of crane.
8. Operating with bent or damaged boom.
9. Non-use of mousing or safety-type hooks.

Every crane must be inspected and tested annually for safe load capacity, in accordance with command policies. The safe load chart should be posted in a prominent place in the cab near the operator, who must familiarize himself with the safe working load and tipping capacity of that particular crane.

Crane operators are responsible for knowing the limitations and capacities of the cranes they operate. You must not attempt, nor will you be required or permitted, to operate a crane either in an unsafe manner or when known to be in an unsafe condition. The operator should promptly report any malfunctioning or other defects in the equipment to his leading petty officer.

You, as an operator, have the authority to stop and refuse to handle loads until you are assured all safety requirements have been met.

All cranes must be equipped with appropriate fire extinguishers which must be maintained ready to use.

Tools and other maintenance items must be kept in the toolbox provided.

Avoid leaving the boom in a raised position with no load in a high wind. Failure to do this could cause the boom to be blown backwards.

In case a load strikes the boom or the boom strikes an object, the boom should be lowered immediately and carefully examined for bent or damaged members. A slight bend in the boom structure can cause it to fail and collapse.

You should never travel and rotate simultaneously with a near-capacity load. If the travel surface is uneven the machine may upset. When necessary to move a near-capacity load, it should be placed on a truck or railroad car and then unloaded at the new location.

When lifting a critical or unstable load, the outriggers should be set. If the outriggers are set and a load should be dropped, the kickback will not tip the crane backwards.

Crane booms should never be operated near high tension powerlines if it can be avoided. If work must be done in their vicinity, contact should be made with the electricians to have the powerlines de-energized before starting work. If this is not possible, then make sure that at no time the boom or hoisting lines come closer than 10 feet of the high tension lines while you are operating the crane. You should not depend on any chain or other grounding device dragging along the ground to give protection against electrical current discharges through the crane. Such a device is not a safe means for grounding a crane and it gives you a false sense of security.

The electrocution hazard created when a crane boom touches a powerline is an extremely serious one. In case a boom or cable does touch a high tension wire, creating a short, you should either stay in the crane KEEPING YOUR HANDS OFF THE CONTROLS, or JUMP CLEAR of the machine. You should never dismount from the machine by climbing down the side, thereby permitting your body to come in contact with the machine and the ground at the same time. You should also warn all other crewmembers not to touch the machine or attachments that are in contact with the high tension line.

VII. WIRE ROPE

You will find that many of the movable parts on cranes and attachments are moved by means of wire rope. We will discuss types of wire rope, their characteristics, construction, and usage. Instruction also is provided on safe working load, use of attachments and fittings, and various procedures applicable to the care and handling of wire rope.

CONSTRUCTION

Wire rope consists of three parts: wires, strands, and core (fig. 24). In the manufacture of rope, a number of wires are laid together to form the STRAND. Then a number

POWER CRANES AND ATTACHMENTS

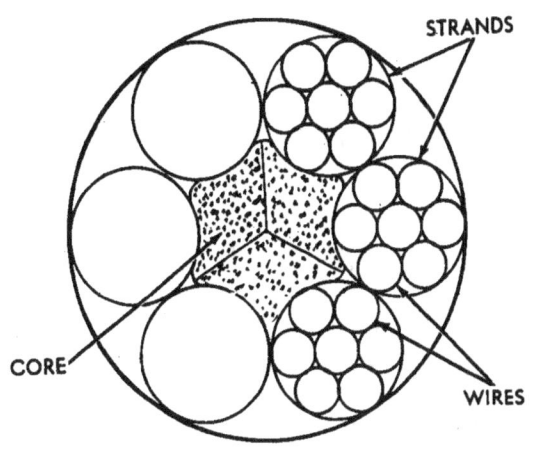

Figure 24.—Parts of wire rope.

of strands are laid together around a CORE, to form the rope.

The basic unit of wire rope construction is the individual wire, which may be made of steel, iron, or other metal, in various sizes. In making a rope, the number of wires to a strand will vary, depending on the purpose for which the rope is intended. Wire rope is designated by the number of strands per rope and the number of wires per strand. Thus, a 1/2" 6 x 19 rope will have 6 strands with 19 wires per strand, but will have the same outside diameter as a 1/2" 6 x 37 wire rope, which will have 6 strands with 37 wires of much smaller size per strand.

Wire rope made up of a large number of small wires is flexible, but the small wires are easily broken so the wire rope is not resistant to external abrasion. Wire rope made up of a smaller number of larger wires is more resistant to external abrasion but is less flexible.

The CORE—the element around which the strands are laid to form the rope—may be a hard fiber (such as manila, hemp, plastic, paper, asbestos, or sisal), a wire strand, or an independent wire rope. Each type of core serves the same basic purpose, that of affording support to the strands laid around it.

A FIBER CORE offers the advantage of increased flexibility. In addition, it serves as a cushion to reduce the effects of sudden strain and acts as a reservoir for the oil necessary for lubrication of the wires and strands to reduce friction between them. Wire rope having a fiber core is used in places where flexibility on the part of the rope is important.

A WIRE STRAND CORE not only provides more resistance to heat than a fiber core, but also adds about 15 percent to the strength of the rope. On the other hand, the wire strand makes the rope less flexible than when a fiber core is used.

AN INDEPENDENT WIRE ROPE CORE is a separate wire rope over which the main strands of the rope are laid. It usually consists of six 7-wire strands laid around either a fiber core or a wire strand core. This type of core gives the rope additional strength, provides support against crushing, and supplies maximum resistance to heat.

Wire rope may be fabricated by either of two methods. If the strands or wires are shaped to conform to the curvature of the finished rope prior to laying up, the rope is termed PREFORMED. If they are not shaped before fabrication, the rope is termed NONPREFORMED. When cut, preformed wire rope tends not to unlay, and it is more flexible than nonpreformed wire rope. With nonpreformed wire rope, the twisting process produces a stress in the wires, and when it is cut or broken the stress causes the strands to unlay. In nonpreformed wire, unlaying is rapid and almost instantaneous, and could cause serious injury to someone not familiar with it.

GRADES OF WIRE ROPE

Wire rope is manufactured in a number of different grades, three of which are: mild plow steel, plow steel, and improved plow steel.

MILD PLOW STEEL rope is tough and pliable. It can stand up under repeated strain and stress, and has a strength of from 200,000 to 220,000 pounds per square inch (psi). These characteristics make its use desirable for cable tool drilling and other purposes where abrasion is encountered.

PLOW STEEL wire rope is unusually tough and possesses great strength. This steel has a tensile strength (resistance to lengthwise stress) of 220,000 to 240,000 psi. This rope is suitable for hauling, hoisting, and logging.

IMPROVED PLOW STEEL rope is one of the best grades of rope available, and most—if not all—of the wire rope used in your work will probably be made of this material. It is stronger, tougher, and more resistant to wear than either plow steel or mild plow steel. Each square inch of improved plow steel can stand a strain of 240,000 to 260,000 pounds. It is especially useful for heavy duty service, such as power cranes with excavating and weight-handling attachments.

WIRE ROPE LAYS

The term LAY refers to the direction of the twist of the wires in a strand and the strands in the rope. In some instances both the wires in the strand and the strands in the rope are laid in the same direction, and in other instances in the opposite direction, depending on the intended use of the rope. Most manufacturers will specify types and lays of wire rope to be used on their particular piece of equipment. Be sure and consult the operator's manual as to proper application.

Five different lays of wire rope currently in use are illustrated in figure 25. The following explanations will help you recognize and identify each of the five types shown.

RIGHT REGULAR LAY: In this type, the wires in the strands are laid to the left, while the strands in the rope are laid to the right.

LEFT REGULAR LAY: In this case, the wires are laid up to the right to make the strands, then the strands are laid up to the left to form the rope. (In this lay, each step of fabrication is exactly opposite from the right regular lay.)

RIGHT LANG LAY: Here the wires in the strands and the strands in the rope are both laid up to the right.

LEFT LANG LAY: With this type, the wires in the strands and the strands in the rope are also laid in the same direction, but in this instance the lay is to the left (rather than in the right lang lay).

REVERSE LAY: The wires in one strand are laid up to the right, the wires in the adjacent strand are laid up to the left; the wires in the next strand are to the right; and so forth, with alternate directions from one strand to the other. Then all strands are laid to the right.

TYPES OF WIRE ROPE

The main types of wire rope used consist of 6, 7, 19, 24, or 37 wires in each strand. Usually, the rope has 6 strands laid around a fiber or steel center.

Two common types of wire rope, 6 x 19 and 6 x 37 rope, are illustrated in figure 11-26. The 6 x 19 type, having 6 strands with 19 wires in each strand, is commonly used for rough hoisting and skidding work where abrasion is likely to occur. The 6 x 37 wire rope, having 6 strands with 37 wires in each strand, is the most flexible of the standard 6-strand ropes. For this reason, it is particularly suitable when small sheaves and drums are to be used, such as on power cranes and similar machinery.

MEASURING WIRE ROPE

Wire rope is designated as to size by its diameter in inches. The true diameter of a wire

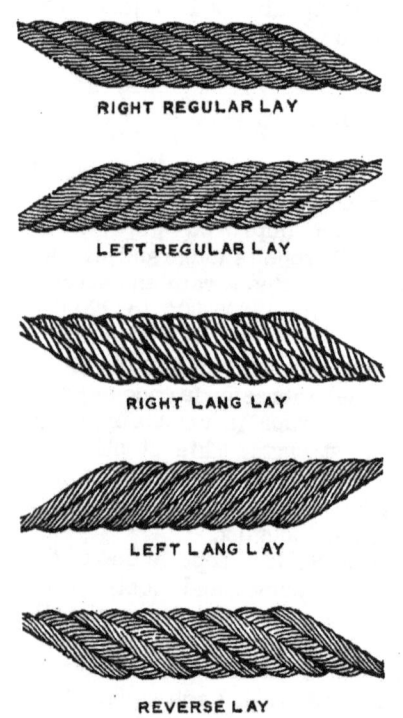

Figure 25.—Wire rope lays.

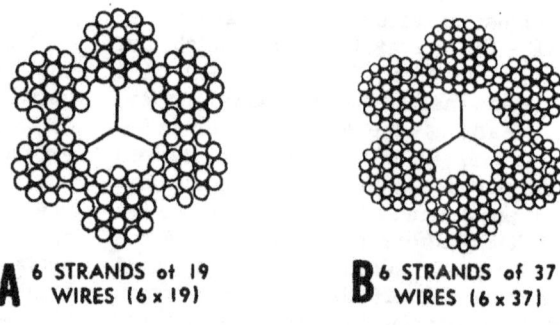

Figure 26.—(A) 6 x 19 wire rope; (B) 6 x 37 wire rope.

POWER CRANES AND ATTACHMENTS

rope is considered as being the diameter of the circle which will just enclose all of its strands. The correct, as well as incorrect, method of measuring wire rope is illustrated in figure 27. Note, in particular, that the RIGHT WAY is to measure from the top of one strand to the top of the strand directly opposite it. The wrong way, as you will note, is to measure across two strands side by side.

Use calipers to take the measurement; if they are not available, an adjustable wrench will do.

To ensure an accurate measurement of the diameter of a wire rope, always measure the rope at three places, at least 5 feet apart. Use the average of the three measurements as the diameter of the rope.

SAFE WORKING LOAD

The term SAFE WORKING LOAD (SWL), as used in reference to wire rope, means the load that can be applied and still obtain most efficient service and also prolong the life of the rope. There are a number of rule-of-thumb formulas which may be used to compute strength of wire rope. The one recommended:

SWL (in tons) = $D^2 \times 4$.

In this formula, D represents the diameter of the rope in inches. Suppose you want to find the SWL of a 2-inch rope. Using the formula above, your figures would be:

SWL = $(2)^2 \times 4$
SWL = $4 \times 4 = 16$

The answer is 16, meaning that the rope has an SWL of 16 tons.

It is important to remember that any formula for determining SWL is ONLY A RULE OF THUMB. In computing the SWL of old rope, worn rope, or rope which is otherwise in poor condition, you should reduce the SWL as much as 50 percent, depending on the condition of the rope.

WIRE ROPE FAILURE

Some of the common causes of wire rope failure are listed below.

1. Using incorrect size, construction, or grade.
2. Dragging over obstacles.
3. Improper lubrication.
4. Operating over sheaves and drums of inadequate size.
5. Overriding or cross-winding on drums.
6. Operating over sheaves and drums with improperly fitted grooves or broken flanges.
7. Jumping off sheaves.
8. Subject to acid fumes.
9. Improperly attached fitting.
10. Allowing grit to penetrate between the strands, promoting internal wear.
11. Subjecting to severe or continuing overload.
12. Excessive fleet angle.

HANDLING AND CARE

To render safe, dependable service over a maximum period of time, wire rope must be given the care and upkeep necessary to maintain it in good condition. Various procedures applicable to the care and handling of wire rope are given in the following subsections.

It is recommended that you not only study these procedures carefully but, it is more important that you also put them into practice on your job. A knowledge of the procedures, as well as experience in using them, will help you do a better job NOW; and in the long run, the life of the wire rope will be longer and more useful.

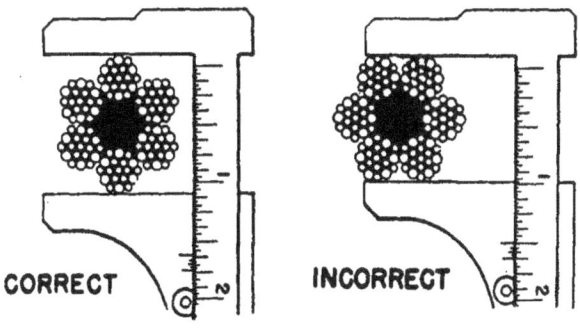

Figure 27.—Correct and incorrect methods of measuring wire rope.

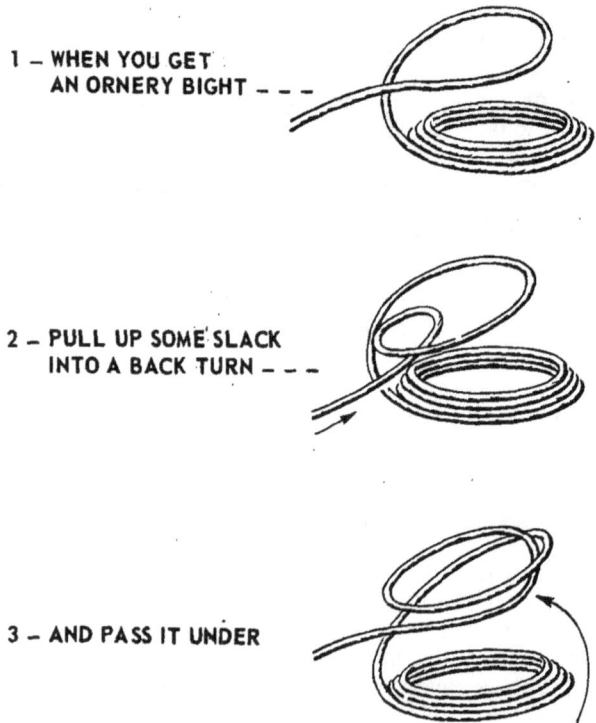

Figure 28.—Throwing a back turn on make wire lie down.

Coiling and Uncoiling

Once a new reel has been opened, it may be coiled or faked down like line. The proper direction of coiling is COUNTERCLOCKWISE for LEFT LAY wire rope and CLOCKWISE for RIGHT LAY rope. Because of the general toughness and resilience of wire, however, it has a tendency now and then to resist being coiled down. When this occurs, it is useless to fight the wire by forcing down the stubborn turn; it will only spring up again. But if it is thrown in a back turn, as shown in figure 28, it will lie down properly. A wire rope, when faked down, will run right off like line; but when wound in a coil, it must always be unwound.

Wire rope has a strong tendency to kink during uncoiling or unreeling, especially if it has been in service for a long time. Keep in mind that a kink can cause a weak spot in the rope, which will wear out quicker than the rest of the rope.

A good method for unreeling wire rope is to run a pipe or rod through the center and mount the reel on drum jacks or other supports so that the reel is off the ground. (See fig. 29.) In this way, the reel will turn as the rope is unwound, and the rotation of the reel will help keep the rope straight. During unreeling, pull the rope straight forward, as shown in figure 29, and try to avoid hurrying the operation. As a safeguard against kinking, NEVER unreel wire rope from a reel that is stationary.

To uncoil a small coil of wire rope, simply stand the coil on edge and roll it along the ground like a wheel or hoop, as illustrated in figure 29. NEVER lay the coil flat on the floor or ground and uncoil it by pulling on the end, because such practice is likely to cause kinks or twists in the rope.

To re-reel wire rope back onto a reel or a drum you may have difficulty unless you remember that it tends to roll in the opposite direction of the lay. A right-lay wire rope, for example, tends to roll to the left.

Closely observe figure 30, which shows drum winding diagrams for selection of the proper lay of rope. When putting wire rope onto a drum, you should have no trouble if you are familiar with the methods of overwinding and underwinding shown in the illustration. When wire rope is run off one reel onto another reel, or onto a winch or drum, it should be run from TOP TO TOP or from BOTTOM TO BOTTOM, as shown in figure 31.

Kinks

If a wire rope should form a loop, never try to pull it out by putting strain on either

Figure 29.—(Left) Unreeling wire rope. (Right) Uncoiling wire rope.

FOR RIGHT LAY ROPE (USE RIGHT HAND)

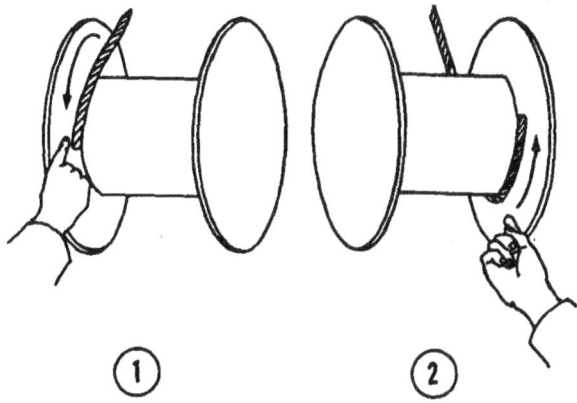

FOR OVERWIND ON DRUM:

The palm is down, facing the drum.
The index finger points at on-winding rope.
The index finger must be closest to the left-side flange.
The wind of the rope must be from left to right along the drum.

FOR UNDERWIND ON DRUM:

The palm is up, facing the drum.
The index finger points at on-winding rope.
The index finger must be closest to the right-side flange.
The wind of the rope must be from right to left along the drum.

FOR LEFT LAY ROPE (USE LEFT HAND)

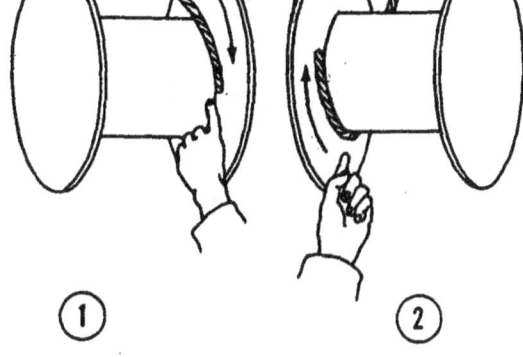

FOR OVERWIND ON DRUM:

The palm is down, facing the drum.
The index finger points at on-winding rope.
The index finger must be closest to the right-side flange.
The wind of the rope must be from right to left along the drum.

FOR UNDERWIND ON DRUM:

The palm is up, facing the drum.
The index finger points at on-winding rope.
The index finger must be closest to the left-side flange.
The wind of the rope must be from left to right along the drum.

If a smooth-face drum has been cut or scored by an old rope, the methods shown may not apply.

Figure 30.—Drum windings diagram for selection of proper lay of rope.

part. As soon as a loop is noticed, uncross the ends by pushing them apart. (See step 1 in fig. 32.) This reverses the process that started the loop. Now, turn the bent portion over and place it on your knee or some firm object and push downward until the kink straightens out somewhat. Then lay it on a flat surface and pound it smooth with a wooden mallet.

If a heavy strain has been put on a wire rope with a kink in it, the rope can no longer be trusted. Replace the wire rope altogether.

Reverse Bends

Whenever possible, drums, sheaves, and blocks used with wire rope should be placed

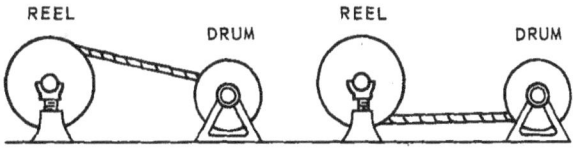

Figure 31.—Transferring wire from reel to drum.

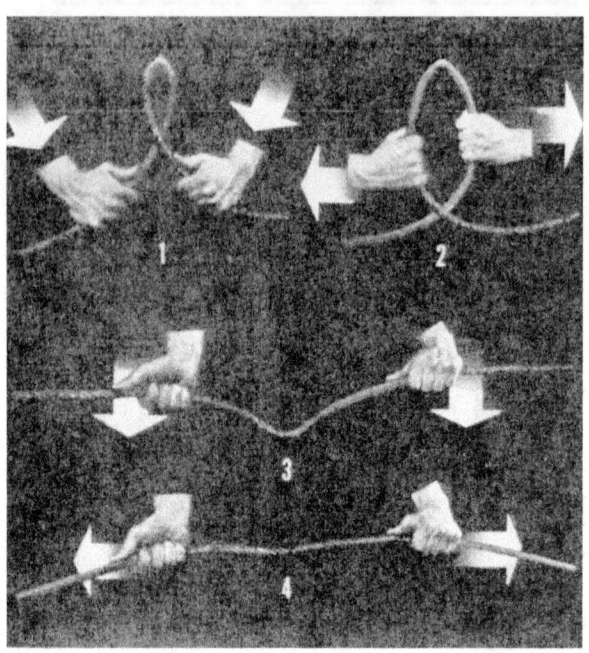

Figure 32.—The correct way to take out a loop in wire rope.

Table 1.—Suggested Minimum Tread Diameter of Sheaves and Drums

Rope diameter in inches	Minimum tread diameter in inches for given rope construction*			
	6 x 7	6 x 19	6 x 37	8 x 19
1/4	10 1/2	8 1/2	---	6 1/2
3/8	15 3/4	12 3/4	6 3/4	9 3/4
1/2	21	17	9	13
5/8	26 1/4	21 1/4	11 1/4	16 1/4
3/4	31 1/2	25 1/2	13 1/2	19 1/2
7/8	36 3/4	29 3/4	15 3/4	22 3/4
1	42	34	18	26
1 1/8	47 1/4	38 1/4	20 1/2	29 1/4
1 1/4	52 1/2	42 1/2	22 1/2	32 1/2
1 1/2	63	51	27	39

*Rope construction is in strands times wires per strand.

so as to avoid reverse or S-shaped bends. Reverse bends cause an unnecessary amount of shifting of the individual wires and strands, increasing wear and fatigue. Where a reverse bend is necessary, the drums and blocks affecting the reversal should be of larger diameter than that ordinarily used and should be spaced as far apart as possible.

Sizes of Sheaves

It is not possible to prescribe an absolute minimum size of wire rope sheaves, owing to the number of factors involved. Experience has shown, however, that the diameter of a sheave should NEVER BE LESS THAN 20 TIMES THE DIAMETER OF THE WIRE ROPE. An exception to this is 6 x 37 wire, for which a smaller sheave can be used because of the greater flexibility of this wire rope. As indicated in table 1, the construction of the wire rope has a great deal to do with determining the minimum diameter of sheaves to be used. The stiffer the wire rope, the larger the sheave diameter required.

Another thing to remember in connection with sheaves and drums is to keep the FLEET ANGLE as small as you can. The fleet angle is formed by running wire rope between a sheave and a hoisting drum whose axles are parallel to each other, as shown in figure 33. Too large a fleet angle can cause the wire to climb the flange of the sheave and may even break the flange. It can also cause the wire to climb over itself on the drum. When setting up the sheave and drum, keep them far enough apart to make the fleet angles small. About 20 times the width of the drum should be the minimum distance between the drum axle and the sheave axle. This will ensure a minimum of 1-1/2 to 2 degrees fleet angle. (The width of the drum is measured from flange to flange.)

Seizing and Cutting

Great care is exercised in the manufacture of wire rope to lay each wire in the strand and each strand in the rope under uniform tension. If the ends of the rope are not secured properly, the original balance of tension will be disturbed and maximum service will not be obtained, because some strands will carry a greater portion of the load than others. Before cutting steel wire rope, place three sets of seizing on

POWER CRANES AND ATTACHMENTS

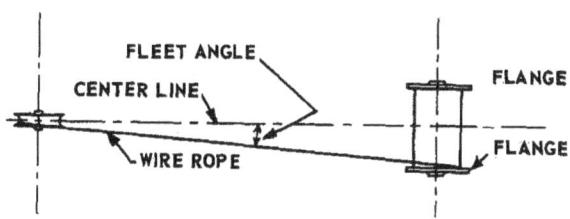

Figure 33.—Fleet angle.

each side of the point where the rope is to be cut. A rule-of-thumb for determining the size, number, and distance between seizing is as follows:

1 x the diameter for the width of the seizing
2 x the diameter for the distance between seizings
3 x the diameter for the number of seizings

For permanent seizings the seizing wire should be inserted through the wire rope by using a pricker to form an opening; the seizing wire is then laid along in the valley between strands for the width of the seizing, and then turns are taken back toward the remaining end.

To make a temporary wire rope seizing, wind on the seizing wire uniformly, using tension on the wire. After taking the required number of turns, as in step 1 in figure 34, twist the ends of the wires counterclockwise by hand, so that the twisted portion of the wires is near the middle of the seizing, as in step 2. Grasp ends with end-cutting nippers and twist up slack as in step 3. Do not try to tighten seizing by twisting. Draw up on seizing as in step 4. Again twist up the slack, using nippers as in step 5. Repeat steps 4 and 5 if necessary. Cut ends and pound them down on the rope as in step 6. If the seizing is to be permanent, or if the rope is 1-5/8 inches or more in diameter, use a serving bar or iron to increase tension on the seizing wire when putting on the turns.

Wire rope can be cut successfully by a number of methods. One effective yet simple method is that of using a hammer-type wire rope cutter (see fig. 35). (Remember that all wire must be seized before it is cut.) For best results in using this method, place the rope in the bottom of the cutter, as illustrated, so that the blade comes between the two central seizings. With the blade down against the rope

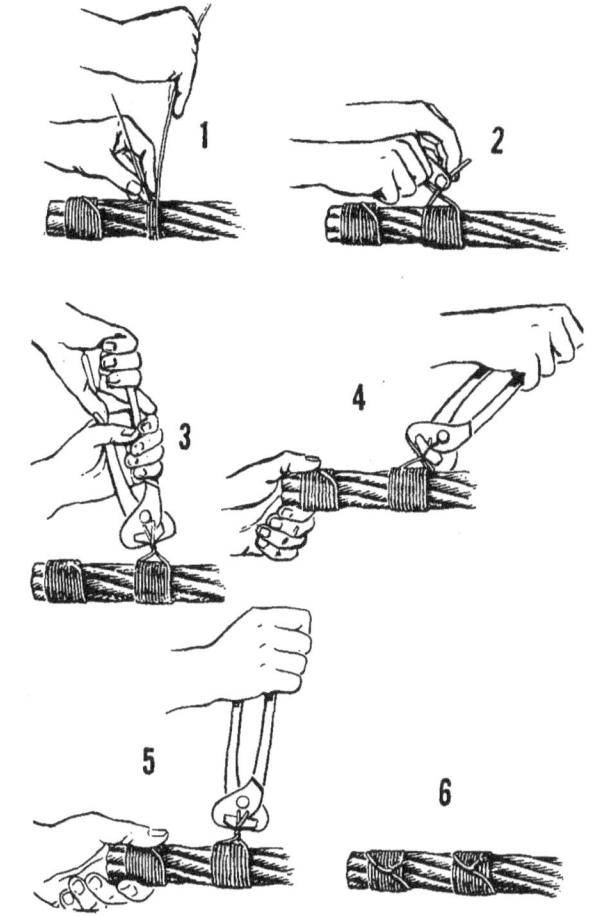

Figure 34.—Putting a seizing on a wire rope.

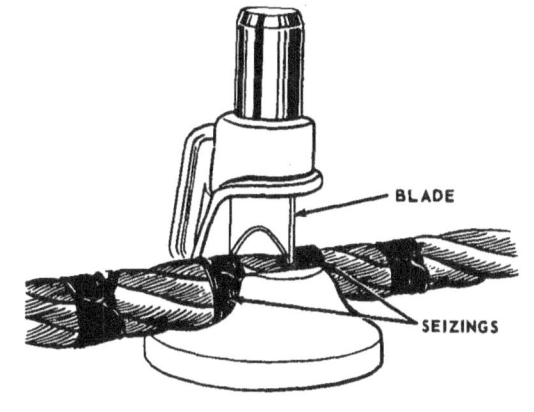

Figure 35.—Hammer-type wire rope cutter.

at the location of the cut, strike the top of the blade sharply several times with a sledge hammer.

Wire rope can be cut easily with a hydraulic wire rope cutter. This device works basically like a hydraulic jack; as you pump the handle, a cutter severs the wire rope.

Bolt cutters are only suitable for cutting wire of fairly small diameter, but the cutting torch will cut wire of any diameter.

Care of Wire Rope

Wire rope bending around winch drums and sheaves will wear like any other metal article, and for this reason lubrication is just as important to an operating wire rope as it is to any other piece of working machinery. The proper functioning of a wire rope depends upon freedom of movement, with a minimum of friction, of the individual wires and strands in relation to one another. Friction caused by lack of lubrication or corrosion, or both, will seriously shorten the service life of the wire rope.

Deterioration caused by corrosion is more dangerous than that caused by wear, simply because corrosion commonly affects the inside wires, and this makes it more difficult to detect by inspection. Deterioration caused by wear can be detected by examining the outside wires of the wire rope, because these wires become flattened and reduced in diameter as the wire rope wears. Any wire rope in which the outside wires are worn to less than 75 percent of their original diameter should be replaced.

Both internal and external lubrication are required to protect a wire rope against wear and corrosion. Internal lubrication can be properly applied only when the wire rope is being manufactured, and manufacturers customarily coat every wire with a rust-inhibiting lubricant as it is laid into the strand. The core is also lubricated in the course of the manufacturing process.

Lubrication applied in the field is designed not only to maintain surface lubrication, but also to prevent the dissipation of the internal lubrication provided by the manufacturer. The Navy issues an asphaltic petroleum oil which must be heated before using. This lubricant is known as LUBRICATING OIL — CHAIN, WIRE ROPE, AND EXPOSED GEAR. There are two types of this oil. Type I, REGULAR, is used when service conditions do not require a rust preventive. This is the case only for interior wires, such as elevator wires, which are not exposed to weather. Type II, PROTECTIVE, is both a lubricant and an anticorrosive. It comes in three grades: Grade A, for use in cold weather (60°F and below); Grade B, for use in warm weather (between 60° and 80°F); and Grade C, for use in hot weather (80°F and above). The oil is issued in 25-lb and 35-lb buckets and in 100-lb drums, and it can be applied with a stiff brush, or by drawing the wire rope through a trough containing hot lubricant as shown in figure 11-36. Frequency of application depends upon service conditions; as soon as the last coating has appreciably deteriorated, it should be renewed.

Never lubricate wire rope being used to operate a dragline and other such attachments that normally bring the wire rope in contact with soils. The reason is that the lubricant will pick up fine particles of the material and the resulting abrasive action will be detrimental to both the wire rope and sheave.

As a safety precaution, always wipe off any excess when lubricating wire rope. This is especially important where hoisting equipment is involved. Too much lubricant is liable to get into brakes or clutches, causing them to fail. While in use, the motion of machinery may sling excess oil around over crane cabs and onto catwalks, making them unsafe to work on.

WIRE ROPE ATTACHMENTS

A considerable number of ATTACHMENTS can be fitted to the ends of wire rope so that the rope can be connected to other wire ropes, pad eyes, or equipment. The attachment used most frequently to attach dead ends of wire ropes to pad eyes or similar fittings on earth-moving rigs is the WEDGE SOCKET shown in figure 37. The socket is applied to the bitter end of the wire rope as shown in the figure. Remove the pin and knock out the wedge first. Then pass the wire rope up through the socket and lead enough of it back through the socket to allow at least 2 inches of the bitter end to extend below the socket upon completing the attachment, as shown in figure 38. Next, replace the wedge, and haul on the bitter end of the wire rope until the bight closes around the wedge as shown in figure 38. A strain on the standing part will tighten the wedge. A great advantage of the wedge socket is the fact that to remove

POWER CRANES AND ATTACHMENTS

Figure 36.—Method of field lubrication.

it you need only to drive out the wedge. It should be noted, however, that the strength of a wedge-type socket is such that the overall strength of a rope having a socket attachment is reduced by about 30 percent, but if one wire rope clip is used, it is only reduced by 20 percent. The safe working load of the rope must, of course, also be reduced accordingly.

The best method for attaching a closed or open socket in the field is by speltering. The term SPELTERING means to attach the socket to the wire rope by pouring hot zinc. (See fig. 39.) Forged steel speltered sockets are as strong as the wire rope itself, and are required on all cranes that are used primarily for lifting personnel, as well as for lifting ammunition, acids, and other extremely dangerous materials. Cranes lifting foodstuff and other general supplies may use forged steel wedge or swaged sockets.

A common method of making an eye in the end of a wire rope is by the use of WIRE ROPE CLIPS like those shown in figure 40. The U-shaped part of the clip, with the threaded ends, is called the U-BOLT; the other part is called the SADDLE (OR RODDLE). The saddle is stamped with the diameter of the wire rope the clip will

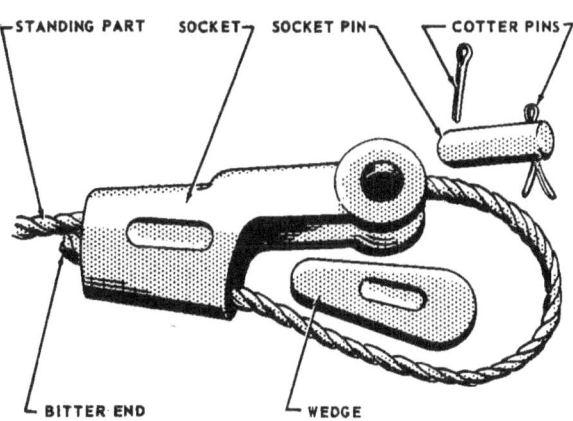

Figure 37.—Parts of a wedge socket.

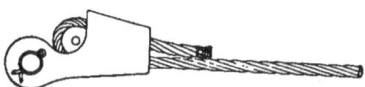

Figure 38.—Wedge socket attached properly.

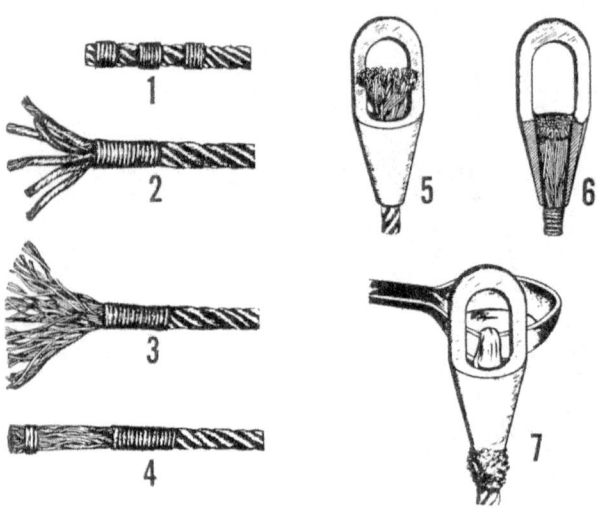

Figure 39.—Speltering a closed or basket socket.

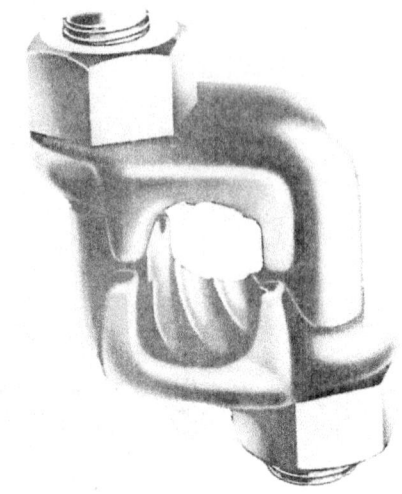

Figure 41.—Twin-base wire rope clip.

fit. Always place a clip with the U-bolt on the bitter end, not on the standing part of the wire rope. If clips are attached incorrectly, the standing part (live end) of the wire rope will be distorted or will have mashed spots.

Following is a simple formula for wire rope clips:

3 x wire rope diameter + 1 = Number of clips
6 x wire rope diameter = Spacing between clips

Another type of wire rope clip is the TWIN-BASE clip shown in figure 41. Both parts of this clip are shaped to fit the wire rope; consequently, the clip cannot be put on wrong and it is less damaging to wire rope than the U-bolt clip. It also allows for a clear 360 degree swing with the wrench when the nuts are being tightened. When an eye is made in a wire rope, the metal fitting called a THIMBLE is usually placed in the eye, as shown in figure 40, to protect the eye against wear.

After the eye made with clips has received an initial heavy strain, the nuts on the clips must be retightened. Periodic checks should be made afterwards for tightness, and also for damage to the rope that might be caused by the clips.

REEVING WIRE ROPES

Usually the manufacturer's manual pertaining to a particular type of power crane and its attachments will tell you the size, length, type, and makeup of each of the wire ropes required for that particular rig. The manufacturer's manual will also contain diagrams, supplemented where necessary by detailed explanatory text, which show exactly how to reeve each wire rope on that rig.

SLINGS

Slings are widely used in the moving and hoisting of heavy loads. Some types of slings can be obtained already made. Slings may be made of fiber line, wire rope, or chain.

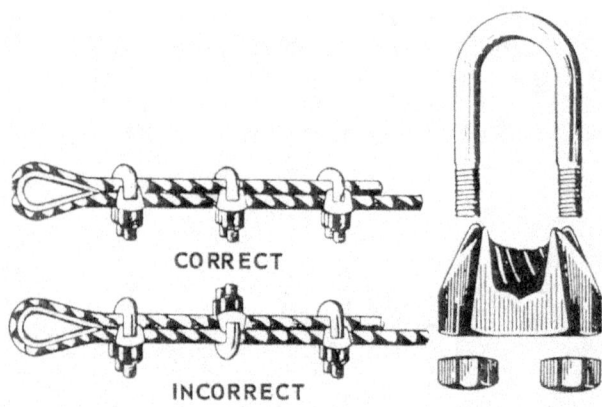

Figure 40.—Wire rope clips.

POWER CRANES AND ATTACHMENTS

FIBER LINE slings offer the advantage of flexibility and more protection of the finished material than is provided by wire rope slings. At the same time, fiber line slings are not as strong as wire rope or chain slings. Furthermore, fiber line is more likely to be damaged by sharp edges on the material being hoisted than is wire rope or chain slings.

WIRE ROPE slings offer advantages of both strength and flexibility. These qualities n.ake wire rope adequate to meet the requirements of many hoisting jobs in steelwork. Thus you will use wire rope slings more frequently than fiber line or chain slings.

CHAIN SLINGS are frequently used in hoisting and moving heavy steel items such as rails, pipes, beams, and angles. They are also especially desirable for slinging hot loads and in handling loads with sharp edges which might cut wire rope.

Using Wire Rope and
Fiber Line Slings

Three types of fiber line and wire rope slings commonly used for lifting a given load are the endless, single leg, and bridle slings.

An ENDLESS SLING, usually referred to simply as SLING, can be made simply by splicing together the ends of a piece of fiber line or wire rope so that an endless loop is formed. An endless sling is easy to handle and can be used as a CHOKER HITCH. (See fig. 42.)

A SINGLE LEG SLING, commonly referred to as a STRAP, can be constructed by forming a spliced eye in each end of a piece of fiber line or wire rope. Sometimes the ends of a piece of wire rope are spliced into eyes around thimbles, and one eye is fastened to a hook with a shackle. With this arrangement, the shackle and hook are removable.

The single leg sling may be used as a choker hitch (fig. 43) in hoisting by passing one eye through the other eye and over the hoisting hook. The single leg sling also is useful as a double anchor hitch (fig. 43). You will find the double anchor hitch desirable for hoisting drums or other cylindrical objects where it is necessary that the sling tighten itself under strain and lift by friction against the sides of the object.

CHOKER HITCH

Figure 42.—Method of using endless sling.

Single leg slings can be used to make various types of BRIDLES. Three common uses of bridles are illustrated in figure 44. Either two or more single slings may be used for a given combination. Also, if an individual sling is not long enough for the job at hand, two of the single slings can be combined to form a longer single sling.

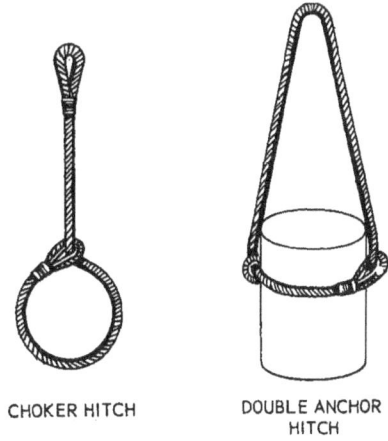

CHOKER HITCH   DOUBLE ANCHOR HITCH

Figure 43.—Methods of using single leg slings.

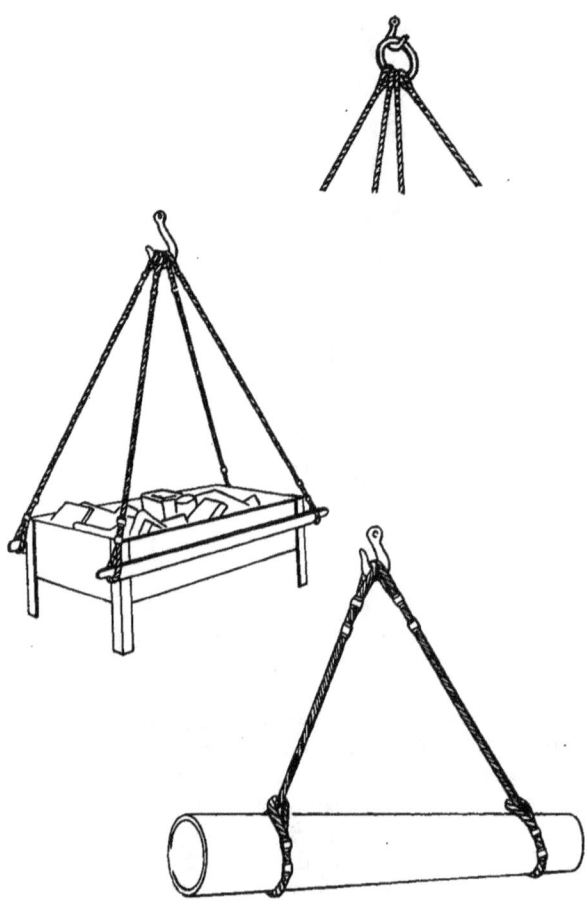

Figure 44.—Bridles.

It is important that protective pads be used when a fiber line or wire rope sling is exposed to sharp edges at the corners of a load. Pieces of wood or old rubber tires are excellent materials for use as padding.

Spreaders and Pallets

In hoisting with slings, the use of SPREADER BARS is often advisable to prevent crushing and damaging the load. Spreader bars are short bars or pipes which have eyes fastened to each end. By setting spreader bars in the sling legs above the top of the load (fig. 45), the angle of the sling leg is changed and crushing of the load, particularly in the upper portion, is avoided.

The use of cargo PALLETS in combination with slings is a big advantage on jobs that involve the hoisting and moving of small lot items. (See fig. 46.) Spreader bars may also be needed frequently to avoid damaging the load when hoisting pallets. The pallet provides a small platform or board on which a number of items can be placed and moved as a unit rather than piece by piece. Palletizing obviously is quicker and easier than moving each individual item separately.

It is advantageous to have matched sets of slings (that is, two or more equal lengths) so that when it is necessary to use more than one to hoist a load the strain will be equal and the load will come up evenly. Also, slings that are of equal length should be marked for ease of identification. Painting the eyes of equal length slings the same color is one way of doing this.

In lifting heavy loads, always make a special effort to ensure that the bottom of the sling legs are fastened to the load in a manner that will prevent damage to the load. To aid in lifting, many pieces of equipment have eyes fastened to them during the process of manufacture. With some loads, though, fastening a hook to the eye on one end of each sling leg provides an adequate means for securing the sling to the load.

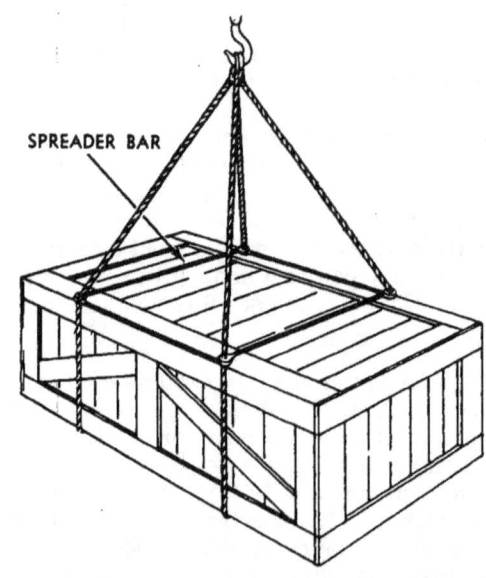

Figure 45.—Use of spreader bars in sling.

POWER CRANES AND ATTACHMENTS

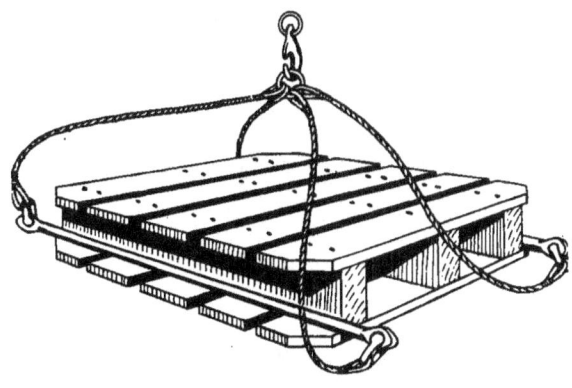

Figure 46.—Pallet.

Frequently, packages of uniform size are palletized when shipping and remain in the original pallet until used. You may not enjoy the luxury of that many pallets in your work. Nevertheless, you will need several pallets for efficient operation. One can be loaded as a previously loaded pallet is being hoisted. After each pallet is unloaded, the hoisting crew returns it for reloading. One set of slings can handle a number of pallets.

When using slings, it is important to remember that the greater the angle from vertical, the greater will be the stress on the sling legs. This is graphically illustrated in figure 47.

Inspecting Wire Rope and Fiber Line Slings

Broken wires are a major defect to look for when inspecting wire rope slings. When 4 percent of the total number of wires in the wire rope are found to have breaks within the length of one lay, the sling is unsafe and should be removed from service immediately. Always make sure that any sling found to be deformed or damaged is also removed from service. Given proper care, a wire rope sling should render service for a long time.

Slings must be inspected frequently and removed from service when defects are disclosed showing that they are no longer safe. Bear in mind that a defective sling may cause serious injury to personnel and extensive damage to equipment in case of failure under load.

Fiber line slings should be checked carefully for signs of deterioration due to exposure to the weather. A close check should also be made to determine whether any of the fibers have been broken or cut by sharp-edged objects.

When inspecting slings, do not overlook the hooks. Examine hooks for cuts, cracks, or signs of distortion.

Using Chain Slings

Steel-length CHAIN SLINGS are available with variable type ends and lengths. One commonly used type is the 1/2-inch sling, obtainable in either 12- or 20-foot lengths.

Before doing any lifting with a chain sling, first place dunnage between the chain and the load to provide a gripping surface. For hoisting heavy metal objects with chain slings, always use chafing gear around the sharp corners on the load to protect the chain links from being cut. As chafing gear, use either planks or heavy fabric. In handling rails, or a number of lengths

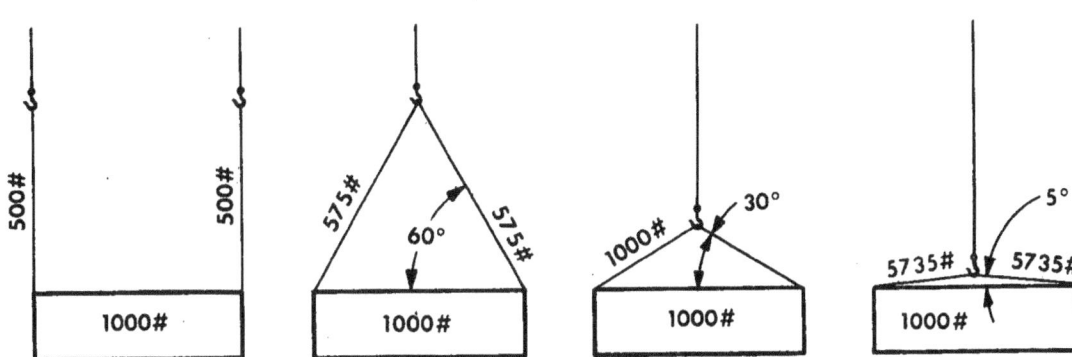

Figure 47.—Stress on sling on various vertical angles.

Figure 48.—Chain sling.

Figure 50.—Drum-handling sling.

of pipe, a round turn should be made and the hook placed around the chain. (See fig. 48.)

In using chain slings, care must be exercised to avoid twisting or kinking of the chain while under stress. This condition might cause failure of the chain, even in handling a light load. Before

Figure 49.—Cargo net in use.

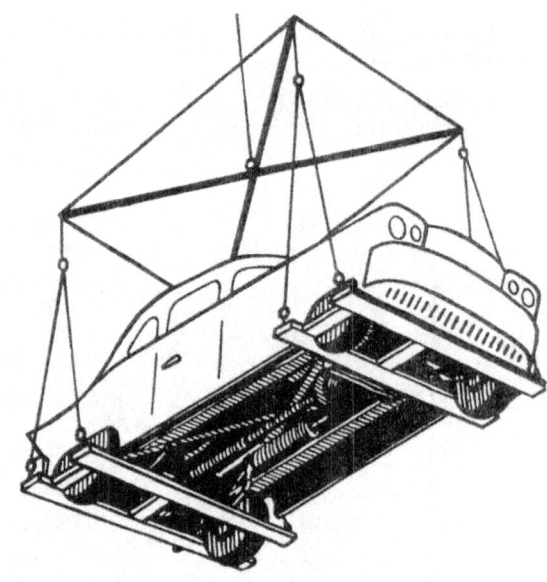

Figure 11-51.—One type of vehicle sling.

POWER CRANES AND ATTACHMENTS

lifting, therefore, make sure that the chain is free from twists and kinks. In addition, see that the load is properly seated in the hook (not on the point) and that the chain is free from nicks or other damage. Avoid sudden jerks in lifting and lowering the load, and always consider the angle of lift when using a sling chain bridle.

Store chains in a clean, dry place where they will not be exposed to the weather. Before storage, it is a good idea to apply a light coat of lubricant to prevent rust.

Makeshift repairs such as fastening links of a chain together with bolts or wire should never be permitted. When links become worn or damaged, cut them out of the chain; then fasten the two adjacent links together using a connecting link. After closing the connecting link, welding will make it as strong as the other links. For cutting small-size chain links, use bolt cutters. For cutting large-size links, use a hacksaw.

Inspection of Chain Slings

Inspection of chain slings is necessary to ensure that they are maintained in safe, operating condition. Obviously, a chain sling that is used continuously for heavy loading should be inspected frequently. It is a good idea, however, that seldom used slings be inspected at least once a month. Bear in mind that chain slings are less reliable than manila or wire rope slings because the links may crystallize and snap without warning.

In making an inspection, examine the chain closely link-by-link, looking for such defects as stretch, wear, distortion, cracks, nicks, and gouges. Under ordinary conditions, wear will be confined to the ends of the links where adjoining links rub together. If wear is detected, each link should be lifted and its cross section measured. Chains should be removed from service when any individual link shows wear greater than 25 percent of the thickness of the metal.

Any link that shows evidence of cracks, distortion, nicks, or cuts should be replaced. However, if a chain shows evidence of stretching or distortion of more than 5 percent in a 5-link section, make sure the entire chain is discarded and destroyed.

The least sign of binding at the juncture points of links indicates collapse in the sides of links, resulting from stretch. Such a condition is dangerous, and the chain should be removed from service.

Nets, Hooks, and Special Slings

Cargo nets are made of fiber line, wire rope, or nylon line. They are efficiently used for handling non-uniform packages. A loaded cargo net is shown in figure 49. Figure 50 through 51 illustrate other special types of slings and hooks in use.

MOBILE CRANES, TOWER CRANES AND DERRICKS

23-8.1 General provisions. (a) *Stability and strength.* Mobile cranes, tower cranes and derricks used in construction, demolition and excavation operations shall be so constructed, placed and operated as to be stable. No component or part of any such crane or derrick shall be stressed beyond its rated capacity as determined by the manufacturer or builder.

(b) *Inspection.* (1) Every mobile crane, tower crane and derrick shall be thoroughly inspected by a competent, designated employee or authorized agent of the owner or lessee of such mobile crane, tower crane or derrick at intervals not exceeding one month. Such inspections shall include but not be limited to all blocks, shackles, sheaves, wire rope, connectors, the various devices on the mast or boom, hooks, controls and braking mechanisms.

(2) A written, dated and signed record of each such inspection shall be completed by the competent, designated employee or authorized agent who made the inspection on an inspection form provided by the commissioner. The most recent record of inspection of a mobile crane, tower crane or derrick shall be posted inside the cab of such crane or derrick under a transparent protective covering or shall be filed in an office on the job site available for examination by the commissioner. Attached to such record of inspection shall be a written designation naming the competent employee or authorized agent. Such attached designation shall be signed by the owner or lessee of such mobile crane, tower crane or derrick.

(3) Every mobile crane, tower crane and derrick shall be inspected before being erected or operated for the first time on any job.

(4) Adjustments and repairs to mobile cranes, tower cranes and derricks shall be made only by competent, designated persons.

(5) A preventive maintenance program shall be established for each mobile crane, tower crane and derrick based on the manufacturer's recommendations. Dated and detailed records of such programs shall be available on the job site for examination by the commissioner.

(c) *Footings.* A firm footing shall be provided for every mobile crane, tower crane and derrick.

(d) *Hoisting mechanism brakes and locking devices.* (1) Every power-operated mobile crane, tower crane and derrick shall be provided with hoisting mechanism brakes capable of sustaining at rest one and one-half times the maximum rated load on a single part line. Hand- or foot-operated brakes shall be provided with a substantial locking device to lock any such brake in engagement. Pedals of foot-operated brakes shall be constructed so that the operators' feet cannot easily slip off. Non-slip pedal surfaces are acceptable for this purpose.

(2) Power-controlled lowering devices, when provided, shall be capable of handling rated loads and speeds in order to provide precision lowering and reduce demands on the brake loads.

Exception: This paragraph does not apply to any mobile crane provided with a clamshell or dragline used in excavation operations.

(3) Electrically-driven mobile cranes, tower cranes and derricks shall be provided with devices which will automatically hold the loads in cases of power failure.

(e) *Load handling.* (1) Mobile cranes, tower cranes and derricks shall not be loaded beyond their rated capacities.

[23-8.1]

(2) Hoisting ropes for concrete buckets used with mobile cranes, tower cranes or derricks shall be provided with safety hooks or closed shackles.

(3) Where slings are used to hoist material of long length, spreader bars shall be used to space and keep the sling legs in proper balance.

(4) Reinforcing rods, conduit and lumber, when of uneven lengths as well as column clamps and similar items which cannot be easily secured to form safe drafts or loads shall be hoisted in boxes. Each such box shall be substantially constructed and supported from its four corners by individual lengths of wire rope having spliced or clipped loops for attachment to the load line. The construction and suspension of each such box shall be capable of holding at least four times the load for which it is intended.

(5) In steel erection, when a load is suspended from a mobile crane, tower crane or derrick at two or more points with slings, the eyes of the lifting legs of the slings shall be shackled together and this shackle or the eyes of the shackled slings shall be placed on the hook. Alternatively, the eyes of the lifting legs may be shackled directly to the hoisting block, ball or balance beam. The eyes may be placed on the lifting hook without shackles if the hook is of the safety type.

(6) No more than one load shall be suspended from the same load line of a mobile crane, tower crane or derrick at one time.

(f) *Hoisting the load.* (1) Before starting to hoist with a mobile crane, tower crane or derrick the following inspection for unsafe conditions shall be made:

(i) The hoisting rope shall be free from kinks.

(ii) Multiple part lines shall not be twisted around each other.

(iii) The hook shall be brought over the load in such manner and location as to prevent the load from swinging when hoisting is started.

(iv) The load is well secured and properly balanced in the sling or lifting device before it is lifted more than a few inches.

(v) If there is a slack rope condition, it shall be determined that the hoisting rope is properly seated on the drum and in the sheaves.

(2) During the hoisting operation the following conditions shall be met:

(i) There shall be no sudden acceleration or deceleration of the moving load unless required by emergency conditions.

(ii) The load shall not contact any obstruction.

(3) The side loading of booms on mobile cranes, tower cranes and derricks shall be limited to freely suspended loads.

(4) Mobile cranes, tower cranes and derricks shall not be used for dragging loads sideways.

(5) Mobile cranes, tower cranes and derricks shall not hoist, lower, swing or travel while any person is located on the load or hook.

(6) Mobile cranes, tower cranes and derricks shall not hoist or carry any load over and above any person except as otherwise provided in this Part (rule).

(7) The operator of any mobile crane, tower crane or derrick shall not leave his position at the controls while any load is suspended nor shall any person be permitted to work or pass under a stationary suspended load.

[23-8.1]

(g) *Limitations on modifications of mobile cranes, tower cranes or derricks.* No load-bearing component or part of any mobile crane, tower crane or power-driven derrick shall be replaced by another component or part nor shall any mobile crane, tower crane or derrick be modified by the addition thereto or the removal therefrom of any load-bearing component or part unless such replacement or modification shall be as certified by either the manufacturer or builder of such crane or derrick or by a professional engineer licensed to practice in the State of New York.

(h) *Cast iron.* Cast iron shall not be used for members or parts of any mobile crane, tower crane or derrick subject to tension or torsion except for brake and clutch drums.

(i) *Guarding moving parts.* Exposed moving components or parts of mobile cranes, tower cranes and derricks such as gears, set screws, projection keys, chains, chain sprockets and reciprocating parts which might constitute a hazard under normal operating conditions shall be guarded and such guards shall be securely fastened in place. Each such guard shall be capable of supporting without permanent distortion the weight of a 200 pound man, unless such guard is located where it is impossible for a person to step or ply his weight on it.

(j) *Protection from the elements.* Friction brakes and clutches of mobile cranes, tower cranes and derricks shall be provided with adequate protection from the elements.

(k) *Wire ropes and reeving accessories.* (1) *Rope safety factors.* Wire rope provided for use on any mobile crane, tower crane or derrick shall be in compliance with the safety factor requirements listed as follows:

(i) For supporting rated loads (including boom suspensions):

(a) The safety factor for live or running ropes that wind on drums or pass over sheaves shall be not less than 3.5.

(b) The safety factor for boom pendants or standing ropes shall be not less than 3.0.

(ii) For supporting the boom and working attachments at recommended travel or transit positions and boom lengths:

(a) The safety factor for live or running ropes shall be not less than 3.5.

(b) The safety factor for boom pendants and standing ropes shall be not less than 3.0.

(iii) For supporting the boom under recommended boom erection conditions:

(a) The safety factor for live or running ropes shall be not less than 3.0.

(b) The safety factor for boom pendants or standing ropes shall be not less than 2.5.

(iv) The safety factors specified in subparagraphs (i), (ii) and (iii) above shall be determined on the basis of rope loads resulting from crane or derrick manufacturers' ratings, with approved reeving, published nominal breaking strengths of new ropes and with load and boom stationary.

(2) *Hoisting rope.* When the hook of the hoist of any mobile crane, tower crane or derrick is resting on the ground or equivalent elevation at least two full wraps of the hoisting rope shall remain on the drum of such crane or derrick.

(3) *Replacement rope.* Replacement ropes for any mobile crane, tower crane or derrick shall be at least the equivalent in strength and grade as the original ropes furnished by the manufacturer or builder of such crane or derrick.

(4) *Eye splices.* Eye splices shall be made in an acceptable manner and rope thimbles shall be used in the eye.

[23-8.1]

(5) *U-bolt clips.* U-bolt clips shall have the U-bolt section on the dead or short end, and the saddle on the live or long end of the rope. Spacing and number of clips shall be in accordance with the manufacturer's recommendation. Clips shall be of drop-forged steel. When a newly installed rope has been in operation for at least one hour, all nuts on the clip bolts shall be re-tightened and they shall be re-checked for tightness at monthly intervals thereafter.

(6) *Special fittings.* Swaged, compressed or wedge-socket fittings shall be applied as recommended by the manufacturer of the rope or fittings or by the manufacturer or builder of the mobile crane, tower crane or derrick.

(7) *Rope inspection.* (i) *Daily.* All running ropes in continuous service on a mobile crane, tower crane or derrick shall be visually inspected at least once every working day.

(ii) *Monthly.* All ropes in use on a mobile crane, tower crane or derrick shall be thoroughly inspected by a competent, designated person at least once a month. A full written, dated and signed report of each such inspection, which shall include the condition of all ropes, shall be kept on file on the job site available for examination by the commissioner. Any rope damage or deterioration which might result in appreciable loss of original rope strength shall be carefully noted and a determination shall be made by the designated person as to whether continued use of such damaged or deteriorated rope constitutes a hazard.

(1) *Lubrication.* (1) *Sheave bearings.* All sheave bearings on mobile cranes, tower cranes and derricks shall be regularly lubricated according to the recommendations of the manufacturers or builders of such cranes or derricks.

(2) *Moving parts.* All moving parts of mobile cranes, tower cranes and derricks for which lubrication is specified, including ropes and chains, shall be regularly lubricated. Lubricating systems shall be frequently checked for proper delivery of the lubricant. Lubricating points shall be accessible without moving guards or other parts.

(m) *Operation near power lines.* The operation of any mobile crane, tower crane or derrick near or around any power line or power facility shall be done only in accordance with the provisions of subpart 23-1 of this Part (rule).

(n) *Use of mobile cranes in concrete work.* In building construction where concrete is raised by mobile cranes, such loads raised to elevations more than 150 feet shall be deposited or discharged only in hoppers or other appropriate facilities which are so located as to permit operation of the boom of any such crane at a minimum load radius.

23-8.2 Special provisions for mobile cranes. (a) *Inspection.* (1) A mobile crane which is moved from one job site to another without dismantling beyond the folding of the boom and such additional dismantling as may be necessary for that purpose is not required to be inspected before being first erected or operated on each job site to which it is moved, providing the monthly inspections are performed on schedule.

(2) The inspection and repair of mobile crane booms shall be made only when such booms are lowered and adequately supported.

(b) *Footings and outriggers.* (1) *Footings.* A firm footing shall be provided for every mobile crane. Where such firm footing is not naturally available, it shall be provided by substantial timbers, cribbing or other structural members sufficient to distribute the load so as not to exceed the safe bearing capacity of the underlying material.

(2) *Outriggers.* (i) Means shall be provided to hold all outriggers of mobile cranes in their retracted positions while such cranes are traveling and in their extended positions when blocked for hoisting.

[23-8.2]

    (ii) Where used on mobile cranes, power-operated jacks shall be provided with means to prevent loss of jack support under load.
    (iii) Each outrigger on a mobile crane shall be visible from its actuating location.
    (iv) Means shall be provided to securely fasten outrigger floats to the outriggers when in use.
 (c) *Hoisting the load.* (1) Before hoisting a load the person directing the lift shall see that the mobile crane is level and, where necessary, blocked.
 (2) Before hoisting any load at a new job site, the boom of a mobile crane shall be test operated to its maximum height.
 (3) Loads lifted by mobile cranes shall be raised vertically so as to avoid swinging during hoisting except when such operations are permitted by the capacity chart. A tag or restraint line shall be used when rotation or swinging of any load being hoisted by a mobile crane may create a hazard.
 (4) When a mobile crane is operated at a fixed radius, the boomhoist pawl or other positive locking device shall be engaged.
 (d) *Mobile crane travel.* (1) A mobile crane traveling to or from one job site to another or traveling on a street or highway shall not carry any jibs, attachments, buckets or other devices or material attached in any way to the boom whether the boom is in the folded position or not.

  Exception: A hydraulic crane where the jib is permanently hinged to the boom or
       any crane where the manufacturer authorizes that the design of such
       crane guarantees the safe transport of the jib or other attachments.

 (2) Mobile cranes shall not travel with suspended loads unless such crane is under the control of a competent, designated person who shall be responsible for the position of the load, boom location, ground support, travel route and speed of movement.
 (3) A mobile crane, with or without load, shall not travel with the boom so high that it may bounce back over the cab.
 (e) *Counterweights for mobile cranes.* Counterweights shall be provided for and used on mobile cranes as specified by the manufacturers or builders of such cranes or by professional engineers licensed to practice in the State. A mobile crane shall not be operated without the full amount of ballast or counterweight in place. Mobile cranes that do not have the ballast or counterweight attached may be operated temporarily with special care when handling light loads. The ballast or counterweight in place on any mobile crane shall not exceed the manufacturer's or builder's specifications.
 (f) *Mobile crane construction.* (1) *Booms.* (i) Booms, boom sections and jibs of every mobile crane shall be constructed of suitable steel and shall be used only for the purposes recommended by the manufacturer or builder of such mobile crane.
  (ii) The boom of any mobile crane shall not be raised from the level of the surface on which the crane rests other than by the use of its own hoisting capabilities. The design, construction and length of any boom shall be such that there is no undue stress imposed on the crane structure or mechanism during such raising operations.
  (iii) Boom stops shall be provided on mobile cranes to prevent overtopping.
  (iv) Any boom extension used on a mobile crane which is not provided by the manufacturer or builder of the crane shall be designed by a professional engineer licensed to practice in the State. A copy of the design plans for such boom extension shall be kept at the job site available for examination by the commissioner.

[23-8.2]

(2) *Braking mechanism.* In addition to the hoisting mechanism brakes required by this subpart, every mobile crane shall be provided with the following:

(i) An adequate braking mechanism for the boom hoist.

(ii) A swing lock or swing brake capable of preventing rotation.

(iii) A brake or other equivalent device adequate to bring the mobile crane to a stop from any travel for which such crane is designed, together with a means of locking such mobile crane so as to hold it stationary.

(3) *Boom sheave guard.* The sheave at the end of a mobile crane boom on which the hoisting rope operates shall be provided with a guard to prevent the rope from leaving the sheave in case of rope slack or any other condition.

(g) *Mobile crane capacity charts.* (1) *Load ratings for mobile cranes.*

(i) Load ratings shall not exceed the percentages listed in Table XVII of this subpart of the tipping loads for mobile cranes.

(ii) The stability of mobile cranes will be influenced by such factors as freely suspended loads, track, wind or ground conditions, condition and inflation of tires, boom lengths and proper operating speeds for existing conditions. All such factors shall be taken into account in determining mobile crane stability.

TABLE XVII
MAXIMUM LOAD RATINGS FOR MOBILE CRANES

Type of Mobile Crane Mounting	Maximum Load Ratings (Percentages of Tipping Loads)
Crawler without outriggers	75
Crawler, outriggers fully extended	85
Truck and wheel mounted (with or without outriggers fully extended)	85

(2) *Mobile crane capacity chart required.* (i) Every mobile crane shall be provided with a capacity chart which shall be posted and maintained clearly legible in the cab of the crane visible to the crane operator from his operating position. Such chart shall set forth the safe loads which may be hoisted by such crane at various lengths of boom at various boom angles and radial distances. Where outriggers are provided, such safe loads shall be set forth on the capacity chart with and without the use of the outriggers. Such chart shall also indicate whether or not such handling accessories as hooks, blocks and slings are included.

[23-8.2]

    (ii) Unless furnished by the manufacturer or builder of the mobile crane, the required capacity chart shall be prepared and certified by a professional engineer licensed to practice in the State and a copy thereof submitted, on request, to the commissioner.
    (iii) No load shall be lifted by any mobile crane that exceeds the relevant maximum specified by its capacity chart.
  (h) Boom *angle indicator.* Every mobile crane having either a boom exceeding 40 feet in length or a maximum rated capacity exceeding 15 tons shall be provided with an approved boom angle indicator. Such boom angle indicator shall indicate the boom angle in degrees and shall be clearly visible to the mobile crane operator from his operating position at all times. Such boom angle indicator shall emit a visible or audible warning signal whenever the boom angle is unsafe.

   Exception: Boom angle indicators are not required to be operative when such
      mobile cranes are used for excavation work with clamshells or
      dragline buckets.

  (i) *Unauthorized operation.* The operator's cab of every mobile crane shall be kept locked whenever the operator is not present. No unauthorized person shall enter the cab of or remain immediately adjacent to any mobile crane in operation. Ignition locks, locking bars or other equivalent devices shall be provided to prevent unauthorized operation of mobile cranes.
  (j) *Operation of a mobile crane with a demolition ball.* In addition to the general requirements of this Part (rule) for mechanical demolition, the operation of a mobile crane with a demolition ball shall be subject to the following provisions:
   (1) The weight of any demolition ball shall not exceed 50 per cent of the safe load capacity of the boom length used at its lowest angle of operation.
   (2) During operation with a demolition ball the swing of the boom shall not exceed 30 degrees from the center line, front to back, of the crane mounting.
   (3) The windows of such crane cabs shall be constructed of shatterproof glass or shall be protected by adequate metal screens.
   (4) The load line and the attachment of the demolition ball to the load line shall be inspected at least twice daily.
   (5) Truck-mounted mobile cranes without outriggers shall not be used with a demolition ball.

23-8.3 Special provisions for tower cranes. (a) *Tower crane erection.* (1) Every tower crane used in construction shall be erected in accordance with the manufacturer's recommendations and under the supervision of a competent, designated person experienced in tower crane erection.
  (2) Prior to the erection of any tower crane the ability of the supporting system, including slabs, foundations and the underlying soil to support the loads intended to be imposed thereon shall be certified by professional engineer licensed to practice in the State.
  (3) Tower cranes shall be erected so that the jibs and counterweights can swing 360 degrees without striking any building, structure or any other object.

[23-8.3]

(4) Prior to initial use, a newly erected tower crane shall undergo a static overload test in the direction of least stability. Such test shall consist of suspending a load at the rated load and at the maximum radius for a period of at least one hour. Subsequent to such test, settlement of the equipment and load-bearing foundation shall be within the limits specified by the tower crane manufacturer. A written report of such test shall be kept on the job site available for examination by the commissioner.

(b) *Tower crane capacity chart.* Every tower crane shall be provided with a capacity chart which shall be posted and maintained legible in the cab of the crane clearly visible to the operator from his operating position. Where a remote control stand is used a duplicate of such capacity chart shall be affixed to such control stand. Such capacity chart shall be furnished by the manufacturer of the crane and shall include a full and complete range of crane load ratings at all stated operating radii for each allowable speed and for each recommended counterweight loading.

(c) *Tower crane construction.* (1) *Limit switches.* Limit switches which shall be sealed against unauthorized tampering shall be provided as follows:

(i) To limit trolley travel at either end of the jib.

(ii) To limit load block upward motion to prevent two-blocking.

(iii) To limit the load being lifted to no more than 110 per cent of the rated load upon completion of the static overload test as specified in paragraph 23-8.3(a) (4) of this section, above.

(2) *Cabs and remote control stations.* (i) Tower crane cabs and remote control stations for such cranes shall be protected from falling objects and material and from the elements.

(ii) Cab windows shall be constructed of transparent safety glazing material and shall provide clear visibility in all directions.

(iii) Cabs and remote control stations for tower cranes shall be heated to a temperature of at least 60 degrees Fahrenheit during cold weather whenever occupied.

(iv) Cabs and remote control stations for tower cranes shall be adequately ventilated.

(3) *Accessibility.* Adequate and safe means of access to and egress from the cabs and machinery platforms of tower cranes shall be provided. Where it is necessary to inspect the jib attachments located on the jib of any tower crane, a footwalk with suitable handrails shall be provided for such inspections.

(4) *Brakes.* In addition to the hoisting brakes required by this subpart, tower cranes shall be provided with the following:

(i) *Slewing brake.* Every tower crane shall be provided with a brake having adequate holding power in either direction to prevent movement of the jib when desired during normal crane operation. Such brake shall be capable of being set in the holding position and kept there without attention from the operator.

(ii) *Trolley brake.* The trolley of every tower crane shall be provided with an automatic brake or device capable of stopping movement of the trolley in case of trolley rope breakage.

(5) *Electrical equipment.* (i) *All* electrical equipment of tower cranes shall be grounded.

(ii) All tower cranes shall be provided with lightning protection.

(iii) All controls of tower cranes shall be of the deadman type.

(iv) In the event of power failure, all tower crane brakes shall be set automatically.

(6) *Climbing jacks.* Where climbing jacks are provided for tower cranes such jacks shall be equipped with over-pressure relief valves, pressure gages and check valves designed to retain pressure in case of hydraulic line failure.

[23-8.3]

(7) *Wind velocity device.* Every tower crane shall be provided with a device for measuring wind velocity. The sensing portion of every such device shall be mounted on the highest point of the crane while the readout of every such device shall be located in the cab or remote control station of the tower crane.

(8) *Counterweights.* Counterweights used on tower cranes shall be in accordance with the manufacturers' recommendations. Counterweights shall be securely fastened to the counter jib to prevent pieces from being accidentally dislodged.

(d) *Inspection and maintenance.* (1) Tower cranes shall be inspected and maintained in accordance with the manfacturers' recommendations.

(2) Where the mast of any tower crane runs through floor openings in the building or other structure in which the crane is mounted and the mast is secured by wedges or braces, such wedges or braces shall be inspected for tightness and dislocation at least twice each working day.

(e) *Operation of tower cranes.* (1) *Operators.* Tower cranes shall be operated only by persons who are qualified in accordance with the provisions of section 23-8.5 of this subpart.

(2) *Operation in windy conditions.* Tower cranes shall not be operated when the wind speed is at any time greater than 30 miles per hour. Tower cranes shall not be raised to new operating levels when the wind speed exceeds 20 miles per hour.

(3) Operation without counterweight prohibited. No tower crane shall be operated without the full amount of ballast or counterweight in place as specified by the manufacturer or builder of the crane or by a professional engineer licensed to practice in the State.

23-8.4 Special provisions for derricks. (a) *Bracing of foot blocks.* The foot blocks of every derrick shall be securely supported and firmly anchored against movement in any direction.

(b) *Guys.* (1) *Number and spacing.* The top of any guy derrick mast more than 25 feet in height shall be steadied by not less than six wire rope guys so spaced as to make the angles between adjacent guys approximately equal.

(2) *Attachment.* Wire rope guys shall be secured by either weldless steel sockets, thimble and splice connections, thimbles with proper size and numbers of rope clips or cast steel guy plates having grooved bearing surfaces of the same shape and size as the wire rope thimbles, using a spliced or wire rope clip attachment.

(3) *Anchoring.* Guys shall be attached to strong permanent con struction or to substantial "dead men" securely anchored in the ground.

(c) *Breast-type derricks.* Breast-type derricks shall be guyed from both the front and rear. Where front guys are not possible because of derrick operation, provisions shall be made to prevent such derricks from tipping over backward. Breast-type derricks which are operated by hand power shall have hand grips securely and positively fastened to the shaft and a ratchet and pawl shall be provided which will hold any load.

(d) *Derrick construction.* (1) *Materials.* The mast, boom, frame and similar parts of a derrick shall be constructed of suitable steel or of selected wood of proper strength and durability.

(2) *Mast fittings.* On derricks which have booms larger than the masts, the gudgeon pins, mast tops and goosenecks shall be securely fastened to the tops of the masts to prevent such parts from pulling out when the booms are raised.

(e) *Derrick capacity charts.* (1) A capacity chart shall be provided for every derrick and such chart shall be posted conspicuously on the job site. Unless furnished by the manufacturer or builder of the derrick, the capacity chart shall be prepared and certified by a professional engineer licensed to practice in the State and a copy thereof shall be submitted, upon request, to the commissioner.

[23-8.4]

(2) A derrick shall not lift any load that exceeds the relevant maximum specified on its capacity chart.

(f) *Derrick boom raising.* The boom of any derrick shall not be raised from the level of the surface on which the derrick rests other than by the use of its own hoisting capabilities. The design, construction and length of the boom shall be such that there is no undue stress imposed on the derrick structure or mechanism during such raising operations.

23-8.5 Special provisions for crane operators. (a) *Finding of fact.* The board finds that the trade or occupation of operating cranes of the type described in subdivision (b) of this section, in construction, demolition and excavation work involves such elements of danger to the lives, health and safety of persons employed in such trade or occupation as to require special regulations for their protection and for the protection of other employees and the public in that such cranes may fall over, collapse, contact electric power lines, dislodge material and cause such material to fall or fail to support intended loads and convey them safely, unless such cranes are operated by persons of proper ability, judgment and diligence.

(b) *Limited application of this section.* This section applies only to mobile cranes having a manufacturers' maximum rated capacity exceeding five tons or a boom exceeding forty feet in length and to all tower cranes operating in construction, demolition and excavation work. The word crane as used in this section refers to tower cranes and to such mobile cranes of the following type: a mobile, carrier-mounted, power operated hoisting machine utilizing hoisting rope and a power-operated boom which moves laterally by rotation of the machine on the carrier.

(c) *Certificate of competence required.* No person, whether the owner, or otherwise, shall operate a crane in the State, unless such person is a certified crane operator by reason of the fact that:

(1) he holds a valid certificate of competence issued by the commissioner to operate a crane; or

(2) he is at least 21 years of age and holds a valid license issued by the Federal government, a State government or by any political subdivision of this or any other State and such license has been accepted in writing by the commissioner as equivalent to a certificate of competence issued by him; or

(3) he is a person who:

(i) is at least 21 years of age and is employed by the Federal government, the State or a political subdivision, agency or authority of the State and is operating a crane owned or leased by the Federal government the State or such political subdivision, agency or authority and h5 assigned duties include operation of a crane;

(ii) is at least 21 years of age and is employed only to test or repair a crane and is operating it for such purpose while under the direct supervision of a certified crane operator; or under the direct supervision of a person employed by the Federal government, the State or a political subdivision, agency or authority of the State and his assigned duties include the operation of a crane;

(iii) an apprentice or learner who is at least 18 years of age and who has the permission of the owner or lessee of a crane to take instruction in its operation and is operating such crane under the direct supervision of a certified crane operator or under the direct supervision of a person employed by the Federal government, the State or a political subdivision agency or authority of the State and whose assigned duties include the operation of a crane.

[23-8.5]

(d) *Application forms and photographs.* An application for a certificate of competence or for a renewal thereof shall be made on forms provided by the commissioner. Upon notice from the commissioner to an applicant that a certificate of competence or a renewal thereof will be issued to him, the applicant must forward photographs of himself in such numbers and sizes as the commissioner shall prescribe, and such photographs must have been taken within 30 days of the request for such photographs.

(e) *Physical conditions. No* person suffering from a physical handicap or illness, such as epilepsy, heart disease, or an uncorrected defect in vision or hearing, that might diminish his competence, shall be certified by the commissioner.

(f) *Experience required.* An applicant for a certificate of competence must be at least 21 years of age and must have had practical experience in the operation of cranes for at least three years and, in addition, have a practical knowledge of crane maintenance.

(g) *Examining board.* The commissioner may appoint an examining board which shall consist of at least three members, at least one of whom shall be a crane operator who holds a valid certificate of competence issued by the commissioner, and at least one of whom shall be a representative of crane owners. The members of the examining board shall serve at the pleasure of the commissioner and their duties will include:

(1) The examination of applicants and their qualifications, and the making of recommendations to the commissioner with respect to the experience and competence of the applicants.

(2) The holding of hearings regarding appeals following denials of certificates.

(3) The holding of hearings prior to determinations of the commissioner to suspend or revoke certificates, or to refuse to issue renewals of certificates.

(4) The reporting of findings and recommendations to the commissioner with respect to such hearings.

(5) The acts and proceedings of the examining board shall be in accordance with regulations issued by the commissioner.

(h) *General examination.* Each applicant for a certificate of competence will, and each applicant for a renewal thereof may, be required by the commissioner to take an appropriate general examination.

(i) *Operating examination.* An applicant who passes the general examination will also be required to take a practical examination in crane operation, except that the commissioner may waive this requirement with respect to an applicant for a renewal of a certificate of competence.

(j) *Contents of certificate.* Each certificate of competence issued shall include the name and address of the certified crane operator, a brief description of him for the purpose of identification and his photograph.

(k) *Term of certificate.* Each certificate of competence or renewal thereof shall be valid for three years from the date issued, unless its term is extended by the commissioner or unless it is sooner suspended or revoked. The commissioner may extend the term of any certificate of competence as he may find necessary to relieve a certified operator of unnecessary hardship.

(l) *Carrying certificate.* Each certified crane operator shall carry his certificate on his person when operating any crane and failure to produce the certificate upon request by the commissioner shall be presumptive evidence that the operator is not certified.

(m) *Renewals.* An application for renewal of a crane operator's certificate of competence shall be made within one year from the expiration date of the certificate sought to be renewed, except that the commissioner may extend the time to make such application to prevent any undue hardship to a certified crane operator.

[23-8.5]

(n) *Suspension, revocation, refusal to renew, denials of certificates, hearings.* (1) The commissioner may, upon notice to the interested parties and after a hearing before the examining board, suspend or revoke a certificateof competence upon finding that the certified operator has failed to comply with an order of the commissioner or that the certified operator is not a person of proper competence, judgment or ability in relation to the operation of cranes, or for other good cause shown.

(2) Prior to a determination by the commissioner not to renew a certificate of competence, the commissioner shall require a hearing before the examining board upon notice to the interested parties.

(3) (i) An applicant whose application for a certificate has been denied by the commissioner may, upon his written request made to the commissioner within 30 days after the mailing or personal delivery to him of a notice of such denial, have a hearing before the examining board.

(ii) Such hearing shall be held by the examining board which shall make its recommendations to the commissioner within three days after such hearing has been concluded. A written notice of the commissioner's decision, containing the reasons therefor, shall be promptly given to the certified operator or applicant, as the case may be, and to any interested parties who appeared at the hearing. Every such hearing shall be held in accordance with such regulations as the commissioner may establish.

POWER-OPERATED EQUIPMENT

23-9.1 Application of this subpart. The provisions of this subpart shall apply to power-operated heavy equipment or machinery used in construction, demolition and excavation operations. These provisions shall not apply to material or personnel hoists, (see subpart 23-6) nor to cranes and derricks (see subpart 23-8).

23-9.2 General requirements. (a) *Maintenance.* All power-operated equipment shall be maintained in good repair and in proper operating condition at all times. Sufficient inspections of adequate frequency shall be made of such equipment to insure such maintenance. Upon discovery, any structural defect or unsafe condition in such equipment shall be corrected by necessary repairs or replacement. The servicing and repair of such equipment shall be performed by or under the supervision of designated persons. Any servicing or repairing of such equipment shall be performed only while such equipment is at rest.

(b) *Operation.* (1) All power-operated equipment used in construction, demolition or excavation operations shall be operated only by trained, designated persons and all such equipment shall be operated in a safe manner at all times.

(2) Operators of power-operated material handling equipment shall remain at the controls while any load is being handled.

(c) *Loading.* Power-operated material handling equipment shall not be loaded in excess of the manufacturer's design live load rating. All loads shall be properly trimmed to prevent dislodgment of any part of such loads during transit.

(d) *Protection of moving parts.* Gears, belts, sprockets, drums, sheaves and any points of contact between moving parts of power-operated equipment or machines when not guarded by location shall be guarded in compliance with this Part (rule) and with Industrial Code Part (Rule No.) 19.

(e) *Refueling.* While refueling, the engines of power-operated equipment or machines shall be stopped except for turbo-charged diesel engines which are refueled through a special connection which prevents exposure of the fuel to the atmosphere. Open flames and any spark producing devices shall be kept a safe distance away from any area where engines are being refueled. Persons shall not smoke or carry lighted smoking materials in such area.

(f) *Engine exhaust.* Steam or exhaust gases from power-operated equipment shall be discharged at a point where such steam or gases will not contaminate the air in a working zone. Such discharges shall be in compliance with any regulations, orders, or laws promulgated by any authority concerned with air pollution.

(g) *Equipment at rest.* The operators of material handling equipment shall not leave such equipment while loads, buckets or blades are suspended. Any such load, bucket or blade shall be brought to rest on blocks, shall be lowered to the ground, grade or equivalent surface or shall be brought to the lowest end of travel of the equipment.

(h) *Roll-over protection required.* (1) *Roll-over protective structure.*

(i) Any new self-propelled earth-moving, excavating or grading equipment or machines, whether mounted on crawlers or wheels, which is sold or offered for sale in the State after January 1, 1973 shall be equipped with an approved roll-over protective structure when such equipment is used or intended to be used at any location in the State subject to the provisions of the Labor Law or of this Part (rule). Such equipment shall include: grader; bulldozer; tractor (prime mover) having a manufacturer's rated flywheel horsepower of 50 or more; front end loader with bucket capacity rated by the manufacturer at one cubic yard or more; scraper and off-highway type hauler having capacities rated by the manufacturers at five cubic yards or more.

[23-9.2]

(ii) Any self-propelled earth-moving, excavating or grading equipment or machines, whether mounted on crawlers or wheels, which has been manufactured after July 1, 1971 and before December 31, 1972, and which is sold or offered for sale in the State, shall be equipped with an approved roll-over protective structure by July 1, 1973, when such equipment is used or intended to be used at any location in the State subject to the provisions of the Labor Law or of this Part (rule).

(iii) Such roll-over protective structure shall be designed, constructed and installed to protect the operator in the event of accidental overturning of such equipment.

(2) *Approved seat belt required.* Any equipment required by this Part (rule) to have an approved roll-over protective structure shall also be provided with an approved seat belt for each seat. Such seat belt shall be used by the operator whenever the equipment is being operated.

> *Exception:* Tractors with pipe-laying equipment installed are not required to be provided with the roll-over protection.

(i) *Riding.* Persons shall not ride on the loads, buckets, blades, slings, balls, hooks, or similar parts of power-equipped equipment or machines.

23-9.3 Conveyors and cableways. (a) *Walkways.* Walkways along and adjacent to conveyor belts shall be kept free of materials and shall be unobstructed for their entire length. Where such walkways are located three feet or more above the ground, grade, floor or equivalent surface such walkways shall be provided with a safety railing constructed and installed in compliance with this Part (rule).

(b) *Trippers.* Where trippers are used to control discharge of materials from conveyors devices for throwing the belt drives into neutral shall be installed at both ends of the runways.

(c) *Spillage.* Where conveyor belts cross over any sidewalk, street, highway, or any other area where persons may work or pass, trays of sufficient size to catch any spillage from such belts shall be installed.

(d) *Overhead protection.* Where persons work or pass directly beneath a conveyor, overhead protection in compliance with this Part (rule) shall be provided.

(e) *Signal system required.* A signal system in compliance with subpart 23-6 of this Part (rule) shall be used in conjunction with conveyors for starting and stopping and for the raising and lowering of loads.

(f) *Riding prohibited.* No person shall ride any conveyor belt or the bucket or load handled by any cableway.

23-9.4 Power shovels and backhoes used for material handling. Where power shovels and backhoes are used for material handling, such equipment and the use thereof shall be in accordance with the following provisions:

(a) *Strength.* Such equipment shall be so constructed, placed and operated as to be stable. Such equipment shall not be stressed beyond their capacities as determined by the manufacturers.

(b) *Inspection.* (1) Such equipment shall be thoroughly inspected by designated persons at intervals not exceeding three months.

(2) Inspection and repair of each such machine shall be performed with the motor stopped and with the boom lowered and adequately supported.

[23-9.4]

(3) A written, dated record of the most recent inspection of each such machine shall be made on a form supplied by the commissioner and shall be signed by the designated person making such inspection. Such written record shall be kept on the job site available for examination by the commissioner.

(c) *Footing.* Firm, level and stable footing shall be provided for each such machine. Where such footing is not otherwise supplied, it shall be provided by substantial timbers, cribbing or other structural members in sufficient numbers and of sufficient size to distribute the load so as not to exceed the safe bearing capacity of the underlying material.

(d) *Hoisting mechanism brakes and locking devices.* (1) Such equipment shall be provided with brakes or equivalent devices capable of sustaining at rest one and one-half times the maximum rated load.

(2) Hand- or foot-operated brakes or equivalent devices shall be provided with substantial locking mechanisms to lock such brakes or equivalent devices while they are engaged.

(e) *Attachment of load.* (1) Any load handled by such equipment shall be suspended from the bucket or bucket arm by means of wire rope having a safety factor of four.

(2) Such wire rope shall be connected by means of either a closed shackle or a safety hook capable of holding at least four times the intended load.

(f) *Limitation on modifications.* No modifications affecting the load handling capacity of such machines shall be made unless the modification is certified by either the manufacturer of the equipment or by a professional engineer licensed to practice in the State.

(g) *Capacity.* No load shall be lifted by such equipment that exceeds the maximum load specified by the manufacturer of such equipment.

(h) *General operation.* (1) Any load lifted by such equipment shall be raised in a vertical plane to minimize swing during hoisting.

(2) Such equipment shall not travel with a suspended load except on surfaces which conform to the requirements of subdivision (c) of section 23-9.4 of this Part (rule).

(3) Ignition locks or equivalent means shall be provided to prevent unauthorized use of such equipment.

(4) Unauthorized persons shall not be permitted in the cab or immediately adjacent to any such equipment in operation.

(5) Carrying or swinging suspended loads over areas where persons are working or passing is prohibited.

(6) Operation near power lines or power facilities shall be in compliance with this Part (rule).

23-9.5 Excavating machines. (a) *Footing.* Excavating machines shall not be used where unstable conditions or slopes of the ground or grade may cause such machines to tilt dangerously. To prevent such unstable conditions, mats of timber or equivalent means to afford stable footings shall be provided.

(b) *Protection of operator.* Where an operator of an excavating machine may be exposed to an overhead hazard, such equipment shall be provided with a cab or equivalent cover affording protection against such hazard.

[23-9.5]

(c) *Operation.* Excavating machines shall be operated only by designated persons. No person except the operating crew shall be permitted on an excavating machine while it is in motion or operation. No person other than the pitman and excavating crew shall be permitted to stand within range of the back of a power shovel or within range of the swing of the dipper bucket while the shovel is in operation. When an excavating machine is not in use, the blade or dipper bucket shall rest on the ground or grade. The operator of an excavating machine shall not leave the controls of such machine at any time when the master clutch is engaged and the engine is operating. Oiling and greasing shall be performed only while an excavating machine is at rest and the master clutch disengaged. The boom or the bucket, dipper or clamshell of a power shovel shall not pass over the seat or cab of a truck or other vehicle while any person is in such seat or cab.

(d) *Operation near power lines or power facilities.* The operation of excavating machines near power lines or power facilities shall be in compliance with this Part (rule).

(e) *Trenching.* Material shall not be pushed manually into the path of trenching machines.

(f) *Stopping or parking excavating machines.* The operator of any excavating machine shall not leave the controls of such machine until he has lowered the bucket or blade into firm contact with the ground or grade surface.

(g) *Backing.* Every mobile power-operated excavating machine except for crawler-mounted equipment shall be provided with an approved warning device so installed as to automatically sound a warning signal when such machine is backing. Such warning signal shall be audible to all persons in the vicinity of the machine above the general noise level in the area.

23-9.6 Aerial baskets. (a) *Equipment inspection.* Prior to the use of an aerial basket the operator shall make a daily inspection of the equipment.

(1) Such daily inspection shall include the following:
 (i) All attachment welds between the actuating cylinders and the boom or pedestal.
 (ii) All pivot pins for security of their locking devices.
 (iii) All exposed ropes, sheaves and leveling devices for both excessive wear and security of attachment.
 (iv) Hydraulic systems for leaks and excessive wear.
 (v) Boom and basket for cracks and abrasions.
 (vi) The lubrication and fluid levels.

(2) A test operation of the boom from the ground controls through one complete cycle shall be performed by the operator. The basket controls shall be tested to make sure that they are in proper working order. The truck driver shall test the truck brakes and other automotive operating accessories.

(3) A record of such inspection and testing which may affect the safe operation of the aerial basket shall be corrected before such aerial basket is placed in operation.

(b) *Aerial basket safeguards.* (1) Where aerial basket controls are so located that they may come into contact with obstructions, such controls shall be protected by guarding or equivalent protection shall be provided.

(2) The lower controls at ground or grade level shall be capable of overriding the controls located in the basket.

(c) *Driving or moving of aerial basket truck.* (1) Aerial basket truck drivers an aerial basket operators shall be competent designated persons who have been trained in the operation and use of such equipment.

[23-9.6]

(2) The instrument panel of the truck cab shall be equipped with an automatic warning device, such as a light or similar device, to warn the driver when the boom is raised.

(3) Driving or moving the aerial basket truck while any person is elevated in the basket is prohibited.

(d) *Truck placement.* Prior to aerial basket operation, the truck shall be placed only on solid ground or equivalent surface to provide a substantially sound footing for the truck wheels and outriggers. The truck shall be so located that both front and rear axles are approximately horizontal, though they may be at different elevations, so that the truck does not lean sideways. Before the operation of the basket, a person stationed on the ground shall, by signaling the truck driver, position the truck and maneuver the empty basket into the proper working position. The basket shall then be returned to the ground or cradled in its traveling position. Such person shall also examine the outriggers for proper positioning and truck stability. Before such outriggers are lowered or extended, such person shall make sure that no obstructions or other persons are in the way.

(e) *Aerial basket operation.* (1) The use of an aerial basket as an anchoring point for a block and tackle, or as a make-shift boom on a straight lift is prohibited.

(2) Aerial basket equipment designed for use as a derrick shall be equipped with an approved boom angle indicator so that the operator will know the boom angle at all times. A capacity chart showing safe loads, boom heights and horizontal reach distances at various boom angles shall be installed next to the operating controls clearly legible to the operator from his operating position.

(3) Before the basket is moved, the operator shall observe the location of all obstructions and any other hazards which may be in the vicinity. The operator shall always face the direction in which the basket is moving or is about to move.

(4) The operation of an aerial basket near power lines or power facilities shall be in compliance with this Part (rule).

(5) All air or oil supply hoses for power tools used from the aerial basket shall be free of any conductive material.

(6) The truck and the aerial basket vehicle shall be adequately grounded at all times when in use or the basket shall be isolated from the truck by insulation.

(7) Where aerial baskets are operated near power lines and power facilities, materials and tools shall not be passed between a person on the ground or grade level and a person in the basket, unless both such persons are wearing high-voltage rubber gloves and other protective equipment, such as rubber sleeves and safety hats or caps. During such use of an aerial basket, persons shall not enter or leave the truck while the boom or basket is near or in contact with electrically energized equipment and no person on the ground or grade level shall be suffered or permitted to touch the truck.

(8) Persons shall enter or leave an aerial basket only when such basket is resting on the ground or grade level or cradled in the traveling position. Persons shall stand clear of the path of the basket and boom when such basket is being lowered. Any movement of the vehicle while persons are elevated in the basket is prohibited.

(9) While persons are in the elevated basket, persons on the ground or grade level shall not enter the area directly beneath such basket except when required by the persons in the basket.

(10) Tools, equipment and materials shall not be thrown from or to the elevated basket.

(11) All tools not in use shall be adequately secured in trays in the baskets, or adequately secured in suitable belt holsters.

(12) Standing on the rim of the basket, placing and standing on boards across the rim of the basket or placing and standing on ladders in the basket is prohibited.

[23-9.6]

(13) Unless in an emergency situation, or upon request of a person in the aerial basket, the controls to lower the boom shall be operated only by persons in the elevated basket.

23-9.7 Motor trucks. (a) *Brake maintenance.* The brakes of every motor truck shall be so maintained that such truck with full load may be securely held on any grade that may be encountered in normal use on the job.

(b) *Blocks.* (1) Provision shall be made to apply wheel blocks to any truck ascending any ramp with a slope steeper than one in 10 to prevent the truck from sliding in case of stall.

(2) No person shall work under the raised body of a dump truck unless such body is securely blocked to prevent accidental lowering.

(c) *Loading.* Trucks shall not be loaded beyond their rated capacities and all loads shall be trimmed before the trucks are moved. Loads that are apt to become dislodged in transit shall be securely lashed in place.

(d) *Backing.* Trucks shall not be backed or dumped in places where persons are working nor backed into hazardous locations unless guided by a person so stationed that he sees the truck drivers and the spaces in back of the vehicles.

(e) *Riding.* No person shall be suffered or permitted to ride on running boards, fenders or elsewhere on a truck or similar vehicle except where a properly constructed and installed seat or platform is provided.

(f) *Dumping.* No person shall be located within the body (load carrying portion) of a truck while the dumping mechanism is being operated.

(g) *Cab protector.* Dump steel bodies which are loaded by mechanical means shall be equipped with suitable steel cab protectors which cover at least the rear quarter of the tops of such cabs.

23-9.8 Lift and fork trucks. (a) *Capacity.* A metal plate with legible etched or stamped figures giving the capacity rating in pounds shall be attached to every lift or fork truck. A pouch firmly secured to the truck and containing a document having the following information may be used as a means of identifying the load rating of the truck: truck make, model, serial number, and load rating in pounds.

(b) *Overloading prohibited.* No lift or fork truck shall be loaded beyond its capacity rating.

(c) *Brakes and load-elevating mechanisms.* Every power-operated fork and lift truck shall be provided with a lockable brake. The load-elevating mechanism shall be capable of being locked at any elevation.

(d) *Hand-lift handles.* Every pallet truck having a hand-lift handle shall be provided with an automatic device to retain the raised load and free the handle until it is re-engaged by the operator.

(e) *Operating surfaces.* No lift or fork truck shall be used on any surface that is so uneven as to make upsetting likely.

(f) *Packaged masonry units.* No masonry units packaged by means of wire or metal tape shall be handled by a lift or fork truck when any part of such wire or tape binding is broken.

(g) *Loose masonry units.* Unless palletized masonry units are securely bound in package form, provisions shall be made to prevent spillage.

(h) *Support of pallets.* Loaded pallets shall be kept level at all times. Masonry units used as pallet supports shall be securely lashed to the pallet and shall be of proper quality and number to provide stable footing for the load. Loose material and other unstable supports for pallets shall not be used.

(i) *Protection of operator.* Every fork lift truck shall be provided with a substantial overhead canopy or screen to protect the operator from falling objects and materials

[23-9.8]

(j) *Prohibited use.* No lift or fork truck shall be in motion when the loaded forks are elevated higher than necessary to clear floor obstructions except as required for positioning to deposit the load.

(k) *Riding on forks.* No person shall stand or ride on the forks of a moving fork lift truck.

(1) *Warning devices.* Every power-operated fork lift truck shall be equipped with a horn, whistle, gong or similar warning device which can be actuated by the operator. Such device shall be clearly audible above the normal noise level in the work area.

23.9.9 Power buggies. (a) *Assigned operator.* No person other than a trained and competent operator designated by the employer shall operate a power buggy.

(b) *Defective machines.* No power buggy shall be operated unless it is in compliance with this Part (rule) and is in good operating condition.

(c) *Mechanical requirements.* (1) *Stability.* Every power buggy shall be so designed and constructed as to withstand without tilting the following:

(i) A 45 degree turn at full rated load and maximum designed forward speed.

(ii) A collision stop against wheel blockage on a level grade at full rated load and one-half maximum designed forward or full reverse speed.

(iii) Lateral traversal of 10 per cent grade slopes at full rated load and maximum designed speed.

(2) *Braking power.* (i) Every power buggy shall be provided with brakes and tire surfaces capable of bringing such buggy to a full stop within 25 feet on a level dry plank surface or frictional equivalent at full rated load and maximum designed speed.

(ii) Brakes shall be capable of being fixed in engagement to hold the full load stationary on a 25 per cent grade.

(3) *Accidental starting.* The controls of every power buggy shall be so arranged, shielded or located that they cannot be accidentally engaged.

(4) *Warning devices.* Every power buggy except those having maximum speeds of three miles per hour and upon which no person rides shall be equipped with an easily operable horn or other audible warning signal. Such audible horn or other signal shall be capable of being heard above the normal noise level in the area.

(5) *Seats and visibility.* Every power buggy of the riding type shall be provided with an operator's seat or standing platform designed and secured to prevent slipping off and so located that the operator may have maximum practicable driving visibility.

(6) *Speed.* Every power buggy of the riding type shall be designed or equipped so that it cannot travel faster than 12 miles per hour on a level surface.

(d) *Operation.* (1) *Parking on grades.* No power buggy shall be left unattended on any grade sufficiently steep to cause such buggy to coast if free of engine and brake resistance.

(2) *Prohibited operation.* No power buggy shall be operated:

(i) at a speed greater than 12 miles per hour;

(ii) when carrying more than its full rated load;

(iii) on insecure or slippery surfaces or on surfaces so inclined or uneven as to endanger stability;

(iv) on grades steeper than 25 per cent; or

(v) on ramps, runways or other surfaces not in compliance with this Part (rule).

(e) *Special requirements for runways and ramps.* Runways, ramps, platforms and other surfaces upon which power buggies are operated shall conform to the following requirements:

(1) They shall be substantially constructed and securely supported, braced and fastened to prevent movement.

[23-9.9]

(2) They shall be constructed to sustain without failure at least four times the maximum load for which they are intended.

(3) The minimum width inside of curbs for any ramp, runway or platform for single lane power buggy traffic shall be two feet wider than the outside width of any power buggy operated thereon and two feet wider than twice such buggy width in places where passing or two lane traffic occurs.

(4) Ramps shall be limited to maximum grades of one on four.

(5) All runways shall be substantially level transversely.

(6) Curbs in compliance with this Part (rule) shall be provided along the edges of surfaces upon which power buggies are operated as follows:

(i) Curbs shall be furnished along all edges which are nearer than 10 feet horizontally to the edge of any unenclosed floor area, shaft or other open space into or through which a fall from such surface of more than 24 inches vertically is possible, except as set forth in subparagraph (iii) below.

(ii) Where curbs are not required because the buggy is operated on a surface not over 24 inches above any floor or equivalent surface below, such lower surface shall be strong enough to sustain the loaded power buggy in event of a fall thereon.

(iii) Curbs may be omitted at actual dumping points more than 24 inches above any floor or equivalent surface below if the edge over which the dumping occurs is provided with bumpers or other means which will effectively stop the buggy from running over the edge while dumping.

23-9.10 Pile drivers. (a) *Footing.* Before placing or advancing a pile driver, the ground shall be inspected and, where necessary for firm and level footing, cribbing or timber mats shall be provided to assure stability for the pile driver. After placing or advancing a pile driver, inspection and correction of the footing shall be made as necessary to maintain such stability.

(b) *Inspection.* All pile driving equipment shall be inspected daily before the start of work and every defect or unsafe condition shall be immediately corrected before pile driving operations are begun.

(c) *Protection of operator.* The operator of every pile driver shall be protected from falling objects or materials, steam, cinders and water by a substantial covering.

(d) *Qualifications of operators.* Each member of the pile driving crew shall be properly instructed in the work he is to perform and the pile driving operation shall be in charge of a trained, designated person who alone shall direct the work and give the operating signals.

(e) *Handling of piles.* The preparation of the piles shall be done at a safe distance from the driving operation. During the hoisting of piles, all persons not actually engaged in operating the equipment and handling the piles shall be kept from the area.

(f) *When not in use.* When any pile driver is not in use the hammer shall be chocked or blocked in the leads or lowered to the ground or grade level.

(g) *Temporary interruption.* The operator of every pile driver shall remain at the controls when the driving is interrupted until the hammer has been chocked or blocked in the leads, or has been lowered and is resting on a driven pile or on the ground.

(h) *Steam and air lines.* Steam and air hose shall be securely fastened in place at couplings and intermediate points to prevent dangerous whipping of such hose in the event of a break. The control valves for steam and air lines shall be located within easy reach of the operator at his operating position.

(i) *Driving plates, cushions and striking heads.* Driving plates, cushions and striking heads shall be securely and positively fastened in such manner as to prevent their dislodgment during the driving operations

[23-9.10]

(j) *Ladders.* A ladder extending from the bottom of the leads to the overhead sheaves shall be permanently attached to the structure supporting the leads.

(k) *Working platforms.* Where a structural tower supports the leads, working platforms consisting of planking at least two inches thick, full size, laid tight shall be provided on all levels of the leads at which it is necessary for persons to work. Such platforms shall be provided with safety railings constructed and installed in compliance with this Part (rule) on all sides, except on the hammer or lead side of the platforms. Where such platforms cannot be provided approved safety belts and lifelines shall be provided.

(1) *Mandril support.* Mandrils shall be attached to the leads by safety chains or cables to prevent dislodging or falling during connection to piles.

23-9.11 Mixing machines. (a) *Charging skips.* Each time before raising or lowering a charging skip, the operator shall make sure that no person is located in the danger area. In addition, there shall be a safety railing constructed and installed in compliance with this Part (rule) on both sides of the charging skip so arranged as to prevent passage of any person under the raised skip.

(b) *Hoppers.* Hoppers into which a person may fall shall be effectively guarded with a substantial iron grating consisting of crossbars of one-half inch round stock or its equivalent, spaced not to exceed five inches between bars. Maximum openings in such grating shall be one square foot in size.

(c) *Bucket hoists.* Where a falling hazard exists at the point where a mixer discharges into a bucket hoist, such point shall be guarded by location, by a safety railing constructed and installed in compliance with this Part (rule) or by other equivalent means.

(d) *Flywheels.* Flywheels and power transmission mechanisms shall be kept covered and guarded against accidental contact.

(e) *Trough type mixers.* The revolving blades of trough or batch type mixing machines shall be guarded with a substantial iron grating consisting of crossbars of one-half inch round stock or its equivalent, spaced not to exceed five inches between bars and located at least five inches above the blades.

BASIC FUNDAMENTALS OF ENGINES, FUELS, LUBRICANTS, AND POLLUTION CONTROL

CONTENTS

		Page
I.	Internal Combustion Engines	1
II.	Fuels and Lubricants	7
III.	Safety in Handling and Storage of Petroleum Products	20
IV.	Filters	23
V.	Environmental Pollution Control	26

BASIC FUNDAMENTALS OF ENGINES, FUELS, LUBRICANTS, AND POLLUTION CONTROL

As an equipment operator, you will be mainly concerned with operation of equipment. In order to perform these duties intelligently, it is important that you fully understand the principles of the internal combustion engine operation and the function of the various components that make up the internal combustion engine. This understanding will make your job easier when simple adjustments or repairs have to be made.

This chapter discusses basic principles of engine operation and explains some of the terminology related to engines. Various types of fuel and lubricants are described and information is given on the safe handling and storage of petroleum products. Information is provided on the types and purposes of filters used on automotive and construction equipment. Various methods are discussed on environmental pollution control so that you may effectively control pollution resulting from the combustion and spillage of fuels.

I. INTERNAL COMBUSTION ENGINES

An internal combustion engine is one in which the fuel burns within the body of the engine. The burning that takes place inside the cylinders produces the energy that turns the crankshaft of the engine. Both gasoline and diesel engines operate on this principle.

Combustion is the act or process of burning. An internal or external combustion engine is defined simply as a machine that converts this heat energy to mechanical energy. To fulfill this purpose, the engine may take one of several forms.

With the internal combustion engine, combustion takes place inside the cylinder and is directly responsible for forcing the piston to move down.

In external combustion engines, such as steam engines, combustion takes place outside the engine. Figure 1 shows, in simplified form, an external and an internal combustion engine.

The external combustion engine requires a boiler to which heat is applied. This combustion causes water to boil to produce steam. The steam passes into the engine cylinder under pressure and forces the piston to move downward.

The transformation of HEAT ENERGY to MECHANICAL ENERGY by the engine is based on a fundamental law of physics which states that gas will expand upon application of heat. If the gas is confined with no outlet for expansion, then the pressure of the gas will be increased when heat is applied. In the internal combustion engine the burning of a fuel within a closed cylinder results in an expansion of gases, thus creating a pressure on top of a piston and causing it to move downward.

In an internal combustion engine the piston moves up and down within a cylinder. This up-and-down motion is known as RECIPROCATING MOTION. This reciprocating motion (straight line motion) must be changed to ROTARY MOTION (turning motion) in order to turn the wheels of a vehicle. A crankshaft and a connecting rod change this reciprocating motion to rotary motion, figure 2.

All internal combustion engines, whether gasoline or diesel, are basically the same. We can best demonstrate this by saying they all rely on three things—AIR, FUEL, and IGNITION.

FUEL contains potential energy for operating the engine; AIR contains the oxygen necessary for combustion; and IGNITION starts combustion. All are fundamental, and the engine will not operate without any one of them. Any discussion of engines must be based on these three factors and the steps and mechanisms involved in delivering them to the combustion chamber at the proper time.

The power of an internal combustion engine comes from the burning of a mixture of fuel and air in a small, enclosed space. When this

ENGINES, FUELS, LUBRICANTS, AND POLLUTION CONTROL

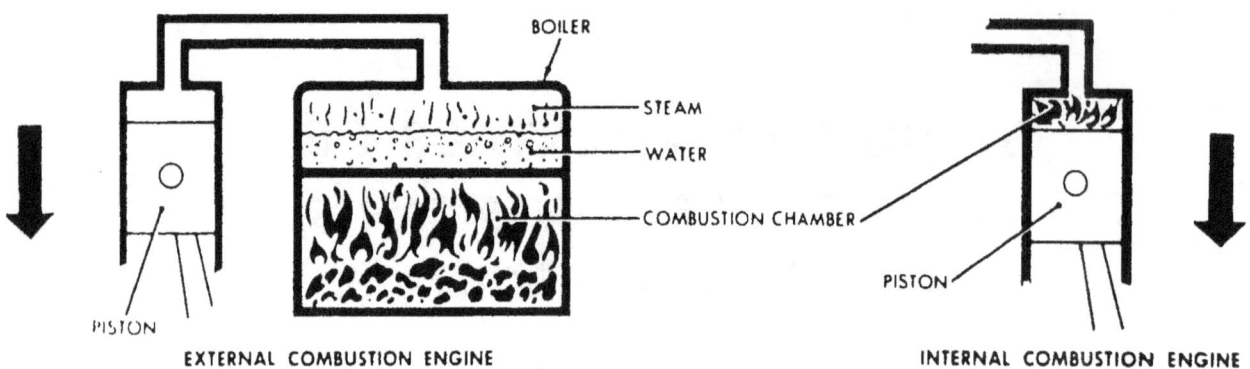

Figure 1.—Simple external and internal combustion engine.

mixture burns it expands greatly, and the push or pressure created is used to move the piston, thereby rotating the crankshaft. This movement is eventually sent back to the wheels to drive the vehicle.

Since similar action occurs in all cylinders of an engine, let's use one cylinder in our development of power. The one-cylinder engine consists of four basic parts as shown in figure 2.

First we must have a CYLINDER which is closed at one end; this cylinder is similar to a tall metal can which is stationary within the engine block. Inside this cylinder is the PISTON,

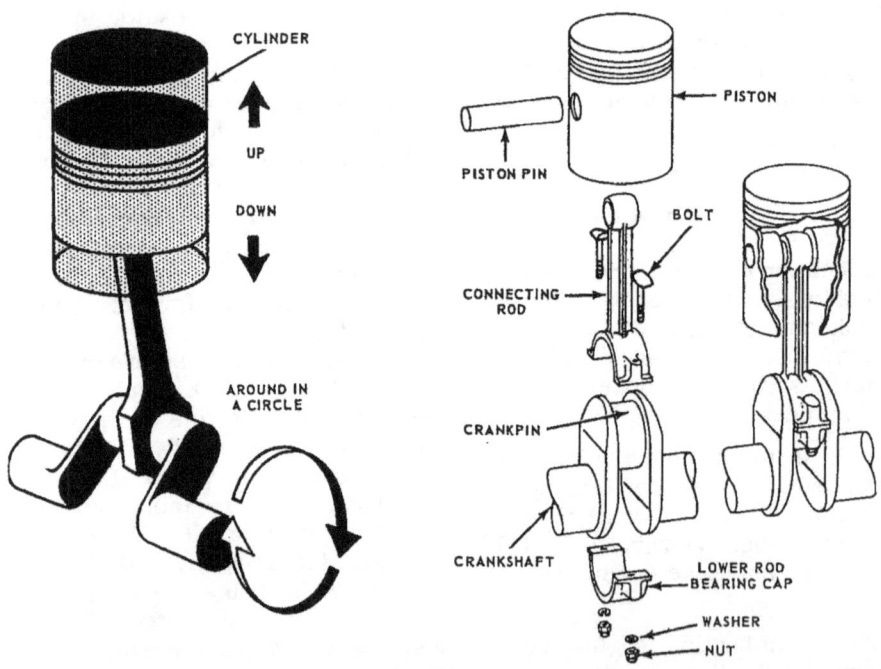

Figure 2.—Cylinder, piston, connecting rod, and crankshaft for one-cylinder engine.

a movable metal plug, which fits snugly into the cylinder, but can still slide up and down easily.

You have already learned that the up-and-down movement of the piston is called reciprocating motion. This motion must be changed to rotary motion so the wheels or tracks of vehicles can be made to rotate. This change is accomplished by a crank on the CRANKSHAFT and a CONNECTING ROD which connects the piston and the crank.

The crank is an offset section of the crankshaft, which scribes a circle as the shaft rotates. The top end of the connecting rod is connected to the piston and must, therefore, go up and down. The lower end of the connecting rod also moves up and down but, because it is attached to the crankshaft, it must also move in a circle with the crank.

When the piston of the engine slides downward because of the pressure of the expanding gases in the cylinder, the upper end of the connecting rod moves downward with the piston, in a straight line. The lower end of the connecting rod moves down and in a circular motion at the same time. This moves the crank which, in turn, rotates the shaft; this rotation is the desired result. So remember, the crankshaft and connecting rod combination is a mechanism for the purpose of changing straight line (or reciprocating) motion to circular (or rotary) motion.

FOUR-STROKE CYCLE
GASOLINE ENGINE

The operating principles of the gasoline and diesel engines are basically the same. Therefore, only the operating cycles of the four-stroke gasoline engine and the two-stroke cycle diesel engines will be discussed.

Each movement of the piston from top to bottom or from bottom to top is called a stroke. The piston takes two strokes (an upstroke and a downstroke) as the crankshaft makes one complete revolution. When the piston is at the top of a stroke (fig. 3), it is said to be at top dead center (TDC). When the piston is at the bottom of a stroke (fig. 4), it is said to be at bottom dead center (BDC).

The basic engine you have studied so far has no provisions for getting the fuel-air mixture into the cylinder or burned gases out of the cylinder. There are two openings in the closed end of a cylinder. One of the openings, permits an intake of air or an intake of a mixture of fuel and air into the combustion area of the cylinder. The other opening permits the burned

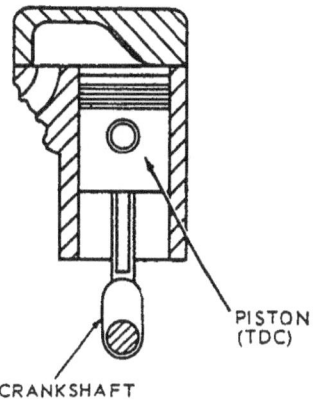

Figure 3. — Piston top dead center (TDC).

gases to escape from the cylinder. The two openings have valves in them. These valves, activated by the camshaft, close off either one or the other of the openings, or both of them during various stages of engine operation. The camshaft has a number of cams along its length that open the valves and hold them open for the correct length of time during the piston stroke. The camshaft is driven by the crankshaft through timing gears, or by means of a timing chain. On a 4-stroke cycle engine (fig. 5) the camshaft turns at one-half crankshaft speed. This permits each valve to open and close once for every two revolutions of the crankshaft. One of the valves, called the intake valve, opens to admit an intake of air or a mixture of fuel

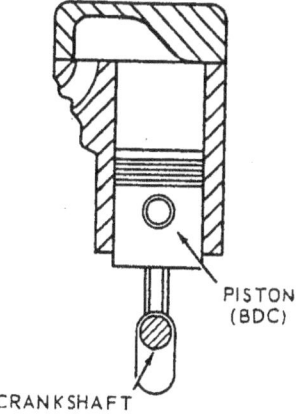

Figure 4. — Piston bottom dead center (BDC).

ENGINES, FUELS, LUBRICANTS, AND POLLUTION CONTROL

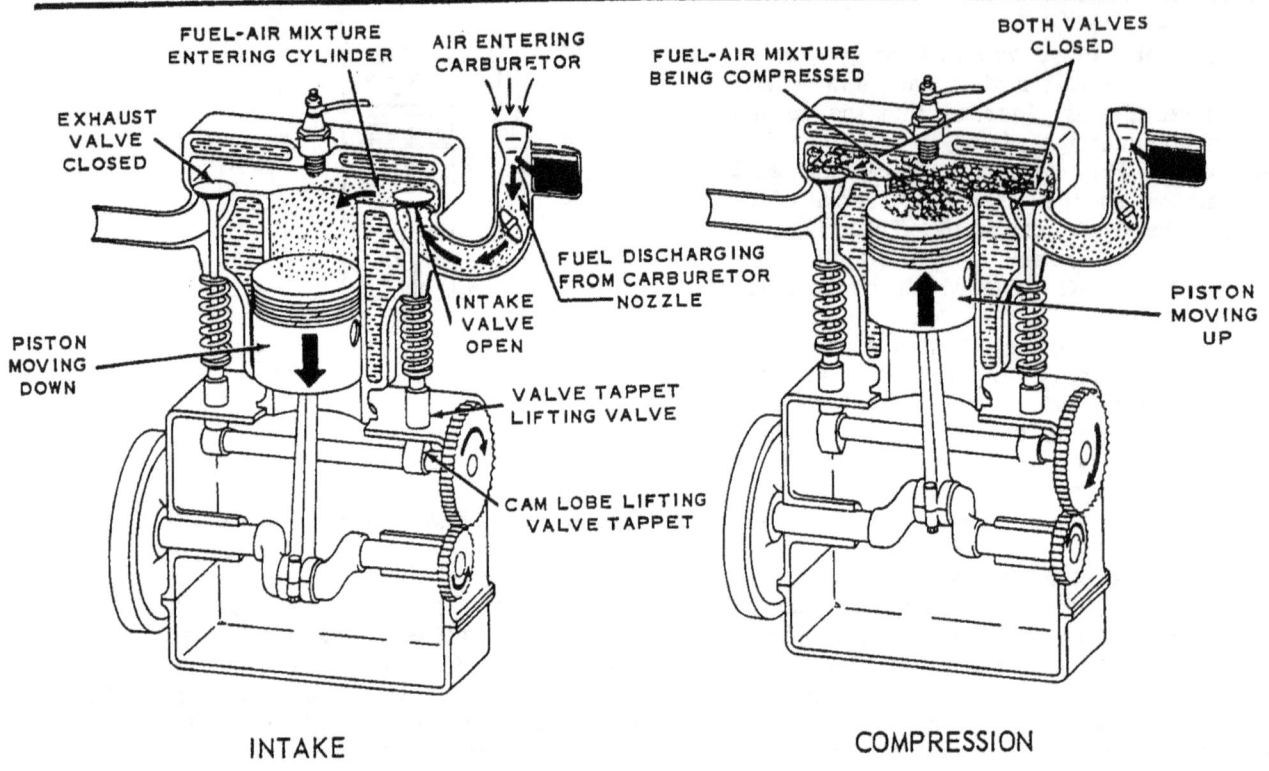
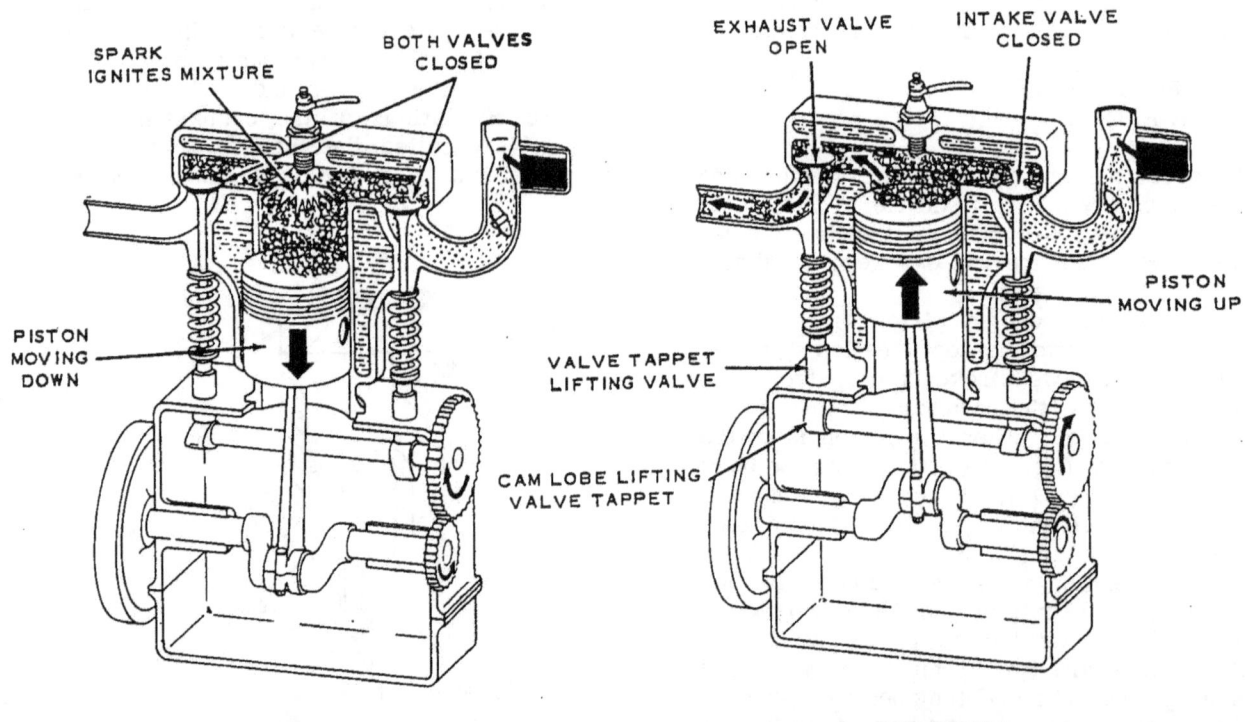

Figure 5.—Four-stroke cycle in a gasoline engine.

and air into the cylinder. The other valve, called the exhaust valve, opens to allow the escape of burned gases after the fuel-and-air mixture has burned.

The following paragraphs give a simplified explanation of the action that takes place within the engine cylinder.

Intake Stroke

The first stroke in the sequence is called the INTAKE stroke (fig. 5). During this stroke, as the crankshaft continues to rotate, the piston is moving downward and the intake valve is open. This downward movement of the piston produces a partial vacuum in the cylinder, and an air-fuel mixture rushes into the cylinder past the open intake valve. This is somewhat the same effect as when you drink through a straw. A partial vacuum is produced in the mouth and the liquid moves up through the straw to fill the vacuum.

Compression Stroke

When the piston reaches bottom dead center at the end of the intake stroke and is therefore at the bottom of the cylinder, the intake valve closes. This seals the upper end of the cylinder. As the crankshaft continues to rotate, it pushes up, through the connecting rod, on the piston. The piston is therefore pushed upward and compresses the combustible mixture in the cylinder; this is called the COMPRESSION stroke (fig. 5). In gasoline engines, the mixture is compressed to about one-eighth of its original volume, which is called an 8 to 1 compression ratio. This compression of the air-fuel mixture increases the pressure within the cylinder. Compressing the mixture in this way makes it still more combustible; not only does the pressure in the cylinder go up, but the temperature of the mixture also increases.

Power Stroke

As the piston reaches top dead center at the end of the compression stroke and therefore has moved to the top of the cylinder, the compressed fuel-air mixture is ignited. The ignition system causes an electric spark to occur suddenly in the cylinder, and the spark ignites the compressed fuel-air mixture. In burning, the mixture gets very hot and tries to expand in all directions. The pressure rises to about 600 to 700 pounds per square inch. Since the piston is the only thing that can move, the force produced by the expanding gases forces the piston down. This force, or thrust, is carried through the connecting rod to the crankpin on the crankshaft. The crankshaft is given a powerful turn. This is called the POWER stroke (fig. 5). This turning effort, rapidly repeated in the engine and carried through gears and shafts, will turn the wheels of a vehicle and cause it to move along the highway.

Exhaust Stroke

After the fuel-air mixture has burned, it must be cleared from the cylinder. This is done by opening the exhaust valve just as the power stroke is finished and the piston starts back up on the EXHAUST stroke (fig. 5). The piston forces the burned gases out of the cylinder past the open exhaust valve.

ENGINE CYCLES

The four strokes (intake, compression, power, and exhaust) are continuously repeated as the engine runs. Now, with the basic knowledge you have of the parts and the four strokes of the engine, let us see what happens during the actual running of the engine. To produce sustained power, an engine must accomplish the same series of events — intake, compression, power, and exhaust — over and over again.

This series of events is called a cycle. Remember that in a 4-stroke cycle engine it takes four complete strokes of the piston to complete one engine cycle, that is, two complete revolutions of the crankshaft. Most engines that you will deal with are of the 4-stroke cycle design.

2-Stroke Cycle Diesel Engine

In the 2-stroke cycle engine, the same four events (intake, compression, power, and exhaust) take place in only two strokes of the piston; one complete revolution of the crankshaft.

The 2-stroke cycle operation shown in figure 6 features the General Motors 71 series. This engine differs in two ways from the 4-stroke cycle engine previously discussed. Not only does it complete the four events in 2-strokes, but it depends upon the heat of compression rather than a spark for ignition. In the two-cycle engine, intake and exhaust take place during part of the compression and power strokes respectively.

ENGINES, FUELS, LUBRICANTS, AND POLLUTION CONTROL

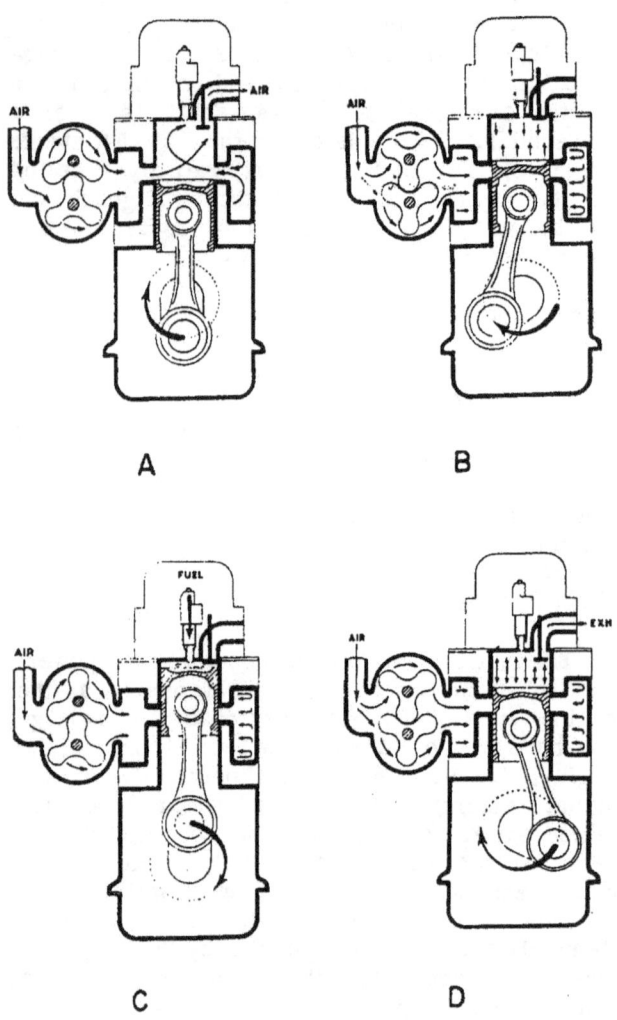

Figure 6.—Events in a 2-stroke cycle, internal combustion engine.

In contrast, a four-cycle engine requires four piston strokes to complete an operating cycle. A blower is provided to force air into the cylinders for expelling the exhaust gases and supply the cylinders with fresh air for combustion. The cylinder walls contain a row of ports which are above the piston when it is at the bottom of its stroke. These ports admit the air from the blower into the cylinder as soon as the top face of the piston uncovers the ports, as shown in view A, figure 6. The indirectional flow of air toward the exhaust valves produces a scavenging effect; this action leaves the cylinder full of clean air when the piston again covers the inlet ports.

As the piston continues on the upward stroke, the exhaust valves (2 per cylinder) close and the charge of fresh air is subject to compression, as shown in view B, figure 6. Shortly before the piston reaches its highest position, the required amount of fuel is sprayed into the combustion space by the cylinder's injector, view C, figure 6; the intense heat generated during the high compression of the air ignites the fine spray immediately and the combustion continues as long as the fuel spray lasts. The resulting pressure forces the piston downward on the power stroke. The exhaust valves are again opened when the piston is about halfway down, allowing the combustion gases to escape into the exhaust manifold, view D, figure 6. Shortly thereafter, the downward movement of the piston uncovers the inlet ports and the cylinder is again swept with clean air, as shown in view A, figure 6. This entire combustion cycle is completed in each cylinder for each revolution of the crankshaft and during two strokes of the piston thus; the term "two-stroke cycle."

4-Stroke Cycle Vs 2-Stroke Cycle

A power stroke is produced every crankshaft revolution within the 2-stroke cycle engine; whereas the 4-stroke cycle engine requires two crankshaft revolutions for one power stroke.

It might appear then that a 2-stroke cycle could produce twice as much power as a 4-stroke cycle of the same size, operating at the same speed. However, this is not true. With some 2-stroke cycle engines, some of the power is used to drive a blower that forces the air-fuel charge into the cylinder under pressure. Also, the burned gases are not completely cleared from the cylinder, reducing combustion efficiency. Additionally, because of the much shorter period the intake port is open (as compared to the period the intake valve in a 4-stroke-cycle is open), a relatively smaller amount of fuel-air mixture is admitted. Hence, with less fuel-air mixture, less power per power stroke is produced in a 2-stroke cycle engine of like size operating at the same speed and with other conditions being the same.

MULTIFUEL ENGINE

The multifuel engine operates on a compression ignition, four-stroke cycle principle similar to conventional four-stroke cycle diesel and gasoline engines. Those pieces of military equipment which are equipped with the multifuel engine are designed to use several different types of fuel, such as gasoline, kerosene, diesel, and (JP) fuels. No modifications or adjustments are necessary when changing grades or types of fuel.

The multifuel engine operation cycle, is shown in figure 7.

STARTING AND STOPPING PROCEDURES FOR GASOLINE AND DIESEL ENGINES

In the previous sections you learned about the operating cycle of the internal combustion engine, and how it is constructed.

In order to make the basic engine operational, it requires the addition of cooling, lubrication, fuel, and electrical systems. Before starting an internal combustion engine, certain pre-start checks must be made to determine if the engine will operate. Check for fuel, coolant, battery condition, loose wires, oil level, and the absence of leaks.

In this chapter, it is infeasible to state the correct procedures for starting and stopping every type of automotive or construction equipment, equipped with a gasoline or diesel engine that is used. Therefore, the procedures explained below apply to typical types of automotive equipment equipped with a gasoline engine. For information on a specific type of automotive vehicle consult the manufacturers operating manual. Procedures for starting and stopping a typical piece of construction equipment equipped with a diesel engine are covered in chapter 9.

Before starting the engine, be sure the hand or parking brake is set, and the gear selector lever is in NEUTRAL. On a vehicle with an automatic transmission, set the lever at N (NEUTRAL) or push in the N (NEUTRAL) button; otherwise the engine will not start. Some vehicles can be started also in P (PARK).

Next, turn on the ignition and depress the accelerator one-quarter of the way toward the floor. If the equipment has a clutch, disengage it before starting the engine to ensure that the vehicle will not move, and to keep the starter from turning the transmission.

If the engine does not have an automatic choke, pull the choke control out about half-way. Using the choke when the engine is warm will cause flooding and will hinder easy starting.

Now operate the starter until the engine begins to fire. The starter on some vehicles may be actuated by pushing in a starter button on the instrument panel; on others, by depressing the starter button on the floorboard. A few engines are started by depressing the accelerator pedal; on others, turning the ignition switch key to the extreme right starts the engine.

If the engine does not start within 10 seconds, stop to see whether you have properly performed all prestarting operations. If it does not start after several attempts, notify your chief.

Caution: Never operate the cranking motor for more than 30 seconds at a time. If the engine fails to start in 30 seconds, allow the cranking motor to cool for 2 to 3 minutes before resuming cranking operation. Prolonged use of the starter wears it out and discharges the battery.

As soon as the engine begins to fire, release the starter knob, or let the ignition switch key snap back to ON position. Release the clutch pedal slowly, if you have depressed it, and push the choke control back in. After the engine is operating smoothly, ease off the throttle, and allow the engine to idle till it warms to the proper operating temperature. The warm-up period allows the oil in the crankcase to circulate and lubricate the engine pistons, bearings, and the cylinder surfaces. Putting a vehicle into motion before the engine is at proper operating temperature will cause undue wear of the moving parts of the engine.

The following are typical procedures for stopping automotive gasoline engines: (1) Allow the engine to operate at low idle for 3 to 5 minutes, (2) check gage readings; for water coolant within normal range, lubricating oil pressure within range, ammeter showing a charge, fuel gage indicating sufficient fule, and air pressure gage (if so equipped) indicating normal air pressure, and (3) turn the electrical system ignition switch to the OFF position.

II. FUELS AND LUBRICANTS

Fuels and lubricants for gasoline and diesel engines are byproducts of petroleum. Petroleum, often called crude oil, means "rock oil." Petroleum products include gasoline, kerosene, diesel fuel, lubricating oils, gear lubricants, and greases. Many different products are added to the raw byproducts to obtain a fuel or lubricant that will perform efficiently in modern equipment.

Crude oil would ruin an engine if the impurities were not removed. The impurities are removed by the refining process, which also

ENGINES, FUELS, LUBRICANTS, AND POLLUTION CONTROL

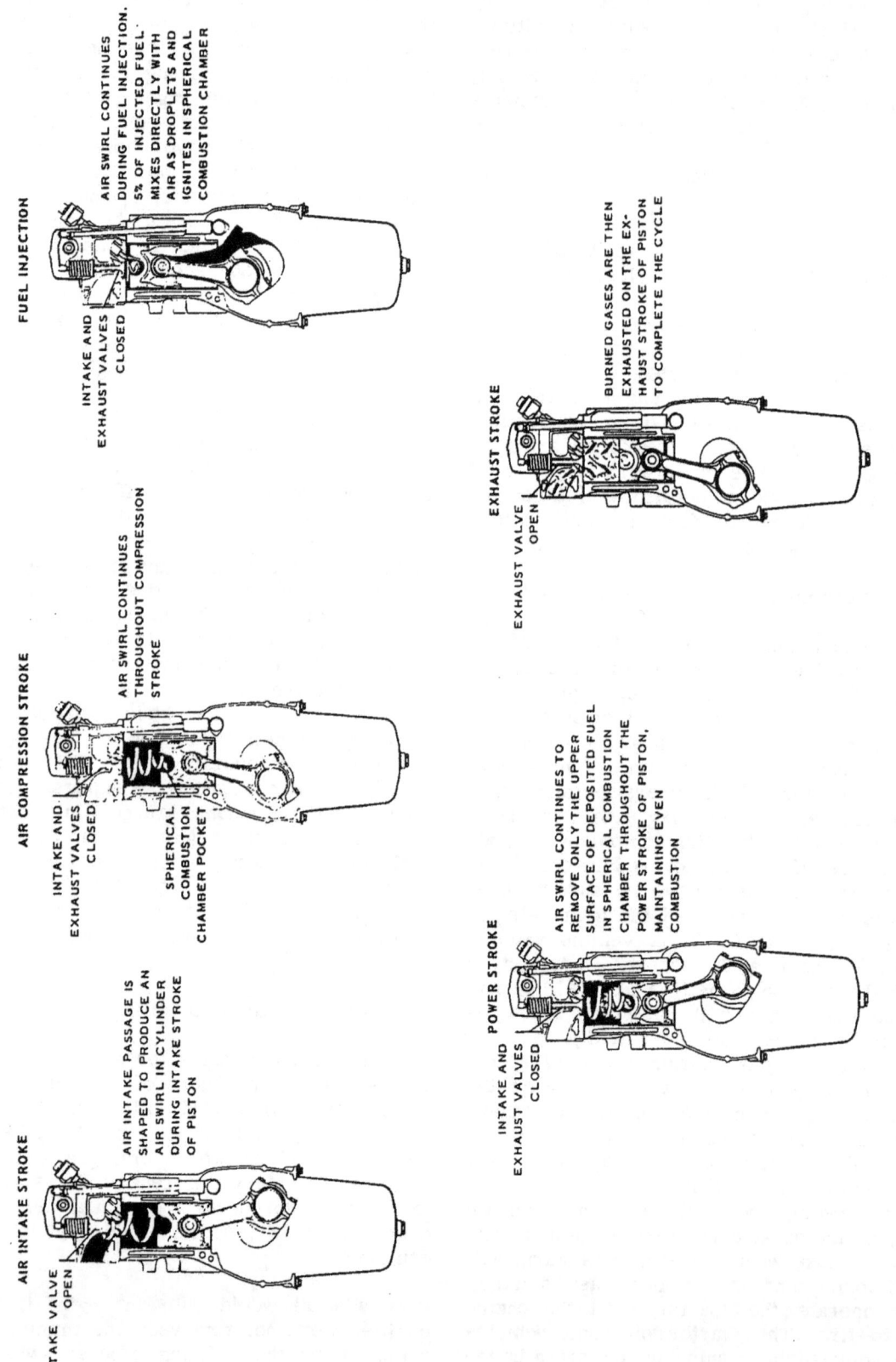

Figure 7. — Multifuel engine operation cycles.

separates the oil into various petroleum products. (See fig. 8.)

You have seen a teakettle boil. Heating the water in the kettle changes it to gas or vapor in the form of steam at a certain temperature. Many kinds of liquids change to gases, or are said to VAPORIZE, at different temperatures. Heating petroleum, which is a mixture of liquids, will change the liquids to gases one by one. Cooling changes each gas back to liquid form through condensation. This process of separating substances from one another is called DISTILLATION.

Distillation drives gasoline vapors from the crude oil first, because gasoline has a lower boiling point and vaporizes before other petroleum products. Substances with higher boiling points, like kerosene and the gas-oil from which we get most of our diesel fuel, are given off next. After the gas-oil has been collected, lubricating oils are distilled, the lightest first (lube distillates), and then the heavier ones (commonly called bottoms). (It is to be noted, bottoms are where we get asphaltic products.) (See fig. 8.)

You will hear also about propane and butane fuels, which are byproducts of natural gas. (Notice in figure 3-8 that gas is taken from a cavity in the earth that is between the oil and the rock formation just above the oil.) These liquids must be collected and stored under pressure because they change into gas when released to the atmosphere. Liquid propane becomes a gas at a temperature of -43°F; liquid butane, at -33°F. Although seldom used as a fuel for automotive equipment, small amounts of these liquid gases have been used to start engines in very cold climates. Some manufacturers believe that internal combustion engines can operate more economically with butane fuel than with gasoline. Gasoline and diesel oil, however, continue to be the most common fuels for internal combustion engines.

PROPERTIES OF GASOLINE

Gasoline contains carbon and hydrogen in such proportions that the gasoline burns freely and liberates HEAT ENERGY. If all the potential heat energy contained in a gallon of gasoline could be converted into work, a motor vehicle could run hundreds of miles on each gallon. However, only a small percentage of this heat energy is converted into power by the engine. Most authorities consider the power losses within the engine to be as follows:

Engine	Percent of Power Loss
Cooling System	35
Exhaust Gases	35
Engine Friction	5 to 10
Total	75 to 80

The question of what is ideal gasoline is more theoretical than practical. Every manufacturer recommends the octane rating of the gasoline he feels is best for the engines he produces. Besides engine design, factors like the weight of the vehicle, the terrain and highways over which it is to be driven, and the climate and altitude of the locality also determine what gasoline is best to use. All other factors being equal, these may be considered as some of the properties of the best gasoline: good antiknock quality, a minimum content of foreign matter, and a volatility which makes starting easy and allows smooth acceleration and economical operation.

Volatility

The blend of a gasoline determines its VOLATILITY—that is, its tendency to change from a liquid to a vapor at any given temperature. The rate of vaporization increases as the temperature of the gasoline rises.

No standard for gasoline volatility meets all engine operating requirements. The volatility must be high enough for easy starting and acceleration. Ordinarily the proper starting mixture is about 15 parts of air to 1 part of fuel, but in very cold weather more fuel must be admitted to the cylinders through the use of the choke in the carburetor for quicker starting. In polar regions, a gasoline of higher volatility makes starting easier; it also helps keep the crankcase from becoming diluted by gasoline seeping past the piston and the piston rings while the engine is being choked.

On the other hand, a gasoline of low volatility brings about better fuel economy and combats VAPOR LOCK (the formation of vapor in the fuel lines in a quantity sufficient to block the flow of gasoline through the system). In the summer and in hot climates, especially, fuels with low volatility lessen the tendency toward vapor lock.

ENGINES, FUELS, LUBRICANTS, AND POLLUTION CONTROL

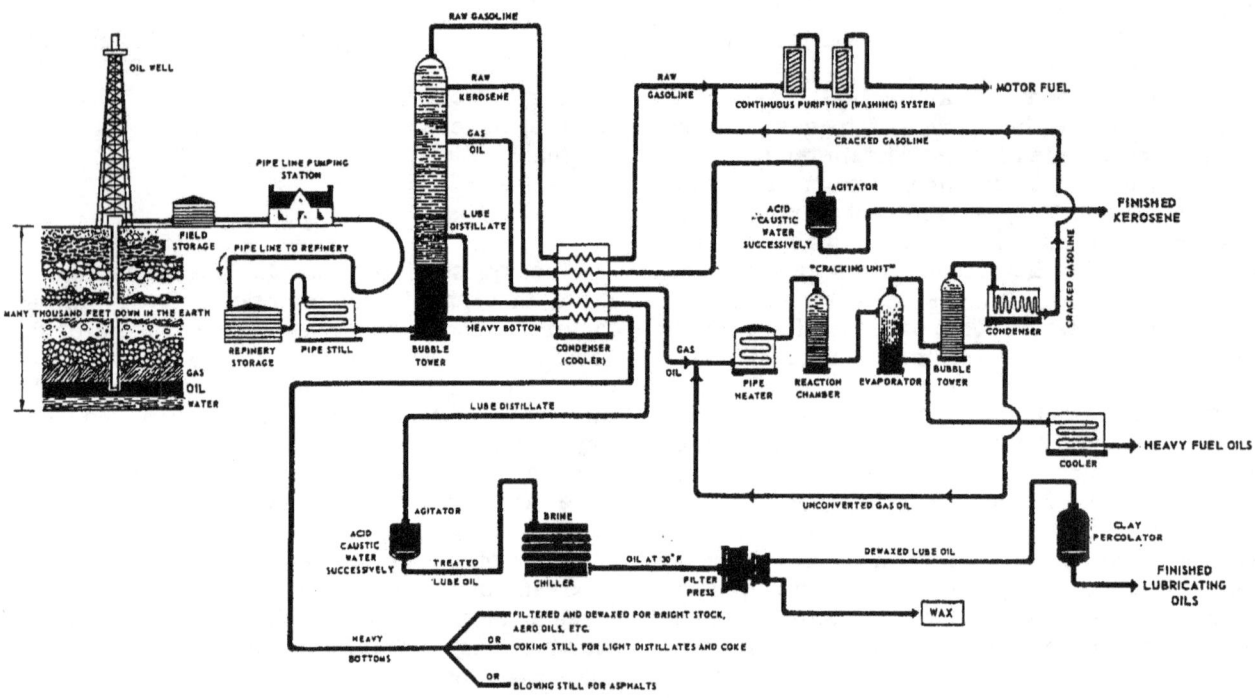

Figure 8.—Typical chart tracing crude oil from well to finished product.

Purity

Engine efficiency depends to some extent on the PURITY of gasoline. Gums and sulfur are removed from crude oil in the refining process. Gums in gasoline cause sticking valves and form hard baked surfaces within the cylinders. Residue unites with moisture to form sulfuric acid, which corrodes engine parts. Modern refining processes have reduced the sulfur and other foreign matter content of gasoline, thus minimizing the damage to engine parts as well as cutting down engine maintenance.

Antiknock Quality and Detonation

Reviewing the process of combustion will help you understand the ANTIKNOCK quality of gasoline. When any substance burns, its molecules and those of the oxygen in the air around it are set into motion, producing heat that unites the two groups of molecules in a rapid chemical reaction. In the combustion chamber of an engine cylinder, the gasoline vapor and oxygen in the air are ignited and burn. They combine, and the molecules begin to move about very rapidly, as the high temperatures of combustion are reached. This rapid movement of molecules provides the push on the piston to force it downward on the power stroke.

In the modern high compression gasoline engines the air-fuel mixture tends to ignite spontaneously or to explode instead of burning. The result is a knock, a ping, or a DETONATION. In detonation the spark from the spark plug starts the fuel mixture burning, and the flame spreads through the layers of the mixture, very quickly compressing and heating them. The last layers become so compressed and heated that they explode violently. The explosive pressure strikes the piston head and the walls of the cylinder, and causes the knock you hear in the engine. It is the fuel, not the engine, that knocks. Besides being an annoying sound, persistent knocking results in engine overheating, loss of power, and increased fuel consumption. It causes severe shock to the spark plugs, pistons, connecting rods, and the crankshaft. To slow down this burning rate of the fuel, a fuel of a higher octane rating must be used.

Octane Rating

The property of a fuel to resist detonation is called its antiknock or OCTANE rating. The octane rating is obtained by comparing the antiknock qualities of gasoline in a special test engine against reference fuels.

Octane numbers range from 50 in cheaper gasolines to over 100 for those required of modern high compression engines. The octane number has nothing to do with the starting qualities, potential energy, or volatility of the fuel.

The octane rating of gasoline can be raised in two ways: by mixing it with another fuel, or treating it with a chemical. In this country a chemical is added to gasoline to improve its octane rating. The most efficient additive used for this purpose is tetraethyl lead compound, which is added to the gasoline with ETHYL FLUID. In addition to the tetraethyl lead, ethyl fluid contains other chemicals that prevent lead deposits from forming within the engine. Lead oxide causes considerable corrosion.

The LEAD CONTENT of ethyl fluid is very poisonous. Ethyl gasoline should be used only for engine fuel and for no other purpose. It should never be used as a cleaning agent.

An engine which does not knock on a low octane fuel will not operate more efficiently by using a fuel of high octane rating. An engine which knocks on a given fuel should use one of a higher rating. If a higher octane fuel does not stop the knocking, some mechanical adjustments are probably necessary. Retarding the spark so that the engine will fire later may end knocking. However, an engine operating on retarded spark will use more fuel and will overheat. It may be less expensive to use a higher priced, high-octane gasoline with an advanced spark than to use a cheap, low-octane gasoline with a retarded spark.

Engine knocking is not always the result of using too low an octane rating; it can be caused by preignition. In preignition the fuel-air mixture begins to burn before the spark occurs. This condition may be caused by an overheated exhaust valve head, hot spark plugs, or glowing pieces of carbon within the combustion chamber. In figure -9, you see the diagrammed course of the fuel-air mixture in the cylinder under circumstances of preignition and detonation, as well as in normal combustion.

DIESEL FUEL

Diesel fuel is heavier than gasoline because it is obtained from the residue of the crude oil after the more volatile fuels have been removed. As with gasoline, the efficiency of a diesel fuel varies with the type of engine in which it is used. By distillation, cracking, and blending of several oils, a suitable diesel fuel can be obtained for almost all engine operating conditions. Slow speed diesels use a wide variety of heavy fuels; high speed diesel engines require a lighter fuel. Using a poor or an improper grade of fuel can cause hard starting, incomplete combustion, a smoky exhaust, and engine knocks.

The properties to be considered in selecting a fuel for a diesel engine are VOLATILITY, CLEANLINESS, VISCOSITY, AND IGNITION QUALITY.

Volatility

The volatility of a diesel fuel is measured by the 90 percent distillation temperature. This is the temperature at which 90 percent of a sample of the fuel has been distilled off. The lower this temperature, the higher the volatility of the fuel. In small diesel engines, a fuel of high volatility is more necessary than in large engines if there is to be low fuel consumption, low exhaust temperature, and little exhaust smoke.

Cleanliness

Cleanliness of diesel fuel is very important. Fuel should not contain more than a trace of foreign substances; otherwise, fuel pump and injector difficulties will develop. Because it is heavier and more viscous, diesel fuel will hold dirt particles in suspension for longer periods than will gasoline. In the refining process, not all foreign matter can be removed, and harmful matter like dirt and water can get into the fuel while it is being handled. Water will cause hard starting and misfiring. Dirt will clog injectors and spray nozzles and may cause an engine to misfire or stop altogether.

Viscosity

The viscosity of fuel is the measure of its resistance to flow. Viscosity is expressed by the number of seconds required for a certain volume of fuel to flow through a hole of a certain diameter at a given temperature. The viscosity of diesel duel must be low enough to flow

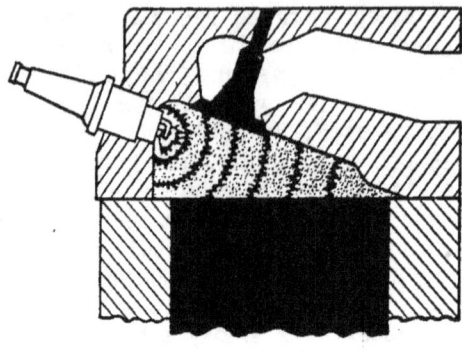
NORMAL

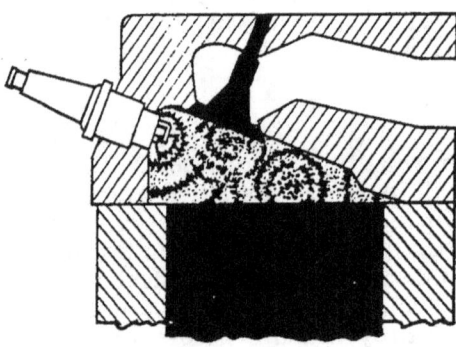
DETONATION

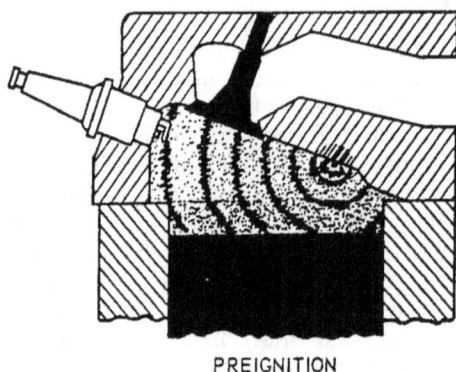
PREIGNITION

Figure 9. — Combustion process.

freely at low temperatures, yet high enough to lubricate the pump and injector plungers properly and lessen the possibility of leakage at the pump plungers and dribbling at the injectors. Viscosity is measured by an instrument (fig. 10) called the SAYBOLT VISCOSIMETER and is expressed in SAYBOLTSECONDS, UNIVERSAL (SSU).

A Saybolt viscosimeter consists of an oil tube, a constant-temperature oil bath which maintains the correct temperature of the sample in the tube, a 60-cc (cubic-centimeter), graduated receiving flask, thermometers for measuring the temperature of the oil sample and of the oil bath, and a timing device.

The oil to be tested is strained and poured into the oil tube. The tube is surrounded by the constant-temperature oil bath. When the oil sample is at the correct temperature, the cork is pulled from the lower end of the tube and the sample flows through the orifice and into the graduated receiving flask. The time (in seconds) required for the oil to fill the receiving flask to the 60-cc mark is noted.

The viscosity of the oil is expressed by indicating three things: first, the number of seconds required for 60 cubic centimeters of oil to flow into the receiving flask; second, the type of orifice used; and third, the temperature of the oil sample at the time the viscosity determination is made. For example, suppose that a sample of lubricating oil is heated to 125°F and that 170 seconds are required for 60-cc of the sample of flow through a Saybolt Universal orifice and into the receiving flask. The viscosity of this oil is said to be 170 seconds Saybolt Universal at 125°F. This is usually expressed in shorter form as 170 SSU at 125°F (or 20 weight oil.)

Other oils have other temperatures that are used for obtaining Saybolt Universal viscosities. Thus, it is important that the temperature be included in the statement of viscosity.

Ignition Quality

The ignition quality of a diesel fuel is its ability to ignite when it is injected into the compressed air within the engine cylinders. Ignition quality is measured by the CETANE RATING of the fuel. A cetane number is obtained by comparing the ignition quality of a given diesel fuel with that of a reference fuel of known cetane number in a test engine. This reference fuel is a mixture of alphamethylnapthalene, which is difficult to ignite alone, and cetane, which

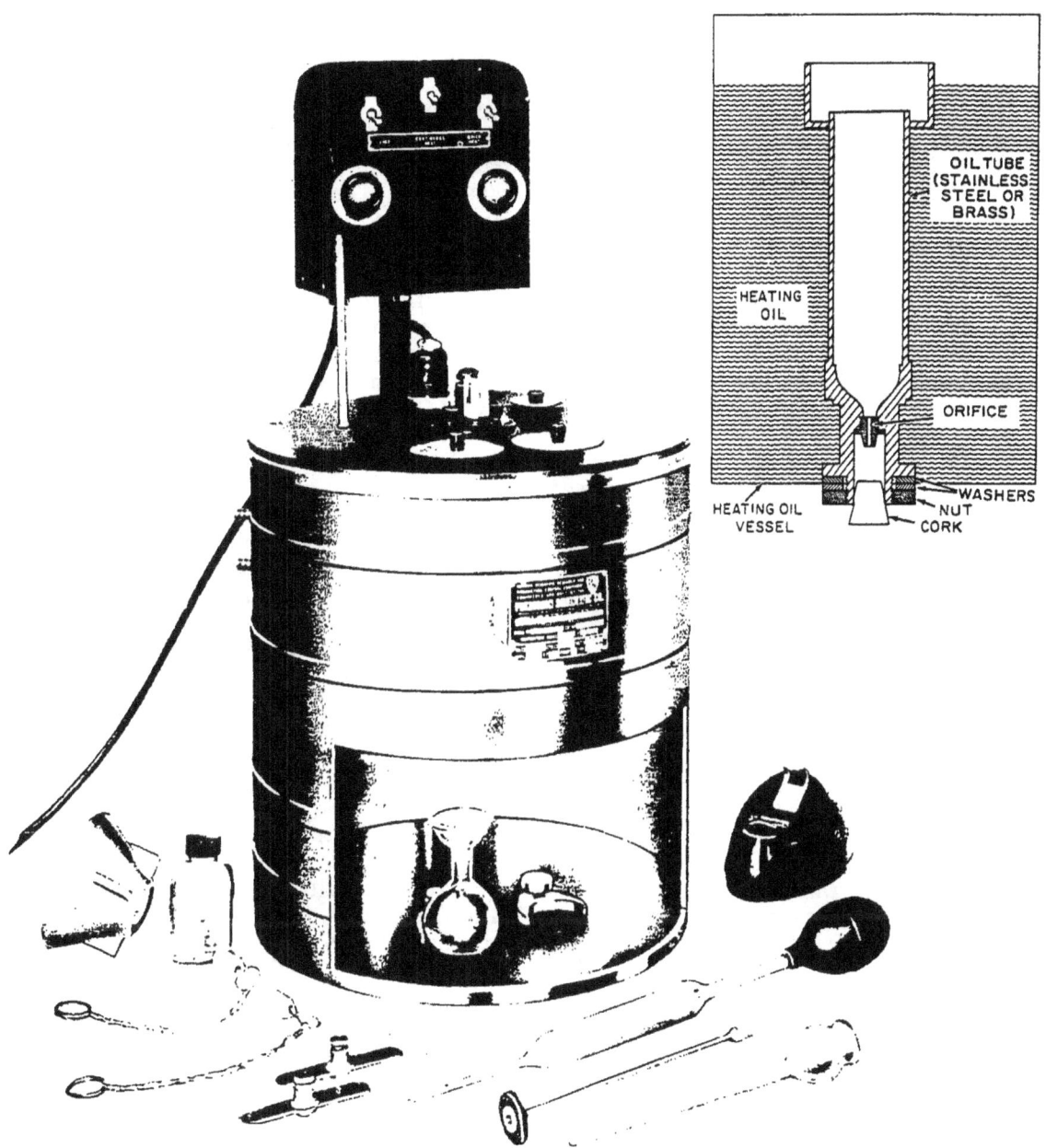

Figure 10.—Saybolt viscosimeter.

will ignite readily at temperatures and pressures comparable to those in the cylinders of a diesel engine. The cetane rating indicates the percentage of cetane in a reference fuel which will just match the ignition quality of the fuel being tested. The higher cetane numbers indicate more efficient fuels. The large slow diesels can use a 30 cetane fuel, but the high speed diesels must use at least a 40 cetane fuel, while some require as high as a 60 cetane fuel.

The ignition quality of a diesel-fuel depends also on its FLASH POINT and its FIRE POINT. The flast point is the temperature to which the fuel vapors must be heated to flash or ignite. The minimum flash point for diesel fuel is 150°

F. A fuel having too low a flash point is dangerous both to handle and to store.

The fire point is that temperature at which the fuel vapors will continue to burn after being ignited. It is usually 10 to 70 degrees higher than the flash point.

You will sometimes hear knocks in diesel engines. They are believed to be caused by the rapid burning of the fuel that accumulates in the delay period between injection and ignition. This delay is known as IGNITION LAG or IGNITION DELAY. When the fuel is injected into the cylinders, it must vaporize and be heated to the flash point to start combustion. The lag between vaporization and flash point depends upon the ignition quality of the fuel and the speed of the engine and its compression ratio. In high speed engines the delay varies from 0.0012 to 0.0018 of a second. Ignition lag decreases with the increase in engine speed because of a swifter air movement in the cylinders that makes the injected fuel heat better.

LUBRICANTS

A lubricant is a substance, usually a thin film of oil, used to reduce friction. There are three types of kinetic friction: sliding friction, rolling friction, and fluid friction. Sliding friction exists when the surface of one solid body is moved across the surface of another solid body. Rolling friction exists when a curved body such as a cylinder or a sphere rolls upon a flat or curved surface. Fluid friction is the resistance to motion exhibited by a fluid.

Fluid friction exists because of the cohesion between particles of the fluid and the adhesion of fluid particles to the object or medium which is tending to move the fluid. If a paddle is used to stir a fluid, for example, the cohesive forces between the molecules of the fluid tend to hold the molecules together and thus prevent motion of the fluid. At the same time, the adhesive forces of the molecules of the fluid cause the fluid to adhere to the paddle and thus create friction between the paddle and the fluid. Cohesion is the molecular attraction between particles that tends to hold a substance or a body together; adhesion is the molecular attraction between particles that tends to cause unlike surfaces to stick together. From the point of view of lubrication, adhesion is the property of a lubricant that causes it to stick (or adhere) to the parts being lubricated; cohesion is the property which holds the lubricant together and enables it to resist breakdown under pressure.

Besides reducing friction and wear, lubricants act as COOLING AGENTS, absorbing heat from the surfaces over which they are spread. This is true particularly of engine oil, which carries heat to the engine sump, where it is dissipated. The water circulating through an oil cooler also helps to reduce this heat (not all engines have oil coolers).

Lubricants are also used as SEALING agents. They fill the tiny openings between moving parts, cushioning them against damage and distortion from extreme heat.

Lubricants are also important as CLEANING AGENTS. Any grit and dirt finding their way into the engine parts often are removed by the lubricants before damage can result. Foreign matter found in old oils and greases in the bottom of the crankcase is evidence of the cleansing quality of lubricants. Some lubricants have chemicals added to make them better cleaners.

The high temperatures, speeds, and cylinder pressures of modern engines have made necessary better grades of lubricating oils. To increase efficiency, certain chemicals, called ADDITIVES, are put into oils. Additives are resistive agents which are used against oxidation and other kinds of metal deterioration. Oil which contains additives specifically designed to help clean the piston rings and other parts of the engine as it lubricates is known as DETERGENT OIL.

It is especially important for you to keep up with the latest developments in lubricants as presented in Navy and other technical publications. Your chief will tell you where you can get this information.

Types of Lubricants and Their Uses

Oils and greases are the two general types of lubricants. The modern high-speed gasoline or diesel engine must be properly lubricated with the proper grades and types of lubricating oils and greases. Present-day refining methods have produced lubricating oils and greases with certain special qualities. In engines operating at high speeds and temperatures, these oils do a better job than ordinary oils can do. Engines operating at low speeds or in cold weather may require an oil with other special qualities.

Greases are used where it is difficult to keep oil in place and where the lubricant is subjected to varying pressures. In some cases, greases are used when centrifugal forces tend to throw the lubricant from moving parts. This is especially true in gear boxes and wheel bearings.

OILS. — Lubricating oils serve four purposes: (1) prevent metal-to-metal contact in moving parts of mechanisms, (2) help carry heat away from the engine, (3) clean the engine parts as they are lubricated, and (4) form a seal between moving parts. Moving parts that do not have enough oil will melt, fuse, or seize after a very short period of engine operation. All gears and accessory drives, as well as other moving parts of the engine subject to friction, must be bathed in oil at all times.

We have seen that viscosity is the resistance of a liquid against flow. It is the most important property of a lubricating oil. A lubricant of high viscosity spreads very slowly. You have heard of car owners using a HEAVY oil in summer and changing to LIGHT oil in winter. The heavy oil used in summer becomes too sluggish in cold weather, while the light oil used in winter flows too easily in hot weather. An oil used in any engine must flow freely and have enough body to resist friction between moving engine parts; it must pass readily through all oil lines and spread effectively over all surfaces that require lubrication.

The temperature of an oil affects its viscosity. The higher the temperature, the lower the viscosity. On a cold morning, the high viscosity or stiffness of the lubricating oil makes an engine hard to turn over.

The viscosity of an oil is figured by the number of seconds which pass while a certain volume flows through a small opening or hole of a definite diameter at a given temperature. The greater the number of seconds, the higher the viscosity. The Society of Automotive Engineers (S.A.E.) has standardized a code of numbers to indicate the viscosity of lubricating oils. You will be using military symbols for these lubricating oils, which are expressed in four digits, as indicated in Table 1. The last three digits indicate the viscosity in number of seconds required for 60 cubic centimeters of oil to flow through a standard opening at a given temperature. The first digit indicates the class and type of lubricating oil. You will use only the lubricant recommended for the particular engine which you service and lubricate. It is advisable to check with your chief from time to time for discontinued and new stocks and changed designations or specification numbers.

Oil is a mixture of many slightly different compounds, and therefore does not have a definite freezing point, but it does thicken as it cools. In order to determine the usefulness of an oil in cold weather, it is tested for its POUR POINT, which is the lowest temperature at which the oil will still flow. The pour point in which you will be interested is the lowest temperature at which the oil on the cylinder walls and bearings will permit the engine to be turned.

While the flash point and the fire point of an oil do not affect its lubricating qualities, they are useful in determining the amount of volatile fluids or compounds in the oil. As you learned concerning diesel oil, the flash point is the temperature at which vapors will ignite, but not sustain a flame. The flash point of a lubricating oil for your entire engine must range from 300°F to 500°F to keep the oil from vaporizing too readily in the crankcase and to make it withstand the heat of the engine. It is used also to determine the fire hazard in shipping and storing the lubricant.

Again, as you previously learned, the fire point is the temperature at which vapors given off continue to burn when ignited. Both the flash point and the fire point must be taken into consideration in the blending of an oil of proper viscosity for the type and condition of the engine in which it is to be used.

From the day that fresh oil is put into the engine crankcase, it gradually begins to lose its effectiveness because of dilution and contamination from engine operation. Gasoline or diesel fuel may dribble into the crankcase oil. Water and sludge also may accumulate. Carbon, gum acids, and dust in the air entering the engine (in the air-fuel mixture) all reduce the effectiveness of any lubricant. It is because of this accumulation of foreign matter that manufacturers recommend regular oil changes, and that regular lubrication is so important in preventive maintenance.

GREASES. — Greases are compounds of oil and soap. The soaps used are not ordinary laundry soaps but animal fats mixed with certain chemicals. The chief purpose of the soap is to provide a body or carrier for the oil that actually does the lubricating.

Grease is used where oil is impractical or unsatisfactory due to centrifugal forces, loads, temperatures or exposure. For instance, it maintains a film at high engine speed and temperature, or when the equipment is idle for long periods of time.

ENGINES, FUELS, LUBRICANTS, AND POLLUTION CONTROL

The chemicals in the grease classify it for a particular purpose or use. CHASSIS GREASES have a lime, sodium, or an aluminum soap base. Chassis greases are distinguished by their shiny, transparent appearance, and are used as a pressure gum lubricant for chassis, U-joints, track rollers, and low temperature ball bearings.

CUP GREASE, or WATER-PUMP GREASE, is a lime-base grease to which water or moisture is added to keep the soap from separating from the oil. The moisture gives the grease a somewhat cloudy appearance, and it will evaporate at a temperature equal to that of boiling water. Lime base greases are not recommended for parts subjected to high temperature. These greases are recommended when moisture resistance is required, and are satisfactory for water pumps and marine stuffing boxes.

WHEEL BEARING or FIBROUS GREASES have a sodium or mixed soap base. These greases only appear fibrous, for there are no actual fibers in them. They are recommended for wheel bearings because they stick or cling to parts. Since they are not water resistant, they can be used only on protected parts.

CABLE GREASE (wire rope and exposed gear grease) is a sticky black oil used to lubricate chains and wire ropes.

The black, tar-like sticky mass called CRATER COMPOUND is used to grease sliding surfaces and exposed gears on heavy duty construction equipment. It is applied by hand or with a brush and cannot be squeezed from between the gear teeth or the sliding surfaces. You will find a can of this grease on nearly every shovel or crane used.

Some form of dry lubricant such as GRAPHITE POWDER is available in the shop, to lubricate small parts and door locks, where a liquid would run off or otherwise be undesirable.

Petroleum refiners have developed greases to meet special lubrication requirements of modern machinery and equipment. Table 2 lists and describes the kinds of greases and their uses for proper maintenance.

CONTAMINATION OF PRODUCTS

A contaminated product is one to which has been added some material not normally present such as dirt, rust, water, or another petroleum product. Such admixture may modify the usual qualities of the product permanently or add new and undesirable characteristics. In either case, the contaminated product may be unsuitable for its intended use. Contamination may result from accident, inability or neglect or follow prescribed procedures, gross carelessness, or sabotage. In most instances contamination of a product can be detected by its unusual appearance, color, gravity, or odor.

Dirt

The causes for the presence of sand, clay, or loam in appreciable quantity in petroleum products should be investigated at once and remedial action taken. It may be the result of carelessness or of sabotage. Most commonly it is the result of inadequate cleaning and inspection of tanks or containers, or the use of muddy water to flush pipelines.

In light fuels such as gasoline, in cans or drums, dirt settles in a few hours. The clear fuel may then be drawn off and the bottom (4 to 10 inches) recovered by filtration through a dry chamois. An alternative is to decant the fuel into larger containers for further settling by pouring off the fuel without disturbing the sediment in the bottom of the container. In bulk tanks the settling may require 12 to 24 hours. The clear fuel may then be run off to clean storage and the bottom layer passed through gasoline filters, if available, or downgraded. Tanks and other containers should be thoroughly cleaned before reusing. In heavier fuels such as diesel oils or JP-5 jet fuel, settling is much less satisfactory. Filtration is recommended if practicable. Otherwise it is usually necessary to downgrade the product. In the case of lube oils and greases, no remedial action can be taken. The product must be downgraded.

Rust

Rust is the common name for the product of corrosion which is formed when unprotected iron or some steel surfaces are subjected to prolonged contact with water or moist air. It is brittle and powders readily. It is insoluble in water and in petroleum products but may form troublesome suspensions because of turbulent flow in pipelines, the churning action produced while pumping into storage tanks, or the rough

Table 1.—Military and Commerical Designation for Gear and Lubricating Oils Used in Equipment Maintenance

General Description	Military Designation and Specification Number	Typical Commercial Designation	Uses
Gear oil. Containing extreme pressure (EP) additives to maintain lubrication under extreme pressure conditions.	Lubricant, Gear, Universal, MIL-L-10324. FSN 9150-259-5443.	E.P. Hypoid Gear Lubricant. Universal Gear Lubricant for very cold climates.	For all gear lubrication including transmission, differentials, hypoid gears, tractor final drives, and steering gear mechanisms in cold climates when the prevailing temperature is below 0° F.
Gear oil. Containing extreme pressure (EP) additives to maintain lubrication under extreme pressure conditions.	Lubricant, Gear, Universal, MIL-L-2105. FSN 9150-577-5842.	SAE 80 EP Hypoid or Universal Gear Lubricant. MA 1327	As above except that it is an SAE 80 gear lubricant for use where the prevailing temperature is between 0° and 32° F.
	FSN 9150-577-5845.	SAE 90 EP Hypoid or Universal Gear Lubricant. MA 1328	As above except that it is an SAE 90 gear lubricant for use where the prevailing temperature is above 0° F.
Mineral Gear Oil, SAE 140. NO ADDITIVES.	Military Symbol 5190. MIL-L-2105. FSN 9150-577-5848.	SAE 140 Mineral Gear Oil. Steam Cylinder Oil. MA 1329	For use in tractor transmissions and final drives only in tropical areas. There are no extreme pressure chemical additives in this oil. DO NOT mix with extreme pressure lubricants. DO NOT use in hypoid gear drives such as truck or passenger vehicle differentials.
SAE-10 Heavy Duty Lubricating Oil.	Military Symbol 9110. FSN 9150-231-9039.	Gasoline and Diesel Engine Oil, SAE-10 and SAE-10W Grades.	For crankcase lubrication in both gasoline and diesel engines requiring an SAE-10 or SAE-10W oil and for general purpose lubrication.
SAE-20 Heavy Duty Lubricating Oil.	Military Symbol 9170. FSN 9150-231-6651.	Gasoline and Diesel Engine Oil, SAE-20 Grade.	For crankcase lubrication in both gasoline and diesel engines requiring an SAE-20 oil and for general purpose lubrication.
SAE-30 Heavy Duty Lubricating Oil.	Military Symbol 9250. FSN 9150-231-6655.	Gasoline and Diesel Engine Oil, SAE-30 Grade. MB 1702	For crankcase lubrication in both gasoline and diesel engines requiring an SAE-30 oil and for general purpose lubrication.
SAE-40 Heavy Duty Lubricating Oil.	Military Symbol 9370. FSN 9150-912-9552.	Gasoline and Diesel Engine Oil, SAE-40 Grade.	For crankcase lubrication in both gasoline and diesel engines requiring an SAE-40 oil and for general purpose lubrication.

ENGINES, FUELS, LUBRICANTS, AND POLLUTION CONTROL

Table 1.—Military and Commerical Designation for Gear and Lubricating Oils Used in Equipment Maintenance—Continued

General Description	Military Designation and Specification Number	Typical Commercial Designation	Uses
SAE-50 Heavy Duty Lubricating Oil.	Military Symbol 9500. FSN 1950-231-9043.	Gasoline and Diesel Engine Oil, SAE-50 Grade. MB 1722	For crankcase lubrication in both gasoline and diesel engines requiring an SAE-50 oil and for general purpose lubrication.
Medium VI Mineral Oil SAE-50. No additives.	Military Symbol 3100. FSN 9150-223-8893.	Mineral Oil SAE-50	For lubrication of certain 2-stroke cycle gasoline engines where prescribed. Mixed with fuel in specified proportions such as outboard motorboat engines. For general purpose lubrication.
Hydraulic Transmission Fluid, Type C-1	EO—Series 3 or MIL-L-45199A. Grade 10. FSN 9150-680-1103.	Lubricating Oil High Output.	For hydraulic systems and certain transmission and converter units as prescribed by the manufacturer.

handling of small containers. Rust is a commonly occurring source of contamination when disused pipelines or containers are employed without proper cleaning. Its prevention in small containers—where it is most likely to occur—is best accomplished by thorough cleaning and subsequent rinsing of the container with a prescribed rust-preventive type oil or solution which will cling to the metal surface in a thin layer and provide temporary protection until the container can be filled with the product to be stored. While empty, the containers should be stored upside down. Active pipelines and large storage facilities do not normally permit the accumulation of rust in appreciable quantity. Rust may be removed from gasoline and heavier fuels by the same methods employed in removing dirt from these products.

Mill-Scale

Mill-scale is a magnetic product formed on iron and some steel surfaces during the manufacturing process. It is largely responsible for the blue-black appearance of such surfaces. It has been observed as a very serious contaminant in bulk products pumped through new pipes during the first few days or weeks of use. The scale is brittle and cracks readily. Corrosion begins at these cracks and proceeds to spread under the scale causing it to flake off. The scale is then carried along by the oil flow and is broken up still further before it reaches terminal storage. Here it may remain suspended for days. Settling is not, therefore, a satisfactory method of elimination. The scale is not removed completely by segregators and consequently, screens are quickly choked. Filtering of such stocks is recommended.

Water

In bulk storage, water can very often be a reason for fuel contamination. Water is sometimes employed as a bottom, to a depth of a few inches, to underlie light products such as gasolines and jet fuels. However, the use of water bottoms should be avoided if at all possible, and only employed when authorized by proper technical authority. It is sometimes used to separate and prevent mixing of products when two products, such as motor gasoline and

Table 2.—Military and Commerical Designations for Greases Used in Equipment Maintenance

General Description	Military Designation and Specification Number	Typical Commercial Designation	Uses
Grease, Chasis—Lime, soda or aluminum soap base grease.	Lubricant, General Mil-G-10924 Mil Sym GAA FSN 9150-530-7369	Chassis Grease, Cup Grease, Pressure Gun Grease, No. 1—Soft.	For general use as a pressure gun lubricant, particularly chassis, universal joints, track rollers, ball bearings operating below 150° F. Lime and aluminum soap base grease types are water resistant.
Grease, Wheel Bearing Soda or mixed soap base grease.	Lubricant, General Purpose, No. 2 (Wheel-Bearing-Chassis Lubricant—WB). VV-G-632 Type B, Grade 2. FSN 9150-531-6971.	Wheel Bearing Grease, No. 2—Medium.	For wheel bearings, ball bearings, and as a pressure gun lubricant when operating temperatures are expected to be above 150° F. DO NOT USE TO GREASE UNIVERSAL JOINTS OR OTHER PARTS HAVING NEEDLE BEARINGS. Not water resistant.
Grease, Ball and Roller Bearing Soda or mixed soap base grease.	Lubricant, Ball and Roller Bearing. Mil-G-18709. FSN 9150-249-0908.	Ball and Roller Bearing Grease, BRB.	BRB and G-18709 suitable for ball and roller bearing lubrication, especially in electric motors and generators and clutch pilot bearings. Not water resistant.
Grease—Water Pump Lime soap base grease.	Lubricant, Water-Pump, No. 4. VV-G-632 Type A, Grade 4. FSN 9150-235-5504.	Water-Pump Grease, No. 4—Hard.	For gland type water-pumps of some engines not equipped with factory lubricated and sealed water pumps. Very water resistant.
Lubricant, Exposed Gear, Chain, and Wire Rope Sticky, viscous, black, residual oil.	Lubricant, Chain and Wire Rope. Mil-G-18458. FSN 9150-530-6814.	Exposed Gear Chain and Wire Rope Lubricant. Gear Grease. Wire Rope Grease No. 2.	For greasing cable, open gears or any open mechanism requiring rough lubrication. Usually heated before applying. Grade B is intended for use in temperate or warm weather and is suitable for open-air or under-water conditions. Not for cables in contact with earth.
		As above, except that it is No. 3 or heavy duty type.	As above except that Grade C is for use in hot weather or for hard service and is suitable for open-air or under-water conditions.

aviation gasoline, are to be pumped through a pipeline, one after the other. Again, this should be avoided if possible as there are better means for segregation of products. The legitimate and necessary uses of water provide ample opportunities for the contamination of light products unless they are controlled by strict adherence to standard operating procedures. Fortunately, water suspended in light products such as gasoline separates rapidly on standing; less rapidly in diesel oil and JP-5 jet fuel. In cold weather this settling may be delayed by the formation of ice crystals, which are lighter than water droplets. In suspension, these crystals may clog filters, fuel lines, or jets in equipment. The most effective precaution against water contamination is to ensure delivery of a well-settled product through a dry line into a dry container. In cold weather, even a small amount of water can cause the freezing of bottom outlet valves in rail tank cars and tank trucks. In the case of packaged products, water may become a contaminant through the use of open or damaged containers, through improper storage and handling methods, and by the breathing which normally occurs in drums and cans. (Breathing is the reverse of vaporization and is caused by a drop in temperature. In breathing, cooled vapors condense to liquids, the interior pressure of the storage tank or container decreases, and air is sucked into the tank or container.)

Water contamination of fuels supplied to consumers in drums or cans can be avoided, when the turnover is rapid, by the application of prescribed methods of inspection, storage, and handling. However, long-term storage in drums, (strategic reserve stocks) cannot fail to result in some contamination. The condensation of some water from the moist air sucked in during the night is inevitable since this water settles and, therefore, is not expelled with product vapors during the heat of the day. During several weeks of storage, this water accumulates in surprisingly large amounts. Not only does it constitute direct contamination, which may have very undesirable consequences if transferred to equipment, but it is the cause of serious additional contamination by rust, and increases container maintenance. For this reason, periodic technical inspection is required and provision must be made for the regular replacement of such stocks at relatively frequent intervals. The length of intervals is determined by climatic and other conditions. Accumulated water can best be removed by decantation, settling, and refilling. Lacking time or facilities for this, a small pump may be employed to remove the lower layers from individual containers.

The most effective and proper protection for lubricants is to keep them well covered, preferably in inside storage. Should damaged containers permit water to contaminate engine or gear oils, the water may remove some of the essential additives. Even more undesirable is the fact that water tends to emulsify in the oil and does not settle out, thus decreasing effective lubricating action. Water can be poured off from greases. When this is done, about an inch of surface grease should also be removed. After removal, the surface grease should be burned or buried.

Commingling of Products

Commingling of products may result from inadequate cleansing of lines or containers; from the use of unmarked or improperly marked containers; and from the mishandling of manifolds. In such cases it can be minimized by supervision sufficient to ensure strict application of the prescribed petroleum handling procedures. Commingling may also result from leaks in tanks or valves aboard tankers, and from leaky valves or insufficient protective facilities in shore installations. These sources can be minimized by proper inspection and maintenance procedures. Nevertheless, serious contamination of one product by another can and does occur occasionally in field operations. This is one of the most compelling reasons for the continuous inspection procedures and the routine testing programs prescribed by the military departments.

Commingling can be negligible or serious depending upon the product contaminated, the contaminating agent, and the amount of contamination. Some of the more important serious effects are:

1. Loss of power in fuels.
2. Increase in volatility (producing a fire or explosion hazard in kerosene or diesel fuels).
3. Increase in gum content.
4. Formation of heavy sludge.

III. SAFETY IN HANDLING AND STORAGE OF PETROLEUM PRODUCTS

Although the handling of petroleum products presents many hazards, both bulk and packaged products can be handled safely and with remarkable freedom from accident if proper precautionary measures are taken. All personnel involved with the receipt, storage, issue, and use of flammable and combustible petroleum products must be familiar with and observe applicable safety precautions.

Precautionary measures must be taken to prevent fire and explosion when handling any petroleum product. The degree of hazard involved depends on the properties of a given product. Therefore, for safe handling purposes, petroleum products are divided into groups or classes according to the temperature at which the product will give off flammable vapors.

Any material which can be ignited easily and which will burn with unusual rapidity is said to be flammable. (The terms flammable and inflammable are identical in meaning, but the former is preferred since the prefix in suggests non flammable.)

All petroleum products, being composed of carbon and hydrogen, will burn and are therefore combustible materials. However, classification for safe handling purposes distinguishes products according to their tendency to burn.

Combustible liquids, according to the National Fire Protection Association (NFPA) Standards, are those liquids having flash points at or above 140°F and below 200°F.

Flammable liquids, according to the NFPA Standards, include all liquid petroleum fuels which give off flammable vapors below temperatures of 140°F.

Volatile products are products which tend to vaporize; that is, give off flammable vapors at comparatively low temperatures are said to be volatile. Because volatile products such as gasoline and JP-4 jet fuels will give off sufficient vapors to be flammable at relatively low temperatures, they are the most hazardous of all petroleum products to handle. For example, gasoline has a flash point of about -45° and JP-4 jet fuel has a flash point slightly higher, while crude oil has a flash point of about 60°F. This varies, however, according to the source of the crude oil. Volatile products such as gasoline and JP-4 jet fuel are normally handled at atmospheric temperatures above -45°F and, therefore, give off sufficient vapors to flash or burn at all times. Products which give off flammable vapors only above 100°F and are relatively nonvolatile are relatively safe to handle at ordinary temperatures and pressures. Such petroleum products as kerosene, JP-5 jet fuel, diesel and light and heavy fuel oils are included in this category.

It is noted, however, that if products such as kerosene, JP-5 jet fuel, diesels and fuel oils are handled at elevated temperatures they are just as hazardous as the volatile products. For example, kerosene, which has a flash point of about 110°F will not ignite at ordinary atmospheric temperatures, but if it is heated above 100°F will give off sufficient flammable vapors to burn or explode. All products which have a flash point above 100°F when heated to temperatures equal to or higher than their flash point, should be treated as volatile products with respect to fire and explosion hazards.

Some precautionary measures to be strictly observed when handling petroleum products are listed below. Most of these precautions apply to the handling of any flammable or volatile product at ordinary temperature, and higher flash or less volatile products at high temperature.

1. Reducing Or Controlling The Discharge Of Vapors
  a. Take care that no spills occur.
  b. Avoid spills from overflow when loading storage tanks by gaging tanks prior to loading.
  c. Never neglect leaks. Make frequent inspections for leaks in tank seams, tank shells, and pipe joints.
  d. If spills or leaks occur, clean them up immediately. Soaked ground should be washed with water or covered with sand or dry earth. The area should be policed until flammable vapor has been eliminated.
  e. When temperatures are excessively high, cool storage tanks by sprinkling, or by playing water over them.
  f. Keep containers for volatile products, whether empty or full, closed tightly.
  g. Beware of empty fuel containers.
  h. Ensure proper ventilation of all enclosed spaces in which vapors may accumulate.

2. Eliminating Sources Of Accidental Ignition
  a. Do not smoke.
  b. Do not carry "strike anywhere" matches or automatic lighters that open and light with a single motion.

ENGINES, FUELS, LUBRICANTS, AND POLLUTION CONTROL

c. Do not perform any mechanical work or repair involving hot work such as burning, cutting, or welding, unless a permit is issued by proper authority.

d. Inspect electrical apparatus frequently and correct any condition likely to cause sparking.

e. Open switches and pull fuses before work is done on electrical equipment.

f. Shut off gasoline tank truck engines during the entire period of filling or discharging unless the truck is designed for engine operation, to drive transfer pumps through a power take-off.

g. Ground flammable fuel hose nozzle to the tank before starting the flow of fuel. Maintain this bond throughout the filling operation.

h. Never load or unload volatile or flammable products during electrical storms.

i. Use only self-closing metal receptacles for discarding oily waste or rags and dispose of such collections daily.

j. Never use volatile petroleum products such as gasoline for any cleaning purpose.

k. Keep gage tape in contact with gage hatch during gaging operations.

l. Immediately remove any clothing which has become soaked with fuels.

3. Safety Precautions For Handling JP-4 Fuel:

In addition to the safety precautions required for handling all volatile fuels, Grade JP-4 fuel, because of its tendency to accumulate and discharge static electricity and its low vapor pressure, requires additional handling precautions. Like other volatile fuels, JP-4 still requires a source of ignition. Unlike the other volatile fuels, the static electricity generated in pumping, transferring and loading JP-4 is an inherrent source of ignition which requires careful handling to control. JP-4 fuel is unique in that its rate of vaporization under most handling conditions will create an atmosphere (vapor/air) well within the explosive range, within the tank above the liquid surface. The atmosphere within a fixed roof tank storing gasoline will normally be too rich to be ignited or to burn within the tank, but in the case of JP-4, any ignition at gaging hatches, or vents will travel into the tank and cause a violent combustion (explosion). This hazard is not normally present in the case of Grade JP-5 fuel because of its relatively high flash point (140°F). To minimize the generation and accumulation of static electric charge in JP-4 fuel, the following procedures and/or precautions are recommended:

a. Do not use overhead fill lines which permit a free fall of product through the air.

b. The entrance of air into fill lines should be minimized or eliminated if practicable.

c. Where feasible the storage of JP-4 in concrete tanks or other poor electrical conducting materials should be avoided.

When handling petroleum products, care must be taken to ensure they do not become contaminated with foreign matter. Since all petroleum products will burn, fire is an ever present hazard. The degree of fire hazard increases as the volatility of the product increases.

Inhaling gasoline vapors may cause headaches, dizziness, nausea, or even unconsciousness. If any of these symptoms are noticed among men handling gasoline or working in an area where gasoline has been spilled, the men should leave the area at once. If anyone has been overcome, he should receive immediate medical attention.

Gasoline may cause severe burns if allowed to remain in contact with the skin, particularly under soaked clothing or gloves. Clothing or shoes through which gasoline has soaked should be removed at once. Gasoline should be washed from the skin with soap and water. Repeated contact with gasoline removes the protective oils from the skin and causes drying, roughening, chapping, and cracking and, in some cases, infections of the skin. Rubber gloves should be worn as protection by persons handling petroleum products.

If gasoline gets into a person's eyes, first aid should be given immediately. Fresh water may be applied, and medical attention should be secured.

If a person swallows gasoline by accident, first aid should be given immediately. Giving the victim warm salty water to induce vomiting is an effective aid. Medical attention should be secured promptly.

Slipping and falling are common accidents which occur when handling petroleum products. This danger is particularly grave while climbing to and from loading racks, storage tanks, or stacks of drums or cans. Tools, pieces of lumber, and other objects should not be left lying where they may cause accidents.

On a hot day, gasoline vapors mixed with air may be flammable for a distance of 20 feet from an open container. By using underground tanks there will be less chance of a fire or an explosion, and less gas will be lost by evaporation. Areas near gasoline storage tanks should ALWAYS BE WELL POSTED WITH WARNING SIGNS.

Gasoline storage tanks should be placed underground and covered with at least 3 or 4 feet of earth. The tanks must be equipped with vent pipes which extend well above the ground (6 to 8 feet) so that the vapors may spread and disappear. (See fig. 11.)

Diesel fuel is not as volatile, flammable, nor as dangerous to handle as gasoline. But it will burn, and in closed unventilated places, diesel vapors can be explosive.

Diesel fuel is generally not stored in the same way as gasoline. Figure 12 shows a typical diesel fuel storage tank. The tank is generally placed above ground on a raised platform. The platform should be high enough to permit the fueling of equipment from the tank by gravity flow. The tank must be provided with an air vent at the top and a drain cock at the lowest point. The outlet for the fuel should be at least 6 inches from the bottom of the tank, so that any water and dirt which have accumulated and settled in the bottom will not be drained into the fuel tanks of the equipment being serviced. The water and sediment that collect in the bottom of the tanks should be drained off daily. When you fill a diesel fuel storage tank, remember to leave enough room for expansion of the fuel. Lubricating oil and greases are furnished in various sizes of containers. More lubricant is wasted because it has become contaminated than for any other cause. All containers should be clearly marked as to their contents and dates received. The lubricants that have been in stock the longest should be used first. Make sure that all openings of lubricant containers are properly secured. This will decrease the chances of lubricants becoming contaminated.

IV. FILTERS

In discussing diesel fuel, it was emphasized that it must be clean for proper diesel engine operation. So important is clean fuel, that besides the precautions observed in handling and storing diesel fuel, manufacturers have built fuel strainers and filters into the fuel systems or diesel engines.

FUEL OIL FILTERS

In addition to a metal strainer, most diesel-fuel systems also contain a filter to remove any remaining small particles of dirt that might clog the injectors. Fuel-oil filters are manufactured in various models by a number of manufacturers. All fuel entering the injectors first passes through the filter elements. The filter elements are made of cotton fiber or mineral wool and glass cloth. After continued use, these filters will become packed with dirt filtered from the fuel, and the flow of fuel to the engine will be reduced to a point where the engine ceases to function properly or stops. Most types of heavy equipment have fuel pressure gages which will indicate when filters are dirty. Filter elements are easily removed and should be replaced with new elements when they start to restrict the flow of fuel to the engine.

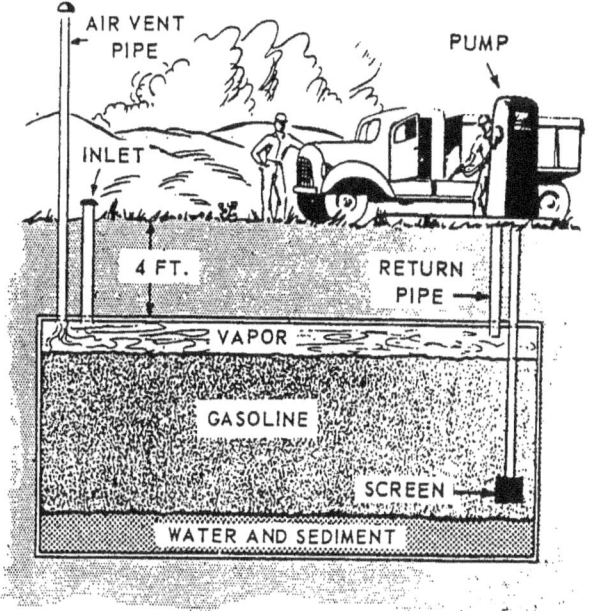

Figure 11. — Underground gasoline storage tank.

ENGINES, FUELS, LUBRICANTS, AND POLLUTION CONTROL

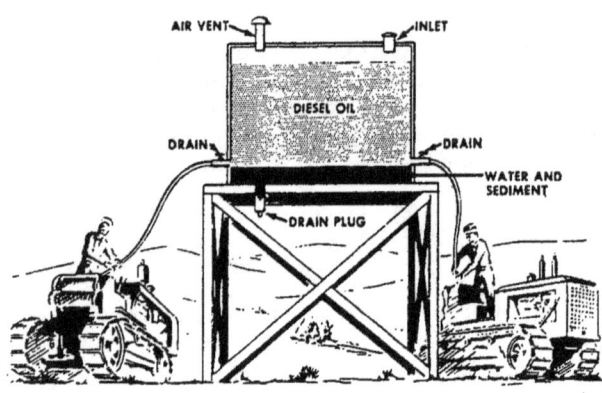

Figure 12.—Storage tank for diesel fuel.

LUBRICATING OIL FILTERS

Most internal combustion engines are equipped with an oil filter. This device filters out the dust, dirt, and grit that enter the oil during operation of the engine.

Construction equipment lubricating oil filters (fig. 13) contain a filtering element for their filtering action. When this filtering element is saturated with solid particles, it ceases to function. It is good practice to replace the element with a new one every time the crankcase is drained and new oil is added. By such replacement you are assured of clean oil and a minimum of wear on engine parts.

The three types of oil filter systems used on automotive engines are the bypass, full-flow, and shunt types. The bypass type of oil filter is bracket mounted to the cylinder head or manifolds with connecting oil lines to the engine. The oil from the oil pump passes through the oil filter and then to the crankcase in the bypass system. The full-flow type of oil filter is integral with the engine. The oil is directed under pressure through the filter and then to the engine bearings. When the oil is too cold to circulate through the filter in the full-flow system, a bypass valve directs the oil around the filter element. The shunt type filters only a portion of the oil at a time, as does the bypass system, but the oil which is filtered is passed directly to the engine bearings.

Bypass systems use three types of filters. They are the throw-away type (fig. 14), the screw-on type of throw-away filter (fig. 15), and the replaceable element type of filter (fig. 16). The full-flow and shunt systems use the replaceable element type of the screw-on type of throw-away filter. A replaceable element for a full-flow type filter is shown in figure 17.

The throw-away type of oil filter is replaced as a complete unit. You have to disconnect the oil line fittings at the filter. Detach the filter from its bracket and remove the brass fitting from its filter housing. Throw away the filter. Place a bolt or plug into the brass fitting when you are removing or installing it. Brass is malleable (easily bent) and may be crushed by excessive wrench pressure.

The screw-on, throw-away type filter is also replaced as a complete unit. You unscrew

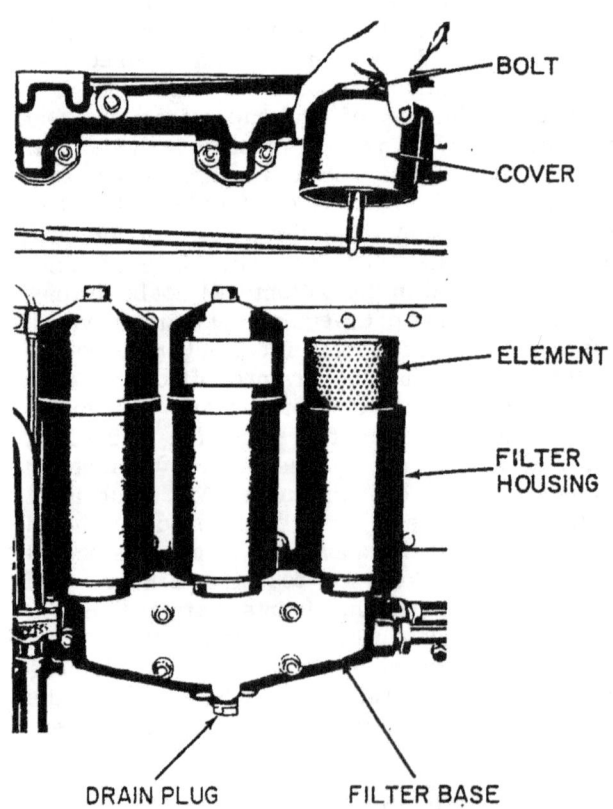

Figure 13.—Lubricating oil filter for construction equipment.

the filter from the base by hand and throw the filter away. Wipe the base clean with a cloth and screw a new filter onto the base by hand, tightening at least half a turn after the gasket contacts the base. Fill the crankcase to the full mark on the dipstick with the proper grade and weight of oil. Start the engine and observe the oil pressure and check for leaks around the oil filter. Stop the engine and add oil to the full level if needed.

To service replaceable element oil filters, you remove the fastening bolt, lift off the cover or remove the filter shell. Remove the gasket and throw it away. When removing the oil filter of the full-flow or shunt type, place a pan under the filter to catch the oil. Take out the old element and throw it away. Throw away the gasket from the top and bottom of the center tube if they are present. Place a pan under the filter and remove the drain plug if the filter is used in the bypass system. Clean the inside of the filter shell and cover. Install metal supports

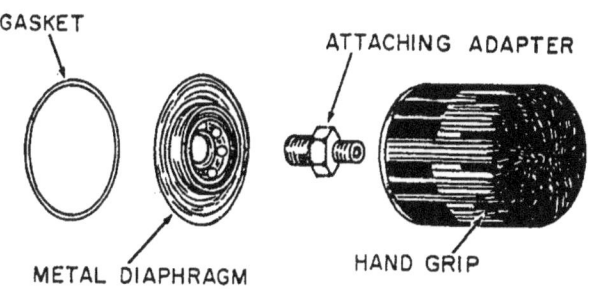

Figure 15. — Screw-on type of throw-away oil filter.

and a new bottom tube gasket. Insert a new element and a new top tube gasket. Insert a new cover or housing gasket (make sure that the gasket is completely seated in the recess). Replace the cover or housing and fasten the center bolt securely. Fill the crankcase to the full mark on the dip stick with the proper grade

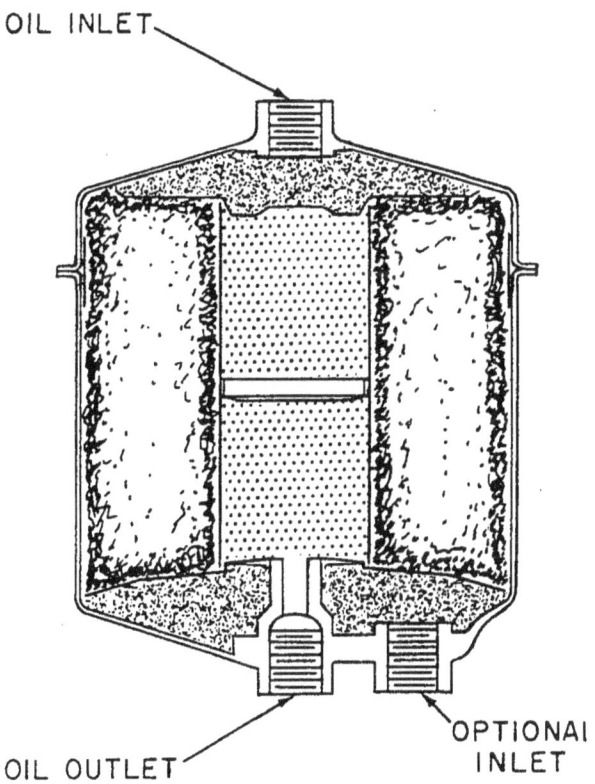

Figure 14. — Sealed type of throw-away oil filter.

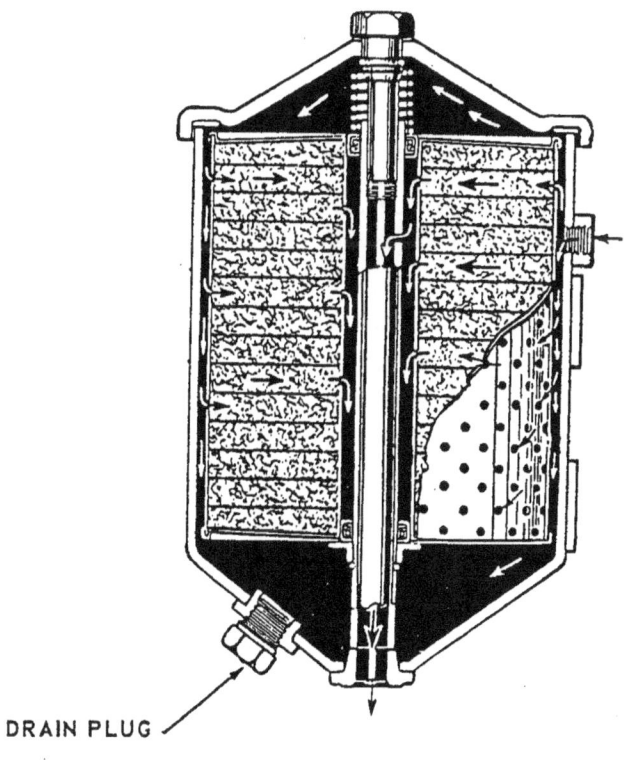

Figure 16. — Replaceable element type oil filter.

ENGINES, FUELS, LUBRICANTS, AND POLLUTION CONTROL

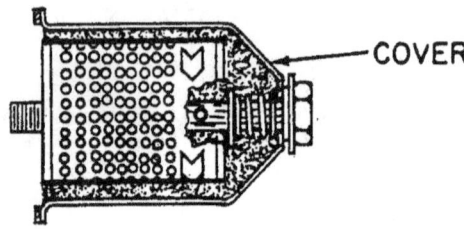

Figure 17.— Replaceable element, full-flow type oil filter.

and weight of oil. Start and idle the engine. Check the oil pressure immediately and inspect the filter for oil leaks. Then stop the engine and check the crankcase oil level and add oil to the full mark. The final step in the procedure is to mark the mileage on the sticker so that the element of the oil filter will be replaced at the proper interval.

DRY-TYPE AIR CLEANERS

The heavy duty dry-type air cleaner illustrated in figure 18 uses a replaceable element. Air enters the cleaner through the air intake cap and screen (1) which prevents chaff and coarse dirt from getting into the air cleaner. After passing through the adapter (3) and rotonamic panel (4), the air is filtered as it passes through the replaceable dry-type element (5) and filter housing (6). The filtered air is then drawn into the engine through the intake manifold.

OIL-BATH AIR CLEANER

The oil-bath air cleaner shown in figure 19 consists of main body, air intake cap, screens, and oil reservoir. Air enters the intake cap and inlet screen (1) which prevent large particles such as dirt, chaff, leaves, and so forth, from entering the air cleaner. After passing down the inlet pipe (2) to the center oil reservoir (3), the air is deflected upward through the screen (4), carrying drops of oil. The oil absorbs dirt from the air as it passes through the screen. The screen is sloped so the air sweeps the dirt laden oil toward the outside of the cleaner where it falls and re-enters the oil reservoir. The clean filtered air is then drawn into the engine through the intake manifold pipe (5).

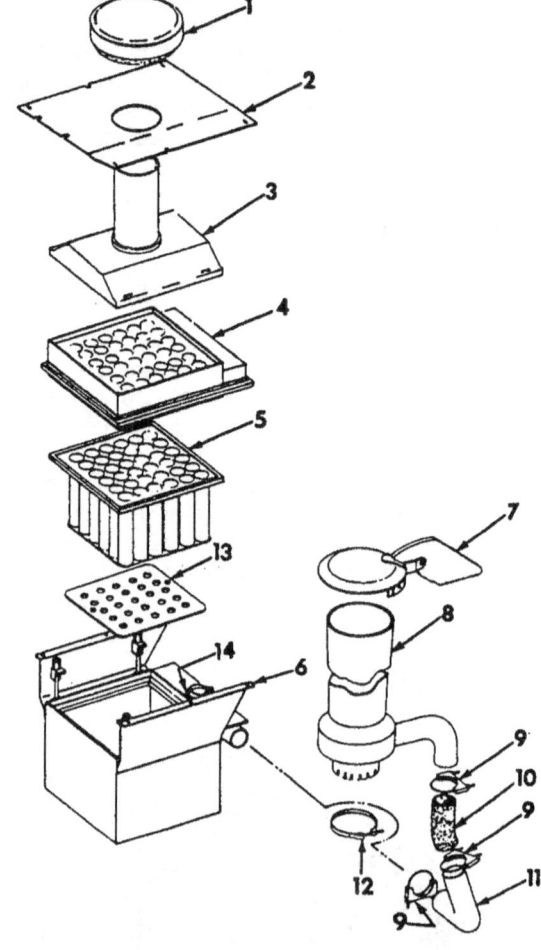

1. CAP, air intake.
2. PANEL, removeable.
3. ADAPTER, intake.
4. PANEL, rotonamic.
5. ELEMENT, filter.
6. HOUSING, air cleaner.
7. CAP, weather.
8. ASPIRATOR.
9. CLAMP.
10. HOSE.
11. ELBOW, exhaust.
12. CLAMP, aspirator.
13. PLATE, support.
14. GASKET.

Figure 18.— Heavy duty dry-type air cleaner.

V. ENVIRONMENTAL POLLUTION CONTROL

Environmental pollution is that condition which results from the presence of chemical, physical or biological agents in the air, water or soil

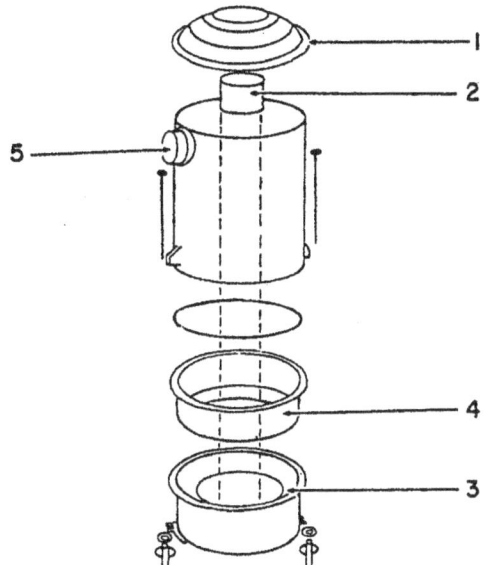

1. Intake cup and inlet screen.
2. Inlet pipe.
3. Center oil reservoir.
4. Screen.
5. Intake manifold pipe.

Figure 19.—Oil bath air cleaner.

which alter the natural environment. This causes an adverse effect on human health or comfort, fish and wildlife, other aquatic resources and plant life, and structures and equipment to the extent that economic loss is produced and recreational opportunity is impaired. Pollution causes nylon hose to disintegrate, masonry to crumble, steel to corrode, and skies to darken. It also damages vegetation, causes illness, and results in the loss of countless work days.

AIR POLLUTION

As an EO, you should be aware of the conditions which cause air pollution when operating equipment, and the efforts being made to minimize or correct these conditions.

When incomplete combustion occurs, unburned hydrocarbons and various other constituents in the basic fuel combine chemically to form some visible, noxious, and harmful byproducts which are emitted into the environment. Some of the fuel components and combustion products which have an adverse effect on the air are carbon monoxide, particulate matter, sulfur, oxides, unburned hydrocarbons, nitrogen oxides, and lead.

CONTROLLING AIR POLLUTION

The most effective means of controlling air pollution caused by fuel combustion is to maintain a well-tuned engine that provides an optimium fuel and oxygen mixture and proper timing; this results in most efficient combustion. Another alternative, not always under control of an operator, is to use only the best grade of fuel available which contains low particulate matter, low water and sulfur content, and other contaminates. Automotive manufacturers now provide systems on engine to return "blowby" (unburned fuel) to the carburetor for combustion, i.e., a pollution control system. Long range research and development is underway in developing systems to remove harmful constituents from engine exhausts, e.g., catalytic filter scrubber systems to remove oxides of sulfur and nitrogen, and others to remove lead.

WATER AND GROUND POLLUTION

In addition to creating a fire hazard, oil and other fuel products pose many possible pollution threats when spilled on the water or ground. Oil products on the ground can infiltrate and contaminate ground water supplies or can be carried into surface water supplies with ground runoff due to rain. Oil products carried into storm or sanitary sewers pose potential explosion hazards. Gasoline seeping into a sewer from a service station created an explosion which demolished several city blocks in a Chicago suburb

Oil on the water surface blocks the oxygen flow from the atmosphere into the water which results in less oxygen in the water for the fish and other aquatic organisms. Fish can be harmed by eating oil or smaller organisms that have eaten the oil. If the fish do not die from the oil coating their gills or from eating the oil, their flesh is tainted and they are no longer suitable for consumption by man. In addition to harming aquatic organisms and contaminating water supplies, oil products foul boats, water front structures, beaches, and in general create an unsightly mess along the waterfront.

ENGINES, FUELS, LUBRICANTS, AND POLLUTION CONTROL

Of all the oil introduced in the world's waters, spent oils from highway vehicles accounted for 37 percent, or 2 million tons in 1969. This is the largest single source of oil pollution, ever greater than tankers (11 percent), other ships (10 percent), offshore oil production (2 percent), refineries and petrochemical plants (6 percent), industrial and all other vehicles (31 percent), and accidental spills (4 percent).

PREVENTIVE MEASURES FOR WATER AND GROUND POLLUTION

During automotive repair, drip pans and an absorbent material should be used to catch all unavoidable spills. Spilled oil or fuels should never be washed down a drain or sewer, unless an immediate fire hazard exists and an oil-water separator is present in the discharge line. Where spills are expected to occur (gasoline fill stands, etc.), absorbent material should be on hand. This material can be sprinkled on spilled oil or fuel, placed in a container, and disposed in a sanitary landfill or other non-polluting manner.

Spent crankcase oil, filters, contaminated fuel should be collected and disposed of in a non-polluting manner. Most naval activities collect and dispose of waste oil periodically through a contractor, by burning in a boiler plant, or reprocessing in an oil reclamation plant. Naval supply fuel farms usually have means to properly dispose of waste oils.

Open vehicle repair or maintenance areas located near water-courses or bodies of water should be landscaped and diked so spilled oil products cannot easily or directly flow into the nearby water.

www.ingramcontent.com/pod-product-compliance
Lightning Source LLC
Chambersburg PA
CBHW081811300426
44116CB00014B/2314